Leaving Certificate English **Higher Level**

Hands-On
Paper 1

The Essential Comprehending and Composing Toolkit

GW00801591

Andrew Mayne

educate.ie

PUBLISHED BY:
Educate.ie
Walsh Educational Books Ltd
Castleisland, Co. Kerry, Ireland

www.educate.ie

PRINTED AND BOUND BY:
Walsh Colour Print, Castleisland

ISBN: 978-1-93698-88-1

Contents

Theme 1: New Frontiers — 1

Theme 2: Artificial Intelligence — 23

Introduction

Welcome to *Hands-On Paper 1 – The Essential Comprehending and Composing Toolkit.*

This book provides you with the tools you need to get to grips with Leaving Certificate English Higher Level Paper 1. It is the only dedicated Paper 1 book to take a thematic approach, offering three texts together at a time, as they would appear on an examination paper.

The *Hands-On Paper 1* toolkit contains everything you require to prepare fully for your examination, including:

- practical examination advice
- answering strategies
- six full sample examination papers
- a range of Comprehending text types – feature article, memoir, speech, novel, interview, opinion piece, visual text, preface, letter, news article
- commentary on different genres
- sample Comprehending questions modelled on recent examinations
- annotated sample answers for all Comprehending question types
- a dedicated Composing section, with information on different composition types
- annotated sample answers for recent Composing examination questions
- grammar advice integrated throughout
- a full spelling and grammar section at the end.

Features

 Discuss questions appear before each paper to encourage you to start thinking about the theme, language styles and text sources before beginning the paper.

 Footnote boxes give information on the key features of different genres of text that can appear in the Comprehending section of the paper.

 Exam Mechanics boxes provide strategies for answering specific examination questions.

 Sample Answers with annotations illustrate how to successfully address a particular question.

 Grammar Guides provide information on key grammar points where they arise.

 Hint boxes provide additional tips and suggestions.

As you work through this book, you will become equipped with the skills and knowledge to be successful in Paper 1.

We hope you enjoy using the *Hands-On Paper 1* toolkit to prepare for your examination.

Examination Advice

English Paper 1 is usually the first written examination and is normally scheduled for 9.30 a.m. on the first Wednesday after the June bank holiday. There are a total of 200 marks available on the paper – half of your final grade for English.

General advice

Timing

The time allocated for the paper is 2 hours and 50 minutes (170 minutes).

A quick calculation reveals something important: 170/200 = 0.85. In other words, there are more marks to achieve than minutes to achieve them. So, if a question is worth 15 marks, you cannot afford to spend 15 minutes on it. The maximum amount of time you could spend on a 15-mark question would be 85 per cent of 15 minutes: 15 x 0.85 = just over 12 minutes.

Furthermore, to allow time for reading through the paper first (20 minutes *maximum*), the amount of time available for answering questions reduces to roughly 75 per cent of the mark allocation, which would be just *under* 12 minutes for a 15-mark question. Depending on how quickly and efficiently you read, your key figure for the minutes to spend on each question will therefore be somewhere between 75 and 80 per cent of the mark allocation.

The timing guidelines given below represent the **maximum** amount of time you should spend. Remember that you always want to have time left over at the end to read through everything and correct your mistakes. Everybody makes mistakes, especially when they are under pressure.

The number one reason why students lose marks is because they have not paid attention to their timing. It is not unusual for an examiner to find long and detailed answers to the comprehension questions (at the beginning of the paper), only to discover barely a page written for the composition (at the end).

Remember that your composition is worth 100 marks. That is one-quarter of your entire English grade. It is vital that you allow yourself adequate time to write your composition; indeed, some students choose to answer this question first.

Before you open your exam paper

The exam superintendent will hand out the exam paper, face up, some minutes before the exam officially begins. There is useful information on the front cover that you can read before the exam even starts. Apart from explaining the structure of the questions, it tells you what **theme** the entire paper is based on. For example, the theme for the 2021 paper was *Reflections on Time*. As you wait for the exam to begin, start thinking about the theme. What does it mean to you? What kinds of texts might have this as a theme? What kinds of compositions might be in a paper based on this theme?

When the exam starts

15–20 mins

Step 1: Read through the entire paper.

1. Read the three sets of Question As and their associated texts. In each case, read the questions first. Simplify the three questions by highlighting or underlining the key words. You should do this because:

   • the questions will reveal a great deal about the text before you even read it, helping you to understand it more clearly

   • on the first read-through of the text, you can already start highlighting and/or annotating the text when you come across obvious evidence that could later help you with the answers.

   The first read-though is not a detailed analysis. Do not get caught up in extensive note-taking. Once you have read everything and selected the questions you will answer, you will come back and read through your chosen text a second or even a third time and make more detailed notes on it.

2. Read the three Question Bs. Remember that you do not need a detailed understanding of each question yet. As long as you are sure you can identify the purpose of, and audience for, each Question B, and you have a good understanding of the style of writing required, you are in a position to decide which Question B you want to attempt.

3. Read all seven Composing questions; keep an open mind at the moment about which one you will answer.

Step 2: Choose what to do in Section I.

Remember you must do one Question A and one Question B from different texts.

• Which Question A will you answer?

• Which Question B will you answer?

• Which text will you leave out altogether?

Remember to spend no more than 20 minutes going through the whole paper and choosing your questions.

> **Hint**
>
> Many students find the most helpful way of making the decision about which Question A to answer is by first choosing which of the Question B tasks they feel most comfortable doing. After that, they choose from the remaining two Question As.

Layout

You are not required to answer the three parts of Paper 1 – Question A, Question B and the Composing question – in any particular order. For the purpose of these guidelines, the parts are addressed in the order they appear. However, if you want to start with your composition or by answering a Question B, that is fine. Just make sure to number your answers clearly.

It is a good idea to start answering each new question on a completely new page. You could even leave a blank page in between questions (see 'Editing', page xi).

Errors

Avoid using correction fluid on errors – it takes too long to dry. Some students indicate errors by putting them inside brackets. However, this can lead to confusion because brackets are recognised punctuation marks and serve a particular purpose. Instead, just cross out mistakes neatly. Inform your examiner where fresh attempts can be found; for example, 'the rest of Question A (iii) is written after the composition'.

Handwriting

Make sure your handwriting is as tidy as you can manage. Bear in mind that your pages will be scanned, so your reader will not have the original page in front of them and will be trying to read off a screen. Examiners must make every effort to decipher the words in front of them, but if those words are so unclear as to be illegible, they can assume they are errors. To ensure your reader's task is as easy as you can possibly make it:

- write in black or blue with a ballpoint pen; never write in pencil – it might not scan properly
- stay within the margins on the page
- avoid squeezing writing onto the very bottom of the page.

Planning

There is plenty of space in the answer booklet for plans, mind maps and spider diagrams. You may choose to remove the centre pages from your booklet and use them for all your planning. Separate sheets have the advantage of not requiring you to flip pages backwards and forwards to consult your plan. If you do fill your booklet, ask the superintendent for more paper – there is no limit on how much you are allowed to use. Remember to hand up all your rough sheets with your answer booklet, including any extra paper or pages removed from your booklet.

Section I – Comprehending (100 marks)

 Question A (50 marks)

Question A (i) (15 marks) is usually a comprehension question, requiring you to find and then present information from the associated text.

Question A (ii) (15 marks) tends to ask your opinion on a particular topic. You may or may not be required to refer to the text in your answer.

For Questions A (i) and (ii), you are expected to make three points in your answer, equating to three separate paragraphs. You may also include a brief introduction to sum up the three points you are going to make. This is not compulsory, but it does show you have fully planned your answer before writing it. Similarly, a short concluding paragraph can sum up the key points of your answer. Some students like to include both an introduction and a conclusion, but normally one or the other will suffice.

The length of your answer will depend on how succinctly (or otherwise) you express yourself. Many students write about three-quarters of a page (around 250 words) for a 15-mark question. Others write more. Remember that it is time, and not space, that determines how much you can write.

Question A (iii) (20 marks) usually requires you to analyse the author's style. You might be asked to find features of a particular genre of writing. Sometimes the question includes key words describing a particular style and then asks if you agree with that assessment of the author's writing.

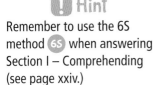

Hint

Remember to use the 6S method 6S when answering Section I – Comprehending (see page xxiv.)

You will be expected to make four separate observations about the writer's style, equating to four separate paragraphs. Make sure you include your assessment of the author's stylistic choices and the effect they have on the piece and/or on you as a reader. As with Questions A (i) and (ii), you can show purposefulness by including a brief introduction that sums up the four points you will be making. A brief conclusion would add cohesiveness.

Question B (50 marks)

(5–10 minutes planning, 30–35 minutes writing)

For Question B, follow the approach described in the Exam Mechanics boxes in this toolkit. First, read the question and highlight the main task. This task will inform your entire answer. It indicates what genre to write in, what your purpose is and what layout/structure to use. Next, identify the audience you will be writing for, which will determine the appropriate style and register. Then, number the points you need to cover to make sure that your answer addresses all aspects of the question.

Question B will ask you to write in a particular style to achieve a particular task for a particular audience. The key to success is to make your writing feel authentic. To do this, you need to be familiar with different styles of writing, and to reproduce the one that is the most appropriate. In some instances, this will mean that you need to be aware of how your writing is laid out on the page. For example, do you need a headline? Would bullet points be appropriate? Your language and diction need to be appropriate too. For example, is some jargon needed?

With any piece of writing, a key consideration is your audience. Who is going to be reading or listening to these words? If you are addressing the President of Ireland, your language will be formal to suit the dignity of the occasion. If you are speaking to your class, your language will be more informal. This is known as your register, and getting it right is crucial.

There will also be specific instructions in the question, which you must follow. Numbering the specific points you need to cover will make sure you do not miss any out.

Section II – Composing (100 marks)

(10 minutes planning, 1 hour writing)

You will be given a choice of seven composition titles, and you must choose one.

The average length of a composition at Higher Level is around 1,000 words. You will need to check for yourself how many pages that equates to in your handwriting. Remember that 1,000 words is an average length. Some students write well in excess of this, while others write less. The length will come down to how quickly and/or efficiently you write.

Several different genres of writing come up in this section. These usually include one (or more) personal essay, short story, speech and article. Other genres that have come up in recent years include discursive essays, descriptive essays, persuasive essays and dialogues. You should have the opportunity to write in each of these genres over the two years you spend completing your Leaving Certificate course, so when it comes to the examination you should know which genres you prefer. Are you able to construct a sound, logical argument? Can you use the techniques of persuasion to good effect? If so, then perhaps the speech option or an opinion piece is the way to go. Perhaps you are more of a creative type, and therefore a short story or descriptive essay would be the right choice.

However, it is unwise to walk into the examination with your composition type already chosen. You may have had success with, say, speech-writing before. But the question on the exam paper may require knowledge of a subject you simply know nothing about. Be prepared to be flexible, and keep an open mind while you consider each Composing question.

Another issue to guard against is the temptation to reproduce a pre-written essay. No matter how successful that essay was when originally composed, there is practically zero chance it will adequately address the specific requirements of a question presented on the day of the exam. Regardless of how well written the piece is, it will be marked according to how well it is tailored to the exact requirements of the exam question, and it is therefore likely to be marked very harshly in terms of its *Purpose* (see page xii).

Editing

If you complete your answers within the maximum time limit, you will have time left over before the exam ends. Do not sit back and congratulate yourself on a job well done, however, because one of the most important tasks is still to be completed.

Go back to the start of your answer booklet and read through everything you have written. No matter how careful you think you have been, you will have made errors. You will often find simple spelling and punctuation mistakes and you may realise that certain phrases are unclear and could be expressed better.

You may wish to take the opportunity to add something to an answer that you felt you did not have time to include earlier. That is why it is a good idea to leave a page between sections and between questions – it gives you space to add material without a lot of fuss and arrows directing the examiner to different parts of your answer booklet. If you do wish to add something somewhere in the body of an answer (as opposed to at the end), then clearly indicate with a large asterisk where the additional paragraph belongs.

Criteria for Assessment: PCLM

When assessing your answers, the examiner uses a specific set of criteria (PCLM) to judge what grade to award you. The four criteria are:

- the clarity of your **PURPOSE**: 30 per cent
- the **COHERENCE** of your delivery: 30 per cent
- how well you use **LANGUAGE**: 30 per cent
- how accurate your **MECHANICS** are: 10 per cent.

It is important to note that the PCLM method is how an examiner determines what mark to award you for every question in Paper 1 (and also Paper 2).

These criteria are used implicitly to grade your answers for Section I, Question A, but they are used explicitly to grade your Section I, Question B and Section II answers. For Question A, the examiner uses the PCLM method to mentally weigh up the strengths of your answers, but they express the grades they have decided on only as marks out of 15 or 20. For Question B and the Composing section, the examiner will complete a PCLM grid (like the one below) next to each answer. These grids show how they calculated your grade.

So, for example, an examiner might fill in a grid like this in the margin next to a composition that has been awarded an H4:

Purpose	21	30
Coherence	20	30
Language	18	30
Mechanics	8	10
Total	67	100

Purpose (P)

This is the first mark awarded, and it determines all the others. Essentially, it is an assessment of how well you have answered the question. The words used under *Purpose* in the marking scheme are 'engagement with the set task', 'relevance, focus, clear aim' and 'understanding of genre'. If the question has asked you to do x, y and z, the examiner must determine whether you have done x, y, and z. And if so, how well you have done them. Let's take a question from the 2021 exam paper as an example:

QUESTION B

You have been invited to write a **feature article**, entitled *Monumental Matters – The Story of Statues*, to appear in the magazine supplement of a weekend newspaper. In your article you should: reflect on the long-established tradition of erecting statues to celebrate or memorialise people, explore some of the reasons why commemorative statues may be controversial, and give your views on continuing this tradition into the future.

When assigning a grade for P, an examiner considers the following:

- Is this piece of writing definitely a feature article? Does it read like a feature article you might come across in the Sunday papers, for example?

 For more information on feature articles, see page 3.

- Does this article do all the other things the question asks, and how well does it do them?
  - Does it reflect on the long-established tradition of erecting statues to commemorate people? What is the quality of that reflection?
  - Does it explore some of the reasons why statues can be controversial? What is the quality of that exploration?
  - Does it give the writer's views on continuing the tradition of commemorating people with statues? Are those views interesting/thought-provoking?

> **Hint**
>
> A successful answer does not necessarily have to deal with all parts of the question equally. But it does have to deal with all of them.

After weighing up all these ideas, the examiner makes a value judgement about the answer's purposefulness using this grading system:

H1	H2	H3	H4	H5	H6	H7	H8
15–14	12	11	9	8	6	5	4–0

So, if the examiner judged the mark P was around the H4 level, they would award either 9 or 10 out of 15. If the style of writing is spot-on, and all the tasks have been completed well, there is nothing to stop an examiner awarding 15 out of 15.

Students tend to lose marks quite heavily if they have not quite 'got' the genre they are supposed to be writing in and/or they leave out one or more of the tasks involved in the question.

The C and L grades cannot be higher than the P grade. So, if you get a low P score, it does not matter how coherent your answer is or how excellent your language usage is, those two grades can at best only equal P.

Coherence (C)

This mark is a judgement of how well you can sustain your writing over the entire answer. For example, do your paragraphs link to each other appropriately and logically? If your task is to write in a particular genre, do you adopt the correct style and use it throughout, or is it a little hit and miss in places? Have you planned your answer carefully so that your ideas are sequenced and you follow a definite train of thought from start to finish?

Students who do not plan their answers tend to fall down here. There might be a powerful opening to a persuasive speech, for example, but then the ideas dry up halfway through. Or worse, the student suddenly realises they have picked the wrong side of a debate to argue for, or they have started writing a short story with no clear idea of how to end it.

Language (L)

This mark is a reflection of how well you communicate using the English language. Is your meaning clear? Can you convey your thoughts accurately? Can you demonstrate flexibility depending on the type of writing you are required to produce? Does your imagery soar from the page?

To score highly here, you need to know and obey the rules of syntax and punctuation. You also need to have a broad vocabulary: not to be able to use big words, but to know the best word to convey a particular idea.

Mechanics (M)

This mark is an assessment of your spelling and grammar. Every mistake is noted. For example, have you kept your tenses consistent? Did you write 'has' when you should have written 'had'?

Having read your entire answer, the examiner will count these mistakes to calculate how many marks (if any) to deduct from the 10 per cent available for M. Four errors will result in one mark being taken off. A further five errors, and the next mark is lost. Six more mistakes will cost another mark, and so on. If you misspell a particular word multiple times, it is counted as only one mistake.

Note: if you have been awarded a Reasonable Accommodation or a Spelling and Grammar Waiver, you will not be assessed under M.

Glossary of Common Examination Terms

Compare	Find the similarities and differences between two examples
Consider	Identify positives and negatives/strengths and weaknesses and justify your position
Contrast	Focus on the differences between two examples
Describe	Give a detailed picture in words; give a full account of an issue
Discuss	Explain something by supplying various different views on the issue; explore lots of different facets of the idea; draw conclusions as well as providing your position on the issue
Effective(ly)	Often phrased as 'how effectively does the writer …', the question is asking you to make a value judgement about how well you think a writer employs a certain feature of writing
Element(s)	Features or aspects – you may be asked to discuss the elements of an author's writing style, for example
Explain	Make clear or plain; justify your position using logic and reason; demonstrate your thinking about a particular issue
Explore	Examine in detail; consider multiple facets of a particular issue; and follow a logical train of thought
Extol	Acclaim, applaud and celebrate – focus on the positives of something and present it in its best light
Feature(s)	Elements or aspects – you may be asked to discuss the features of persuasive language evident in a text, for example
Identify	Pinpoint an idea, a fact or an example
Illustrate	Discuss a point with the use of specific examples; inform and enlighten your reader
Impact(s)	Effects or outcomes – you may be asked to discuss how something affected you, for example
Insight(s)	New knowledge – set out what you learned/discovered that you did not know before
Observation(s)	An idea – you may be asked to comment on a writer's observations about a particular issue, for example (in that case, look for expressions of their opinion)
Outline	Describe or summarise; give an account of
Personal response	Your opinion – discuss how something affected you; consider the implications of something and express your thoughts in relation to it
Refer(ence)	Use textual evidence; provide examples that confirm the point you have made
Reflect	Think deeply about/consider and contemplate the importance of something; relate it to yourself, speculate and discuss
State	Present in a brief, clear form
Support	Back up your argument/discussion with evidence and examples

The Five Language Types

There are five types of language that can be used to categorise writing styles:

- language of information
- language of argument
- language of persuasion
- language of narration
- aesthetic language.

> ## Hint
>
> Depending on the purpose and the audience, there will normally be a combination of language types used. Narrative writing without aesthetic language would be dull and lifeless. Exclusively argumentative language might be a little too cold; exclusively persuasive language would be emotive and unsubstantiated. The trick to writing well is figuring out the right combinations of style to suit the task.

i Language of information

Imagine the set of instructions that comes with a new appliance. You do not want to read a long-winded history of the company or poetic descriptions celebrating the product's design; you just want to know what to do to get the appliance working. So, in an instruction leaflet, you would expect:

- simple language
- only the facts you need
- step-by-step instructions, presented in logical order
- clear headings and subheadings
- bullet points and/or numbering of ideas
- diagrams as necessary.

Informative writing is most obviously characterised by facts, statistics, dates, names, numbers and percentages. Opinions of experts in the field of discussion are relevant, but typically, your own opinion is less so. In an examination, you can make 'facts' up. However, be careful not to invent evidence that is obviously inaccurate. For example, above 85 per cent in any objectively conducted survey would be a remarkable figure. So, producing a statistic like '91 per cent of teenagers have been victims of internet fraud' is simply not believable.

It is likely you will be using the language of information in conjunction with other types of language. For example, an argumentative speech should include pertinent facts, statistics and the opinions of experts to support your argument. An informative essay or an article would require you to convey information clearly and succinctly to your reader. In these instances, you would write your information in clear prose paragraphs.

Language of argument

Like the language of information, the language of argument relies on logic and reason. However, here logic and reason are wielded for a purpose: to convince. The language of argument is carefully structured and presents facts in a way that 'builds' a case, step by step, with one idea per paragraph. Each paragraph should be linked to the one preceding it, so that your text combines into a cohesive and convincing whole. For example, you might use linking words such as 'furthermore', 'nevertheless' and 'therefore'.

A sound argument convinces the audience with well-chosen facts, statistics and expert opinions. If you are in an exam and need to make up an expert's opinion to bolster your argument, remember to state their credentials. Be clear as to why your audience should listen to whatever this person has to say. Do not forget that there is likely to be plenty of information in the exam paper itself that you can use in your argument.

Language of persuasion

Persuasive techniques manipulate an audience by targeting their emotions. Think of some of the adverts you have seen: if you buy a certain brand of deodorant, you will become instantly more attractive; if you wear certain trainers, you will become more athletic. The persuasion here has nothing to do with facts.

Powerful speakers play on the audience's fears, stir their anger and indignation, wrench their heart strings. They use carefully chosen emotive words to conjure up vividly effective imagery. Language is emotive when specific words are chosen for their powerful connotations. For example, instead of 'died', the word 'murdered', 'slaughtered' or 'massacred' would be used.

Tone, structure, word order and rhythm are all employed to build a persuasively written text. Listen to some powerful speakers delivering their speeches. Their words have a kind of musicality to them and their message is hammered home using a variety of techniques. For example:

- **Rhetorical questions:** these are questions posed by the speaker in order to make a point. The answer to a rhetorical question is so self-evident and obvious that it pops into the audience's heads without the speaker having to put it there. In this way, they are halfway to agreeing with you already. Here is Shylock's famous example from Shakespeare's *The Merchant of Venice*:

    If you prick us, do we not bleed?
    If you tickle us, do we not laugh?
    If you poison us, do we not die?
    And if you wrong us, shall we not revenge?

- **Repetition:** in the quotation above, Shylock uses not only rhetorical questions, but also a compelling rhetorical device known as **anaphora**, where the first part of each question is repeated. The whole piece then develops a powerful rhythm. Not all repetition needs to be in the form of anaphora. Another forceful technique is compressing the main idea into a simple maxim and returning to it throughout the speech. For example, in Shakespeare's *Julius Caesar*, Mark Antony makes a speech in which he keeps repeating how 'Brutus is an honourable man' in order to emphasise just how *dis*honourable Brutus is. (This is an example of irony, see page xxii.)

- **Vivid imagery:** mental images are powerful because the ideas they convey are simple and memorable. Consider this excerpt from the famous speech by Martin Luther King: 'I have a dream that one day, down in Alabama, with its vicious racists, with its governor having his lips dripping with the words of interposition and nullification ...'. The image of the governor's 'dripping' lips powerfully conveys the idea of him being hypocritical and deceitful without the speaker having to say so.

- **Triads:** lists of three/rule of three – as threes appeal to the human ear, employing them in persuasive writing lends it a compelling rhythm.

- **Inclusive language:** the speaker makes a point of including the audience with words like 'we' and 'us' in order to implicitly connect them with the speaker's opinion. Anyone disagreeing will automatically no longer be part of 'us'. The audience may be addressed directly as 'you', which is also inclusive.
- **Personal anecdotes:** when a speaker shares of themselves, it tends to develop a certain type of intimacy between them and their audience. Subconsciously, this will encourage the audience to trust the person they are listening to.
- **Hyperbole** (exaggeration), **superlative language** (the best/brightest/most amazing) and **humour** are also useful tools in persuasive writing.

Language of narration

A narrative is a story. Whether that story is fact (as in a personal anecdote) or fiction (a short story), the language of narration is used to tell it. Similar to fiction, personal anecdotes use a narrative voice (likely to be the first person) and tend to include characters, descriptive writing and dialogue. Both types of writing are presented in prose paragraphs. You will always be offered at least one option of writing a short story in Section II – Composing.

 For information on short stories, see page 159.

Aesthetic language

Many interpret aesthetic language to mean language that is beautifully crafted. And indeed, this is often the case. Think about poetic language and carefully crafted imagery; vividly evocative metaphorical language and words chosen for their meaning as well as the sounds they make when combined. However, it may be misleading to think that all aesthetic language is, by definition, beautiful. Have a look at this example, taken from Wilfred Owen's poem 'Dulce et Decorum Est':

> If in some smothering dreams, you too could pace
> Behind the wagon that we flung him in,
> And watch the white eyes writhing in his face,
> His hanging face, like a devil's sick of sin;
> If you could hear, at every jolt, the blood
> Come gargling from the froth-corrupted lungs,
> Obscene as cancer, bitter as the cud
> Of vile, incurable sores on innocent tongues,—

The author is describing something he witnessed on a First World War battlefield. It sickened and disgusted him; in turn, his language sickens and disgusts us. However, the language used is still aesthetic because of its carefully crafted vividness.

The only time not to employ aesthetic language is when the task requires exclusively informative language: where the cold facts need to be presented in an entirely objective and clinical manner. All other types of writing are going to contain some aesthetic devices in order to make the language vivid and memorable. Narrative language in particular relies on aesthetics. However, speeches, articles and discursive essays also need to create vivid and lasting imagery in the mind of the reader.

Summary: Five language types

	Purpose	Features	Suitable genres
Language of information	Communicate information clearly	• Clear, specific, simple language • Necessary information only • Facts and statistics • Expert opinions	• Reports • Leaflets • Guidelines • Manuals
Language of argument	Use logic and reason to convince your audience	• Facts and statistics • Expert opinions • Information presented to build a case	• Debates • Opinion pieces • Letters to the editor • Speeches
Language of persuasion	Use emotion to convince your audience	• Emotive words • Rhetorical questions • Repetition • Triads • Vivid imagery • Inclusive language • Personal anecdotes • Hyperbole • Superlative language • Humour	• Debates • Competition entries • Advertisements • Promotional pitches • Inspirational speeches/talks
Language of narration	Tell a story	• Plot (beginning, middle, end) • Narrative voice • Characters • Descriptive writing • Dialogue	• Short stories • Personal essays • Memoirs • Diary entries
Aesthetic language	Bring your writing to life	• Carefully crafted imagery • Evocative language • Sensual language (appeals to the five senses) • Techniques using the sounds of words and word combinations	• Short stories • Poems • Descriptive essays • Discursive essays • Speeches • Articles

Imagery and Figures of Speech

'Imagery' describes any mental picture conveyed by a writer/speaker into the minds of their readers/audience. The image does not have to be visual, but it will tend to appeal to one of the five senses, or perhaps a combination of them.

Figures of speech (also known as figurative language) are particular techniques employed by writers in order to convey sometimes quite complex images to the reader. You are guaranteed to come across examples of some of these established techniques in the three texts of Section I.

Most examples of figurative language used by an author make good quotes to use when discussing the author's style of writing in response to Question A (iii). If you can:
- recognise where a technique is being used,
- identify the particular technique,
- explain how the technique works
- and discuss the *effect* created by the use of the technique,

then you are a long way down the road to formulating your answer to the 20-mark comprehension question on style.

Remember to use the **QNED** method when discussing figurative language:
> **Q**uote the image
> **N**ame the technique
> **E**xplain how the technique works
> **D**iscuss the effect created by the technique.

The techniques

There are two main categories of figurative language: images that compare things to something else, and images that make use of the sounds words make.

1. Images that compare things to something else

Technique	How it works	Example	Explanation	Discussion
Simile	Compares two things using the words 'like', 'as' or 'than'	'The ship receding with every wave, sometimes standing perpendicularly on her stern and shaking like a palsied man' (Theme 5, TEXT 1)	Compares the ship to a man with palsy (seized with tremors)	It conveys the ship's violent movements in the storm and the helplessness felt by the passengers on board.

Technique	How it works	Example	Explanation	Discussion
Metaphor	Compares two things without using 'like', 'as' or 'than'; it says something is something else	'they had fanned their fictions from the sparks of real life' (Theme 4, TEXT 1)	Compares an author's inspiration for their characters to someone fanning a flame from the embers of a fire	Real life is seen as the glowing 'sparks' of a fire. Some authors base their fictional characters on real people, and from such small sparks of inspiration, the 'fire' of literature can be coaxed into being.
Personification	Particular kind of metaphor where something non-human or non-living is given human or living qualities	'The town is quiet, its breath held.' (Theme 4, TEXT 2)	Describes the town as holding its breath as if it were a living creature	Someone holds their breath if they expect something significant is about to happen. Here, the town itself appears to be waiting in expectation, which creates a sense of anticipation.

2. Images that make use of the sounds words make

Technique	How it works	Example	Explanation	Discussion
Alliteration	Beginning sound of words is repeated	'barrels, boxes, cans, berths' (Theme 5, TEXT 1)	Repeats plosive 'b' sound	It emphasises the noise and chaos on board a ship in a storm.
Assonance	Vowel sound inside words is repeated, usually to create an effective rhythm	'broken only by the hollow lilt of an owl' (Theme 4, TEXT 2)	Repeats long 'o' sound	It evokes the lonely sound of the owl's cry.
Sibilance	Sounds such as 's', 'sh', 'th' and 'f' are repeated, often to create a euphonious (pleasing-sounding) combination of sounds	'in that coast-town of seagulls and steeples, a strange beauty seemed to glitter from its windows' (Theme 4, TEXT 1)	Repeats 's' sound	The words flow from one to the other easily to emphasise the beauty of the image.
Onomatopoeia	Words echo the sound they describe	'My can of spray paint rips into the gentle night, releasing a loud *psssht* into an open mouth of fangs.' (Theme 3, TEXT 2)	'*psssht*' replicates the sound of spray paint being applied	The auditory images (the word 'rips' also metaphorically conveys the suddenness of the sound) make the action more immediate.

Technique	How it works	Example	Explanation	Discussion
Pun	A play on words: where one word can mean different things, or two words sound similar, a pun exploits the word's multiple uses	'Eventually the public pressure was too much, and you had the world's eyes on you, so you started to act. Not acting as in taking climate action but acting as in role-playing.' (Theme 6, TEXT 1)	'act' is used for its different meanings: (1) to put an action into effect, and (2) to perform or play a role	We first interpret the words 'you started to act' favourably, as if the speaker is commending the audience for taking action. However, this is quickly subverted when we understand the second meaning: a strong criticism of their inaction.

Other figurative techniques

Technique	How it works	Example	Explanation	Discussion
Hyperbole	Exaggeration – often used for rhetorical effect	'You have worked so long and hard on it, you know its every line and comma.' (Theme 4, TEXT 1)	Exaggerates the extent to which the author knows the minute details of the novel he is working on	It underscores the exhaustive hard work and constant revision that goes into writing a novel
Apostrophe	Rhetorical device whereby a speaker or writer addresses a third person, not the intended audience	'You [world leaders] are distancing yourself further and further away from us and from reality.' (Theme 6, TEXT 1)	Greta Thunberg is speaking to the assembled members of the Austrian World Summit of 2021, but she constantly addresses a third party, or group referred to as 'the people in power'	By addressing world leaders directly, Thunberg assumes the role of spokesperson for us, the audience. 'We' are characterised as belonging to the right side of the issue, while governments are depicted as being on the wrong side.

Irony

Irony is all about opposites. If it is cold and miserable outside and someone says 'Nice weather we're having', they are being ironic because they mean the opposite of what they say. Understanding irony often depends entirely on the tone of voice used or on the precise context of the statement in question. This is why it can be so difficult to pick up – especially for people for whom English is a second language.

There are three main types of irony that you are likely to come across: dramatic irony, situational irony and verbal irony.

1. Dramatic irony

In this case, a scriptwriter ensures that we, the audience, have information that one (or more) of the characters does not have. This technique is used to great effect when a character speaks and we grasp a deeper significance to the words than the other characters on stage do.

For example, in Shakespeare's *Othello*, the characters constantly refer to Iago as 'honest Iago', not knowing that he is the exact opposite of honest. However, we, the audience, know he is an absolute villain who is lying to everyone, and so we 'get' the dramatic irony.

2. Situational irony

This literary technique involves the author subverting the reader's expectation of how events should play out; often having the opposite happen instead. For example, imagine reading a story where a character is run over by an ambulance. We expect an ambulance to help us if we get injured. We do not expect an ambulance to be the reason for someone's injuries. An example from real life is when the actor Charlie Chaplin once entered a Charlie Chaplin look-alike contest and came third.

Stories can make use of situational irony in order to create a sense of poetic justice. For example, Macbeth's every attempt to avoid the prophecies of the witches, instead of preventing them from coming true, actually makes them come about.

3. Verbal irony

This is where a speaker says the opposite of what they mean. For example, when someone spills coffee on their shirt and says, 'Great! Just what I needed!'

Sarcasm

Verbal irony has a very close relation called sarcasm. Sarcastic comments tend to use irony in the sense that the speaker says the opposite of what they mean. What makes sarcasm different is that it is pointed at someone; it is used to mock; and it has a negative tone.

'Thrift, thrift, Horatio! The funeral bak'd meats did coldly furnish forth the marriage tables.' This is how Hamlet explains the haste with which his mother remarried after the death of his father. 'Thrift' means being sensible with money – so he is saying their quick marriage was a great idea: they saved the expense of catering at the wedding by scheduling it straight after the funeral. But Hamlet's joke is a bitter one because he is devastated by his mother's marriage, and he loathes his uncle who is now her husband – so he is using sarcasm here.

Sarcasm can also be employed while speaking the literal truth. Here is where tone becomes crucial. Imagine a frustrated parent looking at their teenager's room and saying, 'You know, there's an amazing invention called a vacuum cleaner.' These words are true, but the irony resides in the parent's implied meaning that the teenager has never heard of a vacuum cleaner, which is not really the case. The words are sarcastic because they are pointed at the teenager and are meant as a criticism of their untidiness.

6S Answering Strategy

The 6S answering strategy can be used for answering any text-based question. Section I of your exam paper contains three texts and Question A for each text comprises three comprehension questions. You can use the 6S strategy when answering all three of these questions.

The 6S strategy is a step-by step guide to help you to:
- clearly understand the question
- identify which information to use from the text in your answer
- organise the information
- present, explain and discuss the information clearly in your answer.

The strategy involves the following six steps:

6S **Step 1:** Simplify the question by identifying the key words.

6S **Step 2:** Select the required information from the text.

6S **Step 3:** Sort the information by choosing the most useful examples.

6S **Step 4:** State your answer.

6S **Step 5:** Support your answer with the evidence you have selected from the text.

6S **Step 6:** Spell out to your reader how the evidence supports your answer.

To see this method in action, look at any of the Exam Mechanics boxes for Question A answers in this toolkit.

🛈 Hint

The 6S strategy can also be used to answer text-based questions in Paper 2. The only difference is that you will not have the texts in front of you to select from: this step has to be done mentally.

Theme 1
New Frontiers

In this theme we will be looking at people who, in their own ways, have pushed, or are pushing, against boundaries.

The paragraphs below are taken from the three texts we will be exploring over the course of this theme. Take a look at the three samples and discuss the following questions:

Discuss

1. Of which genre of writing is each text an example?
2. What features or styles of writing helped you to identify the genre of each of these samples?
3. Where would you be likely to encounter each of these genres?

Sample 1 – Text 1

There's been research into one-way trips to Mars including 'Mars-One,' the Dutch organization hoping to establish a permanent human colony on the red planet. And more recently, NASA planned a return-trip using its rocket, Space Launch System (SLS).

The SLS mission to Mars — a 40-million-mile trip through a frozen expanse of dark and deathly emptiness — is where Carson plans to be by the time she's 29. The harsh realities and risks of traveling to Mars don't seem to faze Carson at all, not even the real risk of never returning to Earth.

Sample 2 – Text 2

The Shinkansen bullet train from Tokyo to Kakunodate was going so fast it felt like a plane perpetually taxiing on the runway before take-off. It was travelling at such speed that the handwriting in my diary was turning out shaky and uneven. We were flying past conifer forests and Japanese maple trees and snowy mountains. I was writing about the things I had seen in the Tokyo National Museum two days before.

Sample 3 – Text 3

If I had never dropped out, I would have never dropped in on this calligraphy class, and personal computers might not have the wonderful typography that they do. Of course it was impossible to connect the dots looking forward when I was in college. But it was very, very clear looking backward 10 years later.

Again, you can't connect the dots looking forward; you can only connect them looking backward. So you have to trust that the dots will somehow connect in your future. You have to trust in something — your gut, destiny, life, karma, whatever. This approach has never let me down, and it has made all the difference in my life.

SECTION I   COMPREHENDING   (100 marks)

TEXT 1 – A MISSION TO MARS

This text consists of two elements: a feature article about the aspiring astronaut Alyssa Carson that has been taken from the online tech blog site TheNextWeb.com (TNW), and a collection of four posters promoting interplanetary journeys.

> ⚠ **Hint**
>
> Always read with a pen in your hand!
> Before reading a comprehension text like the one below, read the instructions, then all of the questions that follow. Highlight the key words in the questions. Then, when you read the text, you can highlight possible ideas to use in your answers. Reading the questions first will also give you a good idea about what to expect in the text before you start reading it.

Meet Alyssa Carson, the 18-year-old training to become the first human on Mars

At just three years old, Alyssa Carson knew she wanted to be an astronaut, and since then, she's worked tirelessly. Carson could soon become the first human to set foot on Mars – even if it means never returning back to Earth.

'My fascination with space all started when I watched an episode of the cartoon *The Backyardigans* called "A Mission to Mars",' Carson told TNW. '[In that episode] all the friends went on this imaginary adventure in their backyard which eventually brought them to Mars. I had the poster for that episode hung on my bedroom wall for years.'

Growing up, Carson's imagination blew up with questions about space and space travel which eventually led her [to be] America's best chance of landing on Mars. At 16 years old, Carson became the youngest person to have ever graduated from the Advanced Space Academy, the first person to have completed all of NASA's seven Space Camps, and received the certification in applied astronautics. This officially makes Carson certified to do a suborbital research flight and venture into space, all before receiving her driver's permit.

'Technically, I'm allowed to fly into space and just being able to say that, especially in my teens, feels amazing,' Carson said.

So far, the training Carson has done to prepare for a trip to Mars is with Project PoSSUM, a private citizen science organization which works in developing the Final Frontier Space Suit Design, EVA.

[...]

When will humans go to Mars?

A trip to Mars may only seem possible in an episode of *The Backyardigans*, but last year, NASA announced its plans to launch a mission to the red planet by 2030. Since Mars is in our solar system, it's an obvious target for human exploration. Carson's potential mission to Mars will involve searching for lifeforms, understanding the surface and the planet's evolution, and preparing for potential future human colonization.

There's been research into one-way trips to Mars including 'Mars-One,' the Dutch organization hoping to establish a permanent human colony on the red planet. And more recently, NASA planned a return-trip using its rocket, Space Launch System (SLS).

The SLS mission to Mars — a 40-million-mile trip through a frozen expanse of dark and deathly emptiness — is where Carson plans to be by the time she's 29. The harsh realities and risks of traveling to Mars don't seem to faze Carson at all, not even the real risk of never returning to Earth.

On NASA's planned return-trip to Mars, this means Carson would be away from Earth for approximately two to three years, and that's not the scariest part. As Elon Musk, an aspiring carrier of Martian pioneers, said in 2016: 'It's dangerous and probably people will die.' On Monday, Musk said thermal rockets would be 'a great area of research for NASA.' The SpaceX CEO highlighted how the alternative to rocket fuel could mean faster travel times around the solar system.

'The radiation levels in space don't scare me because I've learned about it for so long and it's just become a norm at this point,' Carson said. 'There's always a sense of fear that something could go wrong since no mission to space has ever been 100 percent safe. But I definitely believe that a mission to Mars, and all the benefits we can get from it, outweigh any of the risks.'

One of the main reasons to visit Mars is to colonize the planet since the world's population could increase to 9.9 billion by 2050, according to a report by the Population Reference Bureau (PRB). But questions are being raised around whether humans deserve a second chance at inhabiting a planet given the current climate crisis we're currently living in.

'It's kind of ironic because the things we're doing to Earth, that are actually very harmful to it, are exactly what we need to do to Mars,' Carson explained. 'Since Mars is further away from the sun, it's colder and we need to heat it up. We're doing this on Earth pretty successfully so I guess we have that skill down.'

In the future, Carson hopes humans will inhabit multiple planets, including Jupiter. 'Mars is our first level of learning how to live on new planets and developing those skills on how we can adapt to a new planet.'

[...]

Other than potentially becoming the first human to visit Mars, Carson hopes her journey to space inspires other girls to follow their dreams. 'When I was three and dreamt of being an astronaut and going to Mars, it was probably the most ridiculous dream I could have picked. But the more I've worked towards it, the more of a reality it's becoming,' Carson said.

Footnote on Feature Articles

News articles and feature articles can look similar because they both have **eye-catching headlines** and are considered **non-fiction** writing. Feature articles often focus on a **person or place** that would **appeal to a wide audience**; this is known as a **human interest story**. Feature articles that shine a spotlight on a specific individual are usually written in the **third person**, which allows the writer to incorporate **facts and figures**. The featured individual's opinions can be included as **direct quotations**.

Feature articles give **depth and detail** to particular **newsworthy events** that appeal to a wide audience. For example, TEXT 1 focuses on an individual with popular appeal – a young, female trainee astronaut.

They can also include **sensational or dramatic elements** to engage their readers. For example, TEXT 1 includes a quote from Elon Musk: 'It's dangerous and probably people will die.'

Feature articles can be written in the **past or present tense**. The author of TEXT 1 uses the present tense to give a sense of immediacy.

Poster 1

Poster 2

Poster 3

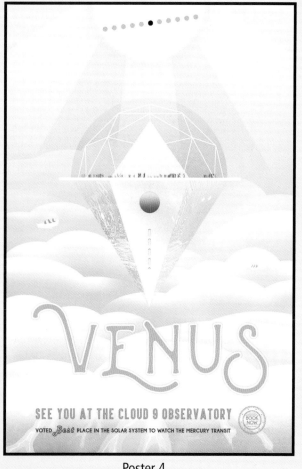

Poster 4

QUESTION A – 50 Marks

(i) Based on your reading of the written element of TEXT 1, what are the three most important qualities Alyssa Carson possesses that make her a suitable candidate for being the first human on Mars? (15)

(ii) We are told that 'Growing up, Carson's imagination blew up with questions about space and space travel'. From the texts you have studied for your Leaving Certificate course*, identify a moment or an episode in a text where you felt your imagination 'blow up with questions'. Explain your choice and give examples of the questions the moment or episode evoked in you. (15)

* Texts specified for study for Leaving Certificate English, including poetry, single texts and texts (including films) prescribed for comparative study.

(iii) Based on your reading of the written element of TEXT 1, discuss four stylistic features that make the extract from the article an engaging and informative piece of writing. Support your response with reference to four stylistic features evident in the text. (20)

Exam Mechanics

QUESTION A (i)

Question A (i) is usually a straightforward comprehension question that requires you to find specific information from the text. Sometimes it will tell you to find three points and sometimes it will not specify a number. Either way, find three points.

The 6S method can be used here to help you to find the relevant information in the text and to write your answer.

For more information on the 6S answering strategy, see page xxiv.

6S Simplify

As the question will set out exactly what you need to find, start by highlighting the key words.

(i) Based on your reading of the written element of TEXT 1, what are the three most important qualities Alyssa Carson possesses that make her a suitable candidate for being the first human on Mars? (15)

Before you start reading the text, you can already make a fairly good guess that you will be looking for anything that describes Carson as brave, resilient, determined, hard-working, particularly gifted or intelligent, etc.

6S Select

As you are reading the text, highlight any references to Carson's personality or character, especially those aspects that you think make her suitable for being the first person to travel to Mars.

6S Sort

You may have highlighted more than three qualities. Here is where the first part of the question comes in: you have been asked to choose the three qualities that are the 'most important'. You have to decide which three you believe are most important, and you will need to be able to explain what makes them the most important.

You do not necessarily have to start your answer with the most important aspect. You may decide to work up to that by discussing the two other important aspects first.

6S State, support and spell out

Your examiner will expect you to answer Question A (i) with three paragraphs. Each paragraph contains three parts. For example, in the first paragraph you will:

!! Hint

Some students like to write an introduction before commencing their answer. However, this is not compulsory. If you do, keep it brief.

1. **State** the first aspect of Carson's character you think is important in making her suitable for travel to Mars.

> The most important quality that Alyssa Carson possesses is her dedication and single-minded pursuit of her goal of being an astronaut.

2. **Support** your idea with a quotation or reference.

> She first made her decision at the age of three, and since then she has 'worked tirelessly' to achieve it. She says that her dream may have been 'ridiculous' at first, but that 'the more I've worked towards it, the more of a reality it's becoming'.

 For advice on how to punctuate quotations properly, see page 29.

3. **Spell out** how your quote supports your idea and why the aspect you have chosen is the most important.

> This demonstrates that over the intervening years it was her hard work and perseverance that brought her dream closer to reality.

Follow this process for each of the three paragraphs of your answer.

 **Sample Answer**

QUESTION A (iii)

A brief introduction demonstrates engagement with the question.

First stated answer. Quotation supports statement.

I found the extract from the article both engaging to read and informative. The subject matter itself is very engaging because the idea of a teenage girl being 'America's best chance of landing on Mars' is particularly appealing. Alyssa Carson is a fascinating high achiever. She is the 'youngest person to have ever graduated from the Advanced Space Academy', she has done 'all of NASA's seven Space Camps' and she has 'received the certification in applied astronautics'.

Spells out why the evidence supports the statement.

She has achieved all this while still being a teenager, which makes her a very interesting person to read about.

Linking phrase connects paragraph two with paragraph one. Second stated answer.

I also found the use of expert quotation very engaging. Elon Musk is a world-famous investor in space travel, and so the inclusion of his observation that 'It's dangerous and probably people will die' makes this article intriguing. We assume that Musk, because of his entrepreneurial activities, has assessed the danger of space flight correctly, and so his words emphasise for us how perilous a mission to Mars would be. The effect of this is that our admiration for Alyssa's courage is amplified still further, making this an engaging article.

Supporting quotation.

Spells out how the quotation supports the statement.

Links paragraph three with paragraph two. Third stated answer.

The sense of danger is enhanced by the writer's use of vivid imagery. 'The SLS mission to Mars — a 40-million-mile trip through a frozen expanse of dark and deathly emptiness' is a particularly evocative image. The repeated heavy 'd' sound in the alliterative 'dark and deathly' adds to the ominous mood by making the emptiness of space seem especially forbidding. The use of vivid imagery deepens our understanding of the dangers Alyssa will face, intriguing us even further.

Fourth stated answer deals with the second key word in the question: 'informative' (the earlier paragraphs discuss the first key word: 'engaging').

The writing is also highly informative. For example, we learn that Alyssa's potential mission will involve 'searching for lifeforms, understanding the surface and the planet's evolution, and preparing for potential future human colonization'. We gain a better understanding of what her mission will entail, and I learned that NASA plans to 'launch a mission to the red planet by 2030' and eventually to colonise Mars. We also discover the necessity for this because the world's population is expected to reach nearly ten billion 'by 2050', a fact I found both surprising and disturbing.

Changed from US spelling because the text is not being quoted directly.

Brief conclusion.

The four stylistic features discussed above show that the style in which this article is written is both engaging and informative.

Theme 1: New Frontiers

QUESTION B – 50 Marks

Imagine that you have decided to embark upon one of the journeys depicted in the four posters on page 4. Write a **letter of application** to the relevant space agency. You should set out the qualities you possess that make you suitable for consideration, as well as why you have chosen this destination, and explain what it was about the particular poster that persuaded you.

Exam Mechanics

QUESTION B

Read the question and highlight the main task. This task will inform your entire answer. It will indicate what **genre** you will be writing in, what your **purpose** is and what **layout/structure** to use. Identify the type of **audience** you will be writing for, which will determine the appropriate **style and register**. **Number the points you need to cover** to make sure that your answer addresses all aspects of the question.

> Imagine that you have decided to embark upon one of the journeys depicted in the four posters on page 4. Write a **letter of application** to the relevant space agency. You should set out the qualities you possess that make you suitable for consideration **(1)**, as well as why you have chosen this destination **(2)**, and explain what it was about the particular poster that persuaded you **(3)**.

Genre: the question asks you to write a letter of application, which means you will be writing a formal letter.

Purpose: the purpose of your letter is to persuade the space agency that you are a suitable candidate to send on your chosen journey.

Layout/structure: formal letters have a strict layout that includes the sender's address, the recipient's address, the date, a formal greeting and a formal sign-off.

Audience: your letter will be read by people who work for the space agency – perhaps your future boss and staff in the human resources department.

Style and register: use a formal style of writing and keep your tone professional.

(1) Use the language of argument to convince the agency that you are suitable for selection and include lots of logical evidence to support your application.

(2) Use the language of persuasion and aesthetic language to explain your choice of destination.

(3) Discuss the visual impact of your chosen poster to demonstrate your visual literacy.

 For information on the different styles of language, see page xvi. For information on how to analyse visual texts, see page 60.

A-Z Grammar Guide

Using numbers in written text

The numbers 1 to 10 should be written out in words: one, two, three, etc. Ordinal numbers should also be written as words: first, second, third, etc. You can see these rules being observed in TEXT 1:

- 'At just three years old ...'
- '... the first person to have completed all of NASA's seven Space Camps ...'

Numbers 11 and above should be shown as numerals. This style can also be seen in TEXT 1:

- 'At 16 years old ...'
- '... a 40-million-mile trip through a frozen expanse ... by the time she's 29.'

Note: any number that starts a sentence is usually written out in words. For example: Twelve people have walked on the moon.

TEXT 2 – TRAVEL WRITING

This text is based on edited extracts adapted from *Elsewhere* by Rosita Boland, a memoir of her travels through Japan, published in 2018.

The Shinkansen bullet train from Tokyo to Kakunodate was going so fast it felt like a plane perpetually taxiing on the runway before take-off. It was travelling at such speed that the handwriting in my diary was turning out shaky and uneven. We were flying past conifer forests and Japanese maple trees and snowy mountains. I was writing about the things I had seen in the Tokyo National Museum two days before.

I had been fascinated to observe a succession of men standing with intense concentration before displays of swords in the Honkan building, the main part of the sprawling museum. There was an entire gallery given over to swords, some of them once used by samurai. To my utterly untrained eye, they all looked more or less the same, but clearly they were not.

I had once changed planes at Amsterdam's Schiphol airport with a colleague en route to an assignment in Asia, and we had gone for sashimi and beer to a sushi place on the airport's concourse. It wasn't a fancy place, or even very large; more a kind of diner set-up with high stools at a counter. We camped out there for almost two hours while waiting for our flight.

For that entire time, a man worked solely on sharpening the blade of one particular knife. He had been at it when we arrived, so who knows for how long he had already been working

on it. He never even looked up at us. He was totally focused on his work. He had some kind of whetstone, and every now and then he stopped, tested the blade's edge with his finger and spent some time staring at the knife, carefully turning it over and over in his hand, regarding the edge from every angle before returning to his minutely precise grinding.

I was transfixed by his dedication and wished I could stay there and keep watching, but our onward flight was called, and we had to go, leaving him bent over the same knife, still at his seemingly unending task. It had the drama and intensity of performance theatre. That was just a routine modern knife in an ordinary sushi place in an airport. Looking into the glass case in Tokyo's flagship museum where historically important swords were displayed, I could scarcely imagine the levels of skilled craftsmanship and the number of hours necessary in honing blades for samurai.

The displays I had spent the most time looking at in the Tokyo museum were of decorative arts; lacquer work, mostly. Every time I thought I had seen the most exquisite of pieces, the next cabinet yielded something even more stunning. There were writing boxes and cosmetic boxes and tea caddies, but what I was struggling to try and write as the shinkansen arrowed northwards through Honshu, was a description of how exceptionally beautiful these objects were.

The lacquerware was sometimes red, a deep sealing-wax red colour, but mainly black. Black with variations of gold and silver decoration. One of the eighteenth-century writing boxes I had looked at was from the Edo period, decorated with golden grasses and mother-of-pearl inlaid flowers. Although the box was eighteenth century, the technique of sprinkled gold designs, called maki-e – so the museum information boards had told me – dated from the eighth century.

[...]

Eventually, I moved on to ceramics. The tea bowls and plates and vases were so delicate and so old. I tried to imagine people deep in the past eating and drinking from these vessels, or arranging flowers in vases destined to long outlive them, regarded by people like me, existing in a world so utterly different from theirs: one of air travel and technology and globalization. It almost hurt my head to think of this museum, as I did of every museum I visited, as a time capsule to the past.

Then, I noticed various pieces that looked different in some way. Beautiful plates and bowls mysteriously veined here and there with gold. A plate with red hollyhocks on a blue background partially rimmed with a golden edge. I looked more closely, puzzled. The gold parts in each piece were irregular, random; not part of the pattern.

And so, I came across kintsukuroi, or 'golden joinery'. This is the Japanese art of repairing broken ceramics with lacquer mixed with powdered gold or silver and understanding that the piece is more beautiful for having been mended. The cracks are thus highlighted, as in the gold rim on the hollyhock plate. The repair work is the opposite of usual mending, where you try to make the joins look invisible. The Japanese aesthetic sees the fact of an object being broken as a transition in the life of the piece, not an ending of its existence or cessation of its original purpose.

It was all this I was trying to record in my diary as the train travelled northwards, towards Kakunodate.

Footnote on Travel Writing

Travel writing is found in dedicated travel magazines and on travel-related websites and also in more mainstream publications such as the Sunday newspapers. The genre includes **feature articles that focus on a specific travel destination**, and also **book-length, memoir-type publications** such as TEXT 2. Travel writing is often written in the **first person**, as is the case with TEXT 2.

The purpose of travel writing can be to **inform and advise** or simply to **entertain**. The travel writer usually aims to **inspire the reader to explore different places** and/or to **convey an appreciation for other cultures**. You can expect the writer to focus on their chosen location's **architecture**, **history**, **traditions**, **food** and any other **must-see attractions**, such as the Tokyo National Museum in TEXT 2.

The genre is defined as **non-fiction prose** and is very often filled with **descriptive imagery**. The author of TEXT 2 endeavours to convey to her readers as vivid a narrative as possible through the use of **aesthetic language**. For example: 'Beautiful plates and bowls mysteriously veined here and there with gold. A plate with red hollyhocks on a blue background partially rimmed with a golden edge.'

According to Katie Diederichs of the travel website *Two Wandering Soles*:

Travel writing should be exciting to read. It should make the reader feel like they are next to you on the powdery beach with a warm breeze tickling their shoulders. They should be able to taste the curry, rich with coconut milk, lime, and lemongrass. They should be able to hear the chaos of the city traffic and smell the sewage wafting from the grimy streets.

QUESTION A – 50 Marks

(i) Based on your reading of TEXT 2, explain three insights you gain into Japanese culture, as witnessed by Rosita Boland. (15)

(ii) In TEXT 2, the author Rosita Boland describes Tokyo National Museum, and all museums she has visited, as 'a time capsule to the past'. Written and visual texts could similarly be described as 'time capsules to the past'. With reference to any text on your Leaving Certificate English course*, identify an image, moment or episode that, in your opinion, vividly transported you to a previous time and/or place. Explain the insight(s) you gained about this time and/or place by engaging with this image, moment or episode. (15)

* Texts specified for study for Leaving Certificate English, including poetry, single texts and texts (including films) prescribed for comparative study.

(iii) Based on your reading of TEXT 2, would you agree that it is the author's narrative and aesthetic style of writing that makes the piece so appealing? Support your response with reference to four stylistic features evident in the text. (20)

Sample Answer

QUESTION A (i)

Identifies the first idea/observation selected to answer the question.	The author recounts the time when she watched a Japanese man sharpen the blade of a knife at a sushi restaurant in Schiphol airport. He worked at this 'precise grinding' for the entire time, 'almost two hours', she was there. She says he was 'totally focused on his work' and she was 'transfixed by his dedication'. She realises that if an ordinary knife at a sushi restaurant requires this level of dedication, then the time and skills involved in honing the blades of samurai swords are 'scarcely' imaginable. This anecdote reveals the dedicated craftsmanship and desire for perfection evident in Japanese culture.
Quotations are used sparingly to support the observation. Short phrases blend with the point being made.	
Addresses the first insight gained into Japanese culture. Note: the paragraph could just as easily state the insight at the start, followed by the supporting evidence.	
A linking statement connects this paragraph with the preceding one. The selected insight is introduced earlier in the second paragraph than in the first.	The author also describes the Japanese appreciation of beautifully crafted objects. When she visited the museum in Tokyo, she viewed 'exquisite' pieces, including ceramics and writing boxes covered in stunning decorations. She was constantly surprised by how 'exceptionally beautiful' these pieces were. The insight gained here is that Japanese culture values and beautifies everyday objects such as cabinets, tea caddies and ceramics, and that it is a culture that surrounds itself with beauty.
Supporting quotations are kept short and structured to flow with the discussion.	
The second insight is stated explicitly, demonstrating a clear response to the question.	

Theme 1: New Frontiers

| A linking phrase connects the third paragraph with the second. | A third insight gained by reading this piece is the concept of *kintsukuroi*, or 'golden joinery'. In Western culture, we tend to repair items in a way that conceals the damage and makes the joins invisible, whereas in Japan, lacquer with gold or silver powder is used to emphasise the cracks. Japanese culture celebrates the repaired object and considers the breakage to be 'a transition in the life of the piece'. Thus, Boland demonstrates how objects are beautifully repaired and valued in Japanese culture. |

Instead of specific quotations, the supporting evidence here is summarised to demonstrate understanding.

A quotation is also provided to support the third insight.

The final sentence returns to address the question explicitly.

Exam Mechanics

QUESTION A (ii)

Question A (ii) is sometimes called the 'wildcard' question and some students have been a little perturbed to find something unexpected here. Whatever comes up, remember: do not panic! You will most likely be asked to discuss your opinion on a topic related to the text. The above example asks you to refer to a text you have studied for Paper 2.

The 6S method can help here. The only difference is that we will not be using the text on the exam paper.

6S Simplify

Simplify the question by highlighting the key words. What is the question asking you to do?

> In TEXT 2, the author Rosita Boland describes Tokyo National Museum, and all museums she has visited, as 'a time capsule to the past'. Written and visual texts could similarly be described as 'time capsules to the past'. With reference to any text on your Leaving Certificate English course, identify an image, moment or episode that, in your opinion, vividly transported you to a previous time and/or place. Explain the insight(s) you gained about this time and/or place by engaging with this image, moment or episode.

For this question, you can answer fully without making any reference to TEXT 2. Instead, you need to:

- **Identify** one key image, moment or episode from one of your studied texts that transported you to a past time and/or place. Remember: *analyse, do not summarise* – you can assume that your examiner knows your texts extremely well.
- **Explain** what it was you learned about this time/place by reading/viewing the text. What new perspective on life in the past – whether it is the distant or recent past – did you get from this text? Give a personal response, clearly explaining the new knowledge you gained about the past from engaging with your chosen text.

6S **Select**

Select **one** image, moment or episode from **one** of your texts. Choose carefully to make sure you have three insights to discuss. Your choice has to 'transport' you to a past time/place, so selecting something that is quite different from our own time and place will provide more elements to discuss. As you have to explain what insight(s) about the past you gained from your chosen image, moment or episode, try to select one that made you think 'that was strange/interesting/unusual', 'I did not know people did that', etc.

> ## Hint
>
> By the end of your Leaving Certificate course, you will have studied:
> - A **Shakespearean play**, which will be full of **images**, **moments** and **episodes** that could **vividly transport you to the past**. The difficulty might be in deciding which moment would be the best to select from your text:
>   - *Othello* – set in Venice and Cyprus in the mid-1500s
>   - *King Lear* – set in England over 2,700 years ago
>   - *Macbeth* – set in Scotland about 1,000 years ago
>   - *Hamlet* – set in Denmark about 700 years ago.
> - **Three comparative texts** (probably a play, a novel and a film), each of which is a substantial work and offers plenty of choice. During your studies, you are likely to have learned about **key moments** in these texts, so why not use one of them?
> - A minimum of **five poets** and a number of poems for each, each of which will be full of **imagery**. Since all were written in the past, all are available for use with this answer. Many will be concerned with particular, and evocative, **places**.

Remember to make your references to your chosen text as specific as possible; quotations will certainly impress your examiner.

6S **Sort**

Once you have selected your image, moment or episode, you will need to sort your ideas concerning it. Why did you choose this one? What about it transports you to a previous time and/or place? What insight(s) did you gain into that time or place?

6S **State, support and spell out**

Your examiner will expect you to answer Question A (ii) with three paragraphs.

1. **State** which text you have chosen (do not forget to give the author's name) and which image, moment or episode you have identified. Give a very brief synopsis of your choice, bearing in mind that this is not a Paper 2 essay question.

   > The text I have studied that vividly transported me to *the past/a different place* is *[insert title]* by *[insert author]*. The *image/moment/episode* I have identified from this text is *[insert brief description]*.

2. **Support** your choice with a reference to your chosen image, moment or episode. Why this particular moment? Why was this the most vivid out of all your possible choices? You do not have to use a quotation here, but if you can supply one, it will demonstrate your textual knowledge.

3. **Spell out** exactly why your chosen image, moment or episode vividly transported you to the past or to a different place AND explain what **insight(s)** you gained from engaging with it. In other words, state what you learned about the past or this place by reading or viewing the text.

   > ## Hint
   >
   > 'Insight' means understanding, wisdom or observation.

Theme 1: New Frontiers

QUESTION B – 50 Marks

A website dedicated to travel writing (both domestic and international) has asked you to contribute an **article** aimed at encouraging young people to explore their own locality more closely. Write the text of the article you would contribute, in which you extol the virtues of your own locality, describe some of its most appealing attractions and inspire your readers to rediscover the area in which they live. Your article could be light-hearted in tone, or serious, or a combination of the two.

Exam Mechanics

QUESTION B

Read the question and highlight the main task. This task will inform your entire answer. It will indicate what **genre** you will be writing in, what your **purpose** is and what **layout/ structure** to use. Identify the type of **audience** you will be writing for, which will determine the appropriate **style and register**. **Number the points you need to cover** to make sure that your answer addresses all aspects of the question.

> A website dedicated to travel writing (both domestic and international) has asked you to contribute an **article** aimed at encouraging young people to explore their own locality more closely. Write the text of the article you would contribute, in which you extol the virtues of your own locality **(1)**, describe some of its most appealing attractions **(2)** and inspire your readers to rediscover the area in which they live **(3)**. Your article could be light-hearted in tone, or serious, or a combination of the two.

Genre: a travel feature article that will be published on a travel website.

Purpose: to encourage young people to explore their local area.

Layout/structure: your article should have an eye-catching headline. As it is for a website, you can include features such as links to other pages. You could include descriptions, quotations, facts and figures as well as your personal opinion.

Audience: your article is aimed at young people and is intended to be published on a travel website, so you can assume that your audience will be young people interested in travel. You could compare some of the attractions in your locality to more well-known tourist destinations that you know will appeal to young people.

Style and register: as your article is describing your local area, it would probably work best to write it in the first person. Your tone can be playful and humorous, serious, or a mix of both.

(1) Use the language of persuasion to praise your local area. Be enthusiastic.

(2) Use aesthetic language to describe the area's best attractions.

(3) Use the language of persuasion to inspire young people to rediscover their own locality.

For information on the different styles of language, see page xvi.

A-Z Grammar Guide

Adjectives

Adjectives are describing words. They add depth and vividness to your writing by offering the reader a more detailed mental image.

In TEXT 2, Rosita Boland was clearly very moved by some of the sights she saw while travelling in Japan. She carefully crafts her language to try to convey those sights to us as mental images. One way she does this is with well-chosen adjectives. For example:

- '**snowy** mountains'
- '**sprawling** museum'
- '**untrained** eye'
- 'vases were so **delicate** and so **old**'
- '**beautiful** plates'.

All colours are adjectives. If you reread TEXT 2, you will notice how rich in colour Boland's descriptions are:

- 'a **deep sealing-wax red** colour'
- '**Black** with variations of **gold** and **silver** decoration'
- '**red** hollyhocks on a **blue** background partially rimmed with a **golden** edge'.

Adjectives are the 'spice' for good writing: they add flavour and texture to your descriptions. But be careful: just like in cooking, too much spice can spoil the dish!

Theme 1: New Frontiers

TEXT 3 – SPEECH: 'YOU'VE GOT TO FIND WHAT YOU LOVE'

This is an extract from the prepared text of a Commencement (graduation) Address delivered at Stanford University, California, on 12 June 2005 by Steve Jobs, then chief executive officer of Apple Inc. and chairperson of Pixar Animation Studios.

I dropped out of Reed College after the first six months, but then stayed around as a drop-in for another 18 months or so before I really quit. So why did I drop out?

It started before I was born. My biological mother was a young, unwed college graduate student, and she decided to put me up for adoption. She felt very strongly that I should be adopted by college graduates, so everything was all set for me to be adopted at birth by a lawyer and his wife. Except that when I popped out they decided at the last minute that they really wanted a girl. So my parents, who were on a waiting list, got a call in the middle of the night asking: 'We have an unexpected baby boy; do you want him?' They said: 'Of course.' My biological mother later found out that my mother had never graduated from college and that my father had never graduated from high school. She refused to sign the final adoption papers. She only relented a few months later when my parents promised that I would someday go to college.

And 17 years later I did go to college. But I naively chose a college that was almost as expensive as Stanford, and all of my working-class parents' savings were being spent on my college tuition. After six months, I couldn't see the value in it. I had no idea what I wanted to do with my life and no idea how college was going to help me figure it out. And here I was spending all of the money my parents had saved their entire life. So I decided to drop out and trust that it would all work out OK. It was pretty scary at the time, but looking back it was one of the best decisions I ever made. The minute I dropped out I could stop taking the required classes that didn't interest me, and begin dropping in on the ones that looked interesting.

It wasn't all romantic. I didn't have a dorm room, so I slept on the floor in friends' rooms, I returned Coke bottles for the five-cent deposits to buy food with, and I would walk the seven miles across town every Sunday night to get one good meal a week at the Hare Krishna temple. I loved it. And much of what I stumbled into by following my curiosity and intuition turned out to be priceless later on. Let me give you one example:

Reed College at that time offered perhaps the best calligraphy instruction in the country. Throughout the campus every poster, every label on every drawer, was beautifully hand calligraphed. Because I had dropped out and didn't have to take the normal classes, I decided to take a calligraphy class to learn how to do this. I learned about serif and sans serif typefaces, about varying the amount of space between different letter combinations, about what makes great typography great. It was beautiful, historical, artistically subtle in a way that science can't capture, and I found it fascinating.

None of this had even a hope of any practical application in my life. But ten years later, when we were designing the first Macintosh computer, it all came back to me. And we designed it all into the Mac. It was the first computer with beautiful typography. If I had never dropped in on that single course in college, the Mac would have never had multiple typefaces or proportionally spaced fonts. And since Windows just copied the Mac, it's likely that no personal computer would have them. If I had never dropped out, I would have never dropped in on this calligraphy class, and personal computers might not have the wonderful typography that they do. Of course it was impossible to connect the dots looking forward when I was in college. But it was very, very clear looking backward ten years later.

Again, you can't connect the dots looking forward; you can only connect them looking backward. So you have to trust that the dots will somehow connect in your future. You have to trust in something — your gut, destiny, life, karma, whatever. This approach has never let me down, and it has made all the difference in my life.

[...]

You've got to find what you love. And that is as true for your work as it is for your lovers. Your work is going to fill a large part of your life, and the only way to be truly satisfied is to do what you believe is great work. And the only way to do great work is to love what you do. If you haven't found it yet, keep looking. Don't settle. As with all matters of the heart, you'll know when you find it. And, like any great relationship, it just gets better and better as the years roll on. So keep looking until you find it. Don't settle.

[...]

Stay Hungry. Stay Foolish.

Thank you all very much.

Footnote on Speeches

The most important thing to remember when assessing or writing a speech is the intended **audience**. The tone, content and style of the speech will be determined by who is going to be hearing it. In TEXT 3, Steve Jobs is addressing a graduating class at Stanford University, so his style is **conversational and informal**. Speeches are usually written in the **first person**.

Speeches often **address the audience directly**. We see this in TEXT 3, when Jobs uses phrases such as: 'You have to trust in something' and 'You've got to find what you love.' This technique involves the audience and allows them to feel part of the discussion.

Anecdotes can be used to make a topic more personal and to build rapport with the audience. In TEXT 3, for example, Jobs refers to his own student days as he knows his audience can relate to those. He uses vivid imagery and details in his anecdotes (sleeping on friends' floors, returning bottles to collect the deposits) to further engage his audience, and figurative language to illustrate his points: 'it was impossible to connect the dots looking forward' (metaphor).

Rhetorical questions can also be used to engage listeners. In TEXT 3, Jobs asks his audience, 'So why did I drop out?'

At the end of a speech, the speaker will usually **sum up the main point**. TEXT 3 does this with a series of pithy messages: 'So keep looking until you find it. Don't settle. ... Stay Hungry. Stay Foolish.'

QUESTION A – 50 Marks

(i) Outline, in your own words, three of the most important pieces of advice Steve Jobs gives to the students at Stanford University at their Commencement Address. Support your answer with reference to the text. (15)

(ii) In TEXT 3, Steve Jobs presents his own narrative in order to inspire and instruct his audience. From the texts you have studied for your Leaving Certificate course*, identify a character, a narrative or a moment that you found inspirational **or** instructive. Explain in detail how and why you found this character, narrative or moment instructive **or** inspirational. (15)

* Texts specified for study for Leaving Certificate English, including poetry, single texts and texts (including films) prescribed for comparative study.

(iii) Based on what you have read in TEXT 3, do you agree that Steve Jobs is both engaging and inspiring in his address to the graduating students? Support your answer with reference to both the content and style of the extract. (20)

Sample Answer

QUESTION A (i)

> Immediately addresses the question and establishes that the most important piece of advice is going to be dealt with first.

> First stated answer.

> Evidence from the text is quoted to support the statement.

> Spells out why this advice is important.

The most important piece of advice Steve Jobs gives to the graduating class of 2005 is to follow their curiosity and intuition. He suggests that everyone has to 'trust in something', whether that's their 'gut, destiny, life, karma, whatever'. He demonstrates how when he 'stumbled' into different things by following his curiosity and intuition, his experiences proved 'priceless later on'. It is important advice because most people simply do not have that kind of courage. Hearing this from someone successful like Steve Jobs might just inspire young people to follow his example.

> Connecting phrase. Second stated answer.

> Spells out why this advice is important.

He also advises his audience to make sure that they do 'great work'. He points out that as work takes up a substantial part of a person's life, the only way to have a rewarding life is to engage in work that is meaningful and important. He says that you have 'to love what you do' because otherwise you will end up feeling unfulfilled and unsatisfied. This is a crucial piece of advice for young people to take on board because it will affect the way they lead the rest of their lives.

> Linking words. Third stated answer.

The third important piece of advice that Steve Jobs gives is to 'keep looking' and not to 'settle'. Another way he phrases the idea is 'Stay Hungry.' He is advising the graduating class against compromising on their dreams or giving up if things become difficult. He dropped out of college and followed his own instincts.

> Spells out why this advice is important.

He did not give up, even though he had to sleep on friends' floors and rely on returning bottles for the deposit money. Many people might have thought him 'Foolish', but his determination and persistence paid off in the end. This is such important advice because so many people would simply give up and take the path of least resistance.

> Brief conclusion.

These are the most important pieces of advice Steve Jobs gives his audience.

Exam Mechanics

QUESTION A (iii)

This part of Question A is the most valuable of the three for a reason. If Question A (i) asks you WHAT the author said, then Question A (iii) asks you to analyse HOW the author said it. That might be a bit more challenging, but do not worry! The best clues as to how to answer are there for you in the question. Read it carefully.

6S Simplify

The question states which two aspects of style to look for by including the key words engaging and inspiring. So, all you have to do is discuss how engaging and inspiring you thought Steve Jobs' speech was.

First, make certain that you know what those key words mean. It is worth taking 30 seconds to write down synonyms (words that mean the same) for both of them. For example:

- Engaging: appealing, captivating, interesting, intriguing, fascinating
- Inspiring: encouraging, heartening, uplifting, stirring, moving.

Then ask yourself two questions:

- How does Steve Jobs make his speech engaging/appealing/interesting, etc. for the graduating students?
- How does he make his speech inspiring/encouraging/heartening, etc. for them?

6S Select

Read through the text to find moments where Steve Jobs makes his speech engaging or inspiring for his audience. Highlight them on the text and make a very brief note in the margin explaining how your chosen example is engaging or inspiring. For example:

| Engaging insight into a public figure and known billionaire. | I returned Coke bottles for the five-cent deposits to buy food with, and I would walk the seven miles across town every Sunday night to get one good meal a week at the Hare Krishna temple. |

| Uses imperative verbs to address audience directly and inspire action. | So keep looking until you find it. Don't settle. |

What other examples can you find of Steve Jobs being (a) engaging and (b) inspiring?

6S Sort

Choose the four strongest examples from the text and decide which order to address them in for your answer. You do not need to follow the order in which they appear in the text.

6S State, support and spell out

Answer Question A (iii) with four paragraphs. Each paragraph contains three parts.

1. **State** what you found engaging/inspiring.

   I found the way that Steve Jobs addresses the graduating students directly to be particularly engaging.

2. **Support** your observation by quoting the example you have chosen.

> Towards the end of the speech, he tells his audience: 'If you haven't found it yet, keep looking. Don't settle. As with all matters of the heart, you'll know when you find it.'

3. **Spell out** what makes it engaging/inspiring. Make sure you include your own response.

> This advice engaged me because it felt as though he was speaking directly to me. The pithy sentences are directed at each member of his audience. The imperative verbs give specific instructions and require action from every person who hears them.

Follow this process for each of the four paragraphs of your answer.

QUESTION B – 50 Marks

▶ In TEXT 3, Steve Jobs extols the value of calligraphy, describing it as 'beautiful, historical, artistically subtle in a way that science can't capture'. Write an **opinion piece**, suitable for publication in a broadsheet newspaper, in which you extol the virtues of art, put forward a reasoned argument to persuade readers that art benefits both individuals and society and give your views on the relationship between art and science.

Sample Answer ▶

QUESTION B

Headline.

Byline (do not give your real name) with a suitable made-up position.

Uses an anecdote to grab the reader's attention.

Pithy statements are a feature of persuasive writing.

Using the information from the text is encouraged.

Lists some benefits to the individual.

Made-up institution.

Opinion – Art Brings Individuals and Communities Together

writes Jane Carroll, teacher of art history, Dublin

The Uffizi Gallery in Florence made world headlines in 2018 when a man suffered a heart attack whilst viewing the famous Botticelli masterpiece *The Birth of Venus*. The man made a full recovery, but his experience was an extreme example of Stendhal syndrome – becoming so overwhelmed by an object of beauty that you become physically unwell. Art has the ability to affect us so powerfully that it can literally knock us off our feet.

Art makes us human. From cave paintings to the elegant typeface of the latest MacBook, the desire to create is an elemental part of who we are. Art stimulates the imagination, encourages creativity and relieves stress. Research conducted by the European Council of Expressive Arts has shown that participation in the arts, whether writing, music or the visual arts, can lead to long-term improvements in health. Participants in the study reported drastically reduced levels of stress and anxiety. Art nourishes our souls.

Rhetorical questions are a feature of persuasive writing.

A triad is another feature of persuasive writing.

Inclusive statement.

Personal anecdote.

Figurative language is a feature of persuasive writing.

Linking statement.

Lists some benefits to society.

Real-world example.

A toddler is never a reluctant artist, so why do so many of us stop creating as we get older? We become self-conscious, unsure, haunted by a suspicion that we are no good at it. But the soul craves an outlet – look at the popularity of colouring books for adults. Art is mindfulness – deep inside, we all know this already. During the long hours working on my thesis, I found that a few minutes of colouring helped to relieve my stress and give my mind a break from my work. It was like recharging my batteries.

Art does not only benefit individuals, it also brings communities together. It can tell a shared story or commemorate a lived experience. For example, back in 2021 the Hugh Lane Gallery's 'Pass Freely' mural represented the people of Ireland's losses during the Covid-19 pandemic. This living piece of art showed a painted figure made of burned matches, each representing a lost life. Poignantly, it was updated with more matches during its lifetime. A public record of a society's collective grief.

Real-world examples strengthen argument.

Art also has a distinguished history as a medium for social change. From the protest songs of Bob Dylan to the satire of Blindboy Boatclub, art has the power to hold up a mirror to society, both reflecting and reforming it at the same time. The graffiti on the Berlin Wall, the murals on Belfast's Falls and Shankill roads, the images of George Floyd and the BLM movement are all mirrors that we hold up to ourselves.

Deals with the final part of the question – the relationship between art and science.

The greatest Renaissance thinker would have found our separation of art and science baffling. Da Vinci the scientist relied upon his art to record his investigations accurately. His creative mind allowed him to dream up literal flights of fancy and express them in his copious notes. He knew that, although they may use different approaches, both science and art ultimately have the same goal: to better understand the world around us.

Conclusion sums up argument.

Returns to opening paragraph to give a sense of closure.

Art is a universal language. It can be a balm to a broken psyche. It can inspire, it can challenge and it can change the world. In high doses, it can be literally overwhelming. So, if you find yourself feeling faint at the Uffizi, remember it is just your soul being nourished.

SECTION II   COMPOSING   (100 marks)

Write a composition on **any one** of the assignments that appear in **bold print** below.

Each composition carries 100 marks.

The composition assignments are intended to reflect language study in the areas of information, argument, persuasion, narration, and the aesthetic use of language.

1. In TEXT 3, Steve Jobs, the CEO of Apple Inc. and chairperson of Pixar Animation Studios, explains how he loves the work that he does.

   Write a personal essay in which you reflect on the things that you love in your life.

2. In TEXT 2, Rosita Boland describes how she struggled to write about the 'exceptionally beautiful' objects in the Tokyo National Museum.

   Write a feature article, suitable for publication in a popular magazine, in which you identify objects that you consider 'exceptionally beautiful' and discuss the value of these objects to society.

3. In the visual element of TEXT 1, various different destinations in space are depicted.

   Write a short story in which a character embarks upon a perilous journey to one of these destinations.

4. In TEXT 3, Steve Jobs revealed how his biological mother 'felt very strongly' that he should be adopted by 'college graduates'.

   Write a discursive essay in which you explore your ideas about the value of third-level education.

5. In TEXT 2, while travelling by train between cities, Rosita Boland describes the samurai swords in the Tokyo National Museum.

   Write a short story, suitable for inclusion in a collection of murder-mystery stories, in which a sword, a train and a diary are central to the narrative.

6. In TEXT 1, we read that 'questions are being raised around whether humans deserve a second chance at inhabiting a planet given the current climate crisis we're currently living in'.

   Write a speech in which you argue for or against the motion: *Humankind should not colonise any other planets before ensuring the future of Earth.*

7. In TEXT 2, Rosita Boland discusses the Japanese technique of *kintsukuroi* or 'golden joinery' where cracks are 'highlighted' so that the piece becomes 'more beautiful for having been mended'.

   Write a descriptive essay in which you capture the beauty to be found in ordinary things.

Theme 2
Artificial Intelligence

Artificial intelligence (AI) is a rapidly developing branch of computer science. It is the attempt to build smart machines that are programmed to think like humans in their reasoning, perception, learning and independent problem-solving.

The paragraphs below are taken from the three texts we will be exploring over the course of this theme. Take a look at the three samples and discuss the following questions:

Discuss

1. Of which genre of writing is each text an example?
2. What features or styles of writing helped you to identify the genre of each of these samples?
3. Where would you be likely to encounter each of these genres?

Sample 1 – Text 1

As I smiled at her, she called over her shoulder: 'Mom! This is her! The one I've been looking for!'

The Mother came slowly towards the arch, then stopped. And for a moment, all three were looking at me: Josie at the front, beaming happily; Manager, just behind her, also smiling, but with a caution in her look which I took as an important signal from her; and then the Mother, her eyes narrowed like people on the sidewalk when they're trying to see if a taxi is free or already taken.

Sample 2 – Text 2

MAG: Because there is no job. Machine/robot is taking over?

EM: There will be fewer and fewer jobs that a robot cannot do better. [...] with automation, there will come abundance. There will be – almost everything will get very cheap. I think the biggest – I think we'll just end up doing a universal basic income; it's going to be necessary. The harder challenge, much harder challenge, is how do people then have meaning. Like a lot of people, they derive their meaning from their employment.

Sample 3 – Text 3

In short, deepfakes work via the use of deep generative modelling. Basically, neural networks of algorithms learn how to create realistic looking images and videos of real (or fictitious) people after processing a database of example images. From being trained on images of a real person, they can then synthesise realistic videos of that person. Ultimately, the same technology can also be used to synthesise the same person's voice, which has led to fears that we're not far from fake yet entirely believable videos of politicians and celebrities doing or saying outrageous things.

SECTION I   COMPREHENDING   (100 marks)

TEXT 1 – KLARA AND THE SUN

This extract is from *Klara and the Sun* by Kazuo Ishiguro. The novel is set in the future and told from the perspective of the robot Klara, an AF (Artificial Friend; designed to be a child's companion). Here, Josie, a teenage girl, and her mother are in a shop to purchase Klara.

As I smiled at her, she called over her shoulder: 'Mom! This is her! The one I've been looking for!'

The Mother came slowly towards the arch, then stopped. And for a moment, all three were looking at me: Josie at the front, beaming happily; Manager, just behind her, also smiling, but with a caution in her look which I took as an important signal from her; and then the Mother, her eyes narrowed like people on the sidewalk when they're trying to see if a taxi is free or already taken. And when I saw her and the way she was looking at me, the fear – the one that had all but vanished when Josie had cried, 'You're still here!' – came back into my mind.

'I didn't mean to take so long,' Josie was saying. 'But I got a little sick. I'm fine again though.' Then she called back: 'Mom? Can we buy her right away? Before someone else comes in and takes her?'

There was silence, then the Mother said quietly, 'This one isn't a B3, I take it.'

'Klara is a B2,' Manager said. 'From the fourth series, which some say has never been surpassed.'

'But not a B3.'

'The B3 innovations are truly marvelous. But some customers feel, for a certain sort of child, a top-range B2 can still be the most happy match.'

'I see.'

'Mom. Klara's the one I want. I don't want any other.'

'One moment, Josie.' Then she asked Manager: 'Every Artificial Friend is unique, right?'

'That's correct, ma'am. And particularly so at this level.'

'So what makes this one unique? This ... Klara?'

'Klara has so many unique qualities, we could be here all morning. But if I had to emphasize just one, well, it would have to be her appetite for observing and learning. Her ability to absorb and blend everything she sees around her is quite amazing. As a result, she now has the most sophisticated understanding of any AF in this store, B3s not excepted.'

'Is that so.'

The Mother was once again looking at me with narrowed eyes. She then took three more steps towards me.

'You mind if I ask her a few questions?'

'Please go ahead.'

'Mom, please ...'

'Excuse me, Josie. Just stand over there a moment while I talk to Klara.'

Then it was the Mother and me, and though I tried to keep a smile on my face, it was not easy, and I might even have let the fear show.

'Klara,' the Mother said. 'I want you not to look towards Josie. Now tell me, without looking. What color are her eyes?'

'They're gray, ma'am.'

'Good. Josie, I want you to keep absolutely silent. Now, Klara. My daughter's voice. You heard her speak just now. How would you say her voice was pitched?'

'Her conversational voice has a range between A-flat above middle C to C octave.'

'Is that so?' There was another silence, then the Mother said: 'Last question. Klara. What did you notice about the way my daughter walks?'

'There's perhaps a weakness in her left hip. Also her right shoulder has potential to give pain, so Josie walks in a way that will protect it from sudden motion or unnecessary impact.'

The Mother considered this. Then she said, 'Well, Klara. Since you appear to know so much about it. Will you please reproduce for me Josie's walk? Will you do that for me? Right now? My daughter's walk?'

Behind the Mother's shoulder, I saw Manager's lips part, as though about to speak. But she said nothing. Instead, meeting my gaze, she gave me the smallest of nods.

So I started to walk. I realized that, as well as the Mother – and of course Josie – the whole store was now watching and listening. I stepped beneath the arch, onto the Sun's patterns spread across the floor. Then I went in the direction of the B3s standing mid-store, and the Glass Display Trolley. I did all I could to reproduce Josie's walk just as I'd seen it, that first time after she'd got out of the taxi, when Rosa and I were in the window, then four days later, when she'd come towards the window after the Mother had removed her hand from her shoulder, then finally as I'd seen her a moment ago, hurrying to me with relieved happiness in her eyes.

[…]

I glanced up and caught sight of the Mother, and something in what I saw made me stop. She was still watching me carefully, but it was as if her gaze was now focused straight through me, as if I was the glass in the window and she was trying to see something a long way behind it.

[…]

'Mom.' This time Josie's voice was hushed. 'Mom. Please.'

'Very well. We'll take her.'

Josie came hurrying to me. She put her arms around me and held me. When I gazed over the child's head, I saw Manager smiling happily, and the Mother, her face drawn and serious, looking down to search in her shoulder bag.

Footnote on Science Fiction Novels

Science fiction (often abbreviated to SF or sci-fi) has been described as 'the literature of ideas'. Writers of sci-fi deal with such **imaginative concepts** as time travel, alien worlds and alien races, robots and cyborgs, spacecraft and far-flung galaxies. They often begin from the premise: *what if?* For example, what if time travel were possible and you could visit your grandparents long before you were born? What would be the consequences? What if robots could be made to have artificial intelligence, feelings and emotions? Would human behaviour seem unusual to them?

Even though their stories tend to be **fantastical and complex**, sci-fi authors are often offering a **veiled commentary** on their own society. The radically different worlds they imagine may be a way of reflecting on and analysing the world they actually live in. For example, George Orwell imagined a horrifyingly dystopian future in his novel *Nineteen Eighty-Four* based on observation and criticism of his own society in 1948.

Any book or film that tries to imagine an alternative, future world to the one we live in can be classified as science fiction. So, *Star Trek* fits this definition; as do *Jurassic Park, Inception* and the *Avengers* series of films. Other examples include *The Handmaid's Tale* by Margaret Atwood, *The War of the Worlds* by H. G. Wells, *The Hunger Games* by Suzanne Collins and *Divergent* by Veronica Roth. You may have read these or seen the films and/or television series based on them.

QUESTION A – 50 Marks

(i) Based on your reading of TEXT 1, what impression did you form of 'the Mother'? Support your response with reference to the text. (15)

(ii) TEXT 1 is an example of writing in the science fiction genre. Explain why this genre has a wide and enduring appeal. Make three points in your response. (15)

(iii) Identify four features of good storytelling evident in TEXT 1. Discuss how the features you have identified add to your enjoyment of the extract. Support your response with reference to the extract. (20)

Sample Answer

QUESTION A (i)

Introduction answers the question without supporting quotations.

From reading TEXT 1, the impression I formed of 'the Mother' is that she is shrewd, can be quite intimidating and seems to be hiding some kind of secret.

First point.

'The Mother' appears to be very shrewd and cautious. This aspect of her character is made obvious in the way she

Supports point with direct and indirect reference to TEXT 1.

questions Manager about Klara – 'This one isn't a B3, I take it' – and then quizzes Klara and asks her to perform Josie's walk. It shows that 'the Mother' is not someone who makes an expensive

Sums up point by explaining what this evidence shows.

purchase without thinking it through.

Connecting word.

Secondly, it is clear that 'the Mother' can be an intimidating person and expects to get her own way. The way she looks at

Second point.

Klara causes the robot to feel fear: 'though I tried to keep a smile on my face, it was not easy, and I might even have let

Three pieces of evidence to support point.

the fear show'. 'The Mother' seems comfortable issuing demands – telling her daughter to keep silent, and speaking quite briskly to Manager: 'But not a B3.' Her assertiveness suggests that she is

Sums up point.

used to having her demands met.

Connecting word.

Finally, 'the Mother' appears to be quite concerned about something and perhaps has some sort of secret. This possibility

Third point.

is suggested by the strange way she looks at Klara – 'as if her gaze was now focused straight through me'. She also remains

Two pieces of evidence to support point.

'drawn and serious' when agreeing to the purchase. This unusual reaction for a mother buying her daughter a present and making her very happy in the process suggests she has some greater concerns or worries. Her complex behaviour makes 'the Mother'

Sums up point.

a very interesting character, as we wonder what she is thinking.

Exam Mechanics

QUESTION A (ii)

6S Simplify

As we have seen elsewhere, Question A (ii) can be a little unpredictable. This example asks you to discuss the genre of science fiction, explaining what you think makes this genre appealing to a wide audience and why its appeal is enduring (has lasted for a long time). As the question explicitly asks you to make three points, you should plan to develop three paragraphs.

6S Select

You have about ten minutes to write this answer, so take a minute to jot down the strongest ideas you can come up with as to why lots of people read/watch science fiction and have been doing so for quite some time. Start by thinking about examples of science fiction that you have read or watched and what made them appealing.

Science fiction is popular/has enduring appeal because:
- Escapism – people enjoy a change from day-to-day life
- Writers comment on their society by imagining an alternative
- Raises public awareness of possible consequences of developing technologies
- Sci-fi has been written and enjoyed for decades – give famous examples.

Remember, you can use TEXT 1 to help you answer this question, but there is nothing in the question that says you have to use it.

6S Sort

Look through the ideas you jotted down and identify which ones you will be most comfortable writing about. Decide on your strongest three points and the order in which you will discuss them.

6S State, support and spell out

You must answer this question with three paragraphs (four if you opt to write an introduction, which is not compulsory but does show purposefulness). Each paragraph should:

1. **State** a reason why science fiction has a wide and enduring appeal.

   Science fiction has enduring appeal because for many decades its writers have been exploring important social issues.

2. **Support** your observation by referring to specific examples.

   In the 1940s, George Orwell imagined a dystopian future where society itself is designed to repress human freedoms in *Nineteen Eighty-Four.* In the 1980s, Margaret Atwood's *The Handmaid's Tale* explored the need to guard personal rights and gender equality by portraying an oppressive version of the near future.

3. **Spell out** exactly why your chosen examples appeal to so many.

   Such powerful social commentary continues to attract a wide audience to science fiction.

Follow this process for each of the three parts of your answer.

QUESTION B – 50 Marks

In TEXT 1, we meet Klara, a type of robot called an AF (Artificial Friend). Imagine that a company producing AFs has commissioned you to promote its latest model at an annual convention of toy retailers. Write the text of the **verbal pitch** you will deliver in which you: give a brief overview of some of this model's best features by explaining how it is an improvement on previous models, convince the retailers to stock your company's merchandise and offer advice on how best to market this model to the public.

Exam Mechanics

QUESTION B

Read the question and highlight the main task. This task will inform your entire answer. It will indicate what **genre** you will be writing in, what your **purpose** is and what **layout/ structure** to use. Identify the type of **audience** you will be writing for, which will determine the appropriate **style and register** to use. **Number the points you need to cover** to make sure that your answer addresses all aspects of the question.

In TEXT 1, we meet Klara, a type of robot called an AF (Artificial Friend). Imagine that a company producing AFs has commissioned you to promote its latest model at an annual convention of toy retailers. Write the text of the **verbal pitch** you will deliver in which you: give a brief overview of some of this model's best features **(1a)** by explaining how it is an improvement on previous models **(1b)**, convince the retailers to stock your company's merchandise **(2)** and offer advice on how best to market this model to the public **(3)**.

Genre: a verbal pitch (a presentation that will be delivered out loud).

Purpose: to persuade/convince your audience to buy or accept something.

Layout/structure: a verbal pitch is presented on the page in the same way as any talk or a speech.

Audience: practically everyone in your audience owns or works in a toy shop and is a toy expert. You work for a toy company, so you are a toy expert too.

Style and register: use the language of persuasion and the language of argument in your pitch and include plenty of toy-related jargon to appeal to your audience of toy experts.

(1) There are two parts to this task – you must **(a)** describe your model's new features and **(b)** explain how they are an improvement on previous models. This particular model will have specific selling points to help it compete with other brands of AF. Is it smarter? More reliable? More empathetic? Less synthetic-looking? Perhaps it can be programmed to play sports, or it has a repertoire of jokes?

(2) Convincing the retailers to buy is not a stand-alone task, it is the purpose of the entire pitch. When you are explaining the features of the model, for example, you should do so in a manner that makes the model sound as desirable as possible. Some of the best features may be new, but others may always have been unique selling points for your brand.

(3) Your advice might include telling the delegates how best to highlight the unique selling points of the new model when they display it in their shops. What promotional materials should they use? How should it be displayed?

A-Z Grammar Guide

Using dialogue

Dialogue can be complicated, especially if many characters are speaking. The appropriate use of punctuation will guide the reader. Always observe the following conventions (accepted rules) when writing dialogue:

- Use speech marks to indicate the start and the end of a unit of speech.
- Use a punctuation mark before the speech marks are closed. When the closing speech mark comes at the end of the speaker's sentence, use a full stop, an exclamation mark or a question mark. If the speaker's sentence is unfinished, use a comma.
- Start a new line to indicate a change of speaker. This convention helps the reader to follow the conversation with a limited number of reminders as to who is speaking. Dialogue becomes tedious when 'he said' and 'she said' are repeated too often. A competent writer is able to judge when it is necessary to indicate the speaker.

Take a look at the following example from TEXT 1:

The voice of the narrator (the words inside the speech marks are spoken by the Mother).	'Klara,' **the Mother said**. 'I want you not to look towards Josie. Now tell me, without looking. What color are her eyes?'
The question mark indicates the end of the Mother's sentence (a question) and is placed before the speech marks are closed.	'They're gray, ma'am.'
New speaker, new line. As it is clear that Klara is answering the question, there is no need to state that she is the speaker.	'Good. Josie, I want you to keep absolutely silent. Now, Klara. My daughter's voice. You heard her speak just now. How would you say her voice was pitched?'
	'Her conversational voice has a range between A-flat above middle C to C octave.'

If you look again at the first bit of dialogue above, the author could have arranged it differently. For example:

'Klara, I want you not to look towards Josie. Now tell me, without looking. What color are her eyes?' the Mother said.

Discuss

Which version do you think is more effective? Why?

Use more specific words than 'said' to make your writing more vivid and expressive. Try out each of the alternatives below and see how the meaning changes.

She took him by the hand and looked deep into his eyes. 'I love you,' she _____.

joked	begged	sniggered
blurted	stammered	sneered
groaned	promised	reassured
yelled	cried	insisted
whispered	spat	laughed
pleaded	murmured	sighed
snapped	demanded	mouthed

Write out each of the following sentences. Insert the correct punctuation marks and fill in the blank with a suitable alternative to 'said'.

1. We were having such a lovely time _____ Michael. Why would you spoil things by bringing up the past

2. This bread is delicious, but I will never make that tomato soup again _____Diane.

3. Would you like to go to Cork for the whole summer _____ Jacob.

4. The city looks so beautiful at night Stella _____.

5. You're walking dirt all over my clean floor _____ Dad.

TEXT 2 – INTERVIEW: THE SHAPE OF THE WORLD TO COME

This text has three elements: two images and an edited extract from an interview with Elon Musk, CEO of Tesla Inc. and founder of SpaceX. The interview took place in front of an audience at the World Government Summit in 2017 and was conducted by Mohammad Al Gergawi.

Image 1

Image 2

Mohammad Al Gergawi (MAG): This is the largest global government summit. We have over 139 governments here. If you want to advise government officials to be ready for the future, what are three things or three [pieces of] advice you can give them?

Elon Musk (EM): Well, I think the first bit of advice would be to really pay close attention to the development of artificial intelligence. I think this is – we need to just be very careful in how we adopt artificial intelligence and to make sure that researchers don't get carried away. Because sometimes what happens is a scientist can get so engrossed in their work, they don't necessarily realise the ramifications of what they're doing. So I think it's important for public safety that governments keep a close eye on artificial intelligence and make sure that it does not represent a danger to the public.

Let's see, secondly, I would say we do need to think about transport in general, and there's the movement towards electric vehicles, sustainable transport. I think that's going to be good for many reasons; but again, not something that happens immediately. That'll happen slower than the self-driving vehicles. So that's probably something that happens over 30 or 40 years, the transition to electric vehicles. So thinking about that in context, the demand for electricity will increase dramatically. So currently, in terms of total energy usage in the world, it's about one-third electricity, about one-third transport,

about one-third heating. So, over time, that will transition to almost all – not all, but predominantly – electricity, which means that the demand for electricity will probably triple. So it's going to be very important to think about how do you make so much more electricity.

MAG: Seems they have an easy job. That's it, there are no more challenges for them?

EM: These things do play into each other a little bit, but what to do about mass unemployment? This is going to be a massive social challenge and I think ultimately we will have to have some kind of universal basic income. I don't think we're going to have a choice.

MAG: Universal basic income.

EM: Yes, universal basic income. I think it's going to be necessary.

MAG: So it means that unemployed people will be paid across the globe?

EM: Yeah.

MAG: Because there is no job. Machine/robot is taking over?

EM: There will be fewer and fewer jobs that a robot cannot do better. And I want to be clear, these are not things that I wish would happen, these are simply things that I think probably will happen. And so, if my assessment is correct and they probably will happen, then we need to say what we are going to do about it. And I think some kind of a universal basic income is going to be necessary.

Now, the output of goods and services will be extremely high. So with automation, there will come abundance. There will be – almost everything will get very cheap. I think the biggest – I think we'll just end up doing a universal basic income; it's going to be necessary. The harder challenge, much harder challenge, is how do people then have meaning. Like a lot of people, they derive their meaning from their employment. So if you don't have – if you're not needed, if there's not a need for your labour, how do you – what's the meaning? Do you have meaning? Do you feel useless? That's a much harder problem to deal with.

And then how do we ensure that the future is going to be the future that we want, that we still like? You know, I mean I do think that there's a potential path here which is – I'm really getting into the science fiction or sort of advanced science stuff – but having some sort of merger with biological intelligence and machine intelligence. To some degree,

we are already a cyborg. You think of like the digital tools that you have – your phone, your computer, the applications that you have, like the fact that … you can ask a question and instantly get an answer from Google or from other things, and so you already have a digital tertiary layer. I say 'tertiary' because you can think of the limbic system*, kind of the animal brain or the primal brain, and then the cortex, kind of the thinking, planning part of the brain, and then your digital self as a third layer. So you already have that, and if somebody dies, their digital ghost is still around: all of their emails and the pictures that they posted in their social media – that still lives, even if they die.

So over time I think we'll probably see a closer merger of biological intelligence and digital intelligence.

* The limbic system is a set of brain structures in the forebrain. It supports a variety of functions including emotion, behaviour and long-term memory.

Footnote on Interviews

The most obvious indicator that you are reading an interview is that there are at least two 'voices': the **interviewer** (who asks the questions) and the **interviewee** (who answers them). There could be multiple interviewees, perhaps in the form of a panel discussion. There could be multiple interviewers also. TEXT 2 conforms to the standard model of one interviewer (Mohammad Al Gergawi) and one interviewee (Elon Musk).

Interviewees tend to be selected on the basis of their expertise in a certain field, or perhaps because they are a celebrity and a sufficient number of people are interested in hearing their thoughts on a range of topics.

An interview is different from a speech in that an interviewee rarely has prepared notes and so their words tend to **conform to the patterns of natural and unscripted speech**. There will be pauses and hesitations. They will use 'fillers' such as 'um', 'you know' and 'like'. There will probably be instances where they leave a sentence grammatically incomplete. We see this in TEXT 2: 'There will be – almost everything will get very cheap.'

When writing the text of an interview, it is important to think carefully about the kinds of questions an interviewer would ask. A good interviewer encourages the interviewee to elaborate by asking **open-ended questions** that require thought and explanation to answer. For example, instead of 'Did you enjoy the film?', ask 'What did you enjoy about the film?' and, if appropriate, follow up with questions seeking more clarity or challenging the interviewee to justify their position.

QUESTION A – 50 Marks

(i) Based on your reading of TEXT 2, explain three insights you gain into Elon Musk's hopes and/ or fears for the future. Support your answer with reference to the text. (15)

(ii) The extract of the conversation with Elon Musk used for TEXT 2 is an example of an interview. The interview was conducted at the World Government Summit (WGS) held annually in Dubai. The WGS brings together government leaders from around the world to focus on the issues of technology and innovation. Explain why you think interviews with personalities such as Elon Musk have a wide appeal. (15)

(iii) Based on your reading of TEXT 2, do you agree that Elon Musk is a knowledgeable and credible speaker? Support your response with reference to four features of Musk's comments in TEXT 2. (20)

Sample Answer

QUESTION A (ii)

Introduction summarises the main points to be discussed – this demonstrates a purposeful (planned) answer.	The personality and reputation of a guest speaker are the primary reasons that they will attract a large audience. Their expertise in specific fields will also ensure that a great many people will be interested in what they have to say.

Refers to the question – indicates a purposeful answer.

Elon Musk, as a personality, is a world-famous success story. He is one of the world's richest self-made business people. He is the founder and CEO of SpaceX, as well as being the CEO of Tesla. He is clearly a highly intelligent and capable individual. People tend to want to learn from listening to successful and knowledgeable personalities like Musk.

Connecting words.

Another reason for the appeal of the interview with Musk is the range of topics covered. Musk is a proven expert in the fields of economics and technology, and both these subjects interest the WGS audience immensely. He discusses his prediction that a 'universal basic income'

Supporting quotation.

for everybody will one day be necessary because automation is leading to the loss of employment for people all over the world. This issue

Refers to the question – writer is staying on task.

has potentially enormous financial consequences for his audience of government leaders, and his thoughts on it will be listened to attentively.

Connecting words.

Musk also has a huge knowledge base in the field of technology. This topic has a wide appeal because technology affects practically everyone

Refers to the 'wide appeal' of the question.

in the world. Many people are worried about the possible consequences of AI, and many countries are currently experiencing the transition to electric vehicles. Both of these issues are covered in the interview.

Uses terms linking to 'wide appeal'.

These are also topics that will intrigue a global audience because they are issues with direct consequences for many millions of people.

QUESTION B – 50 Marks

In TEXT 2, Elon Musk envisages a time when humans integrate closely with machines, even becoming 'cyborgs'. The two images in TEXT 2 represent artists' ideas about what such a future might look like. Write the text of a **talk** you would deliver on a national radio station in which you discuss what you see as the likely future of humankind and its relationship with technology. You should describe the future you think is most likely, and outline both the positives and the negatives of how you see such technology developing.

Exam Mechanics

QUESTION B

Read the question and highlight the main task. This task will inform your entire answer. It will indicate what **genre** you will be writing in, what your **purpose** is and what **layout/ structure** to use. Identify the type of **audience** you will be writing for, which will determine the appropriate **style and register** to use. **Number the points you need to cover** to make sure that your answer addresses all aspects of the question.

> In TEXT 2, Elon Musk envisages a time when humans integrate closely with machines, even becoming 'cyborgs'. The two images in TEXT 2 represent artists' ideas about what such a future might look like. Write the text of a **talk** you would deliver on a national radio station in which you discuss what you see as the likely future of humankind and its relationship with technology **(1)**. You should describe the future you think is most likely **(2)**, and outline both the positives **(3a)** and the negatives of how you see such technology developing **(3b)**.

Genre: a talk on a national radio station (such as RTÉ Radio 1 or Newstalk).

Purpose: a radio talk should entertain and inform; in this case, it must discuss the future and humankind's relationship with technology.

Layout: as long as it reads like a talk on the radio, you are free to present your text in whatever fashion feels the most authentic to you. You might choose the form of an interview; in which case the question-and-answer format of TEXT 2 may be helpful – having your interviewer ask questions containing the key words (or synonyms of them) in the numbered tasks will ensure that your answer remains purposeful and focused. Questions serve as clear markers that you are staying on track and dealing with all the required points. If you prefer to deliver the text of your talk with a single voice, you can still pose rhetorical questions to yourself. For example:

So, what will be the downside of this new technology? Well, I predict the following two outcomes if we go down this road …

Structure: a talk should have a clear introduction, body and conclusion.

- **Introduction:** listen to any radio programme and you will hear the presenters start with a greeting such as 'Good morning/Hello and welcome to …' and provide their name(s). Your introduction should do the same and should establish your credentials. Why should the nation listen to what you have to say? Are you an expert in the field of technology? (Careful – if you're not clued-up on technology, this could be very difficult to do convincingly!) Perhaps you are a Leaving Cert student with an interest in technology and are representing the opinions of today's youth? If you are a guest, your host will most likely introduce you to the audience and briefly explain what you are going to talk about (or ask you to do that). If you are alone, you have to do the introduction yourself.
- **Body:** address all parts of the question. You do not have to deal with them all equally, and you do not have to do them in the order in which they appear.
- **Conclusion:** if you are a guest, thank the host for inviting you; if you are a broadcaster, thank your audience for listening. Most radio items end with the presenter mentioning what is coming up next (such as the news).

Audience: a national radio station will have an audience of tens (or hundreds) of thousands of listeners. You may find it useful to imagine yourself as a guest on an existing radio programme, and if so, your audience may include an interviewer who is an actual broadcaster.

Style and register: your awareness of audience and your level of authenticity need to be sustained throughout the talk (mentioning the listeners at appropriate moments will help). You might try interacting with listeners or encouraging them to get in contact via a text number/phone-in line. Keep any such interactions on topic and make sure they are helping you to deal with the tasks.

(1) The question requires you to *discuss* the likely future of humankind and its relationship with technology. Why do you see the future of humanity the way you do?

(2) *Describe* your vision of the future of humankind and technology. What will this future look and feel like?

(3) Suggest some of the likely **(a)** positive and **(b)** negative consequences of these technological developments.

A-Z Grammar Guide

Phrases, clauses, sentences

TEXT 2 reproduces spoken English, which often contains word combinations that are not, strictly speaking, grammatically correct. In general, we write sentences that conform to the rules of grammar.

Phrases and clauses are two of the building blocks of sentences:

- A **phrase** is a combination of words that does not make a complete sentence. For example: 'A walk in the park', 'The bane of my life'.
- A **clause** is a combination of words that contains a finite verb, which means it could be used as a sentence on its own but is called a clause when it is contained within a longer sentence. For example: 'Elon Musk, **who is the CEO of Tesla**, spoke at the WGS in 2017.'

There are four types of **sentence**:

1. **Simple sentences** contain one subject (who/what is doing the action of the sentence) and one verb (the action itself). For example: Artificial intelligence is dangerous.

2. **Compound sentences** are created by joining two simple sentences together using a conjunction. For example: Artificial intelligence is dangerous, **so** world governments must monitor their scientists.

3. **Complex sentences** occur when phrases and/or clauses are included to add information or develop meaning. For example: Artificial intelligence, where machines are designed to think like humans, is dangerous.

4. **Complex-compound sentences** are a combination of compound and complex sentences. For example: Artificial intelligence, where machines are designed to think like humans, is dangerous, **so** world governments, through their respective domestic security agencies, must monitor their scientists.

When you combine sentences and add clauses, your sentences can quickly become clumsy. Remember: **the more complicated the idea you are trying to express, the simpler your sentences should be to express it**.

Rules for sentence structure

The two basic rules for sentence structure are:

1. A sentence should comprise a **complete thought or idea**.
2. All sentences must have a **finite verb**.

For more information on verbs, see page 56.

What is a 'complete thought'? Compare these two examples and decide which one is NOT a sentence:

1. Julia's team lost the football match.
2. Because Julia's team lost the football match.

You can most likely tell that the second example is incomplete: the word 'Because' implies that there is something more to be added. For this reason, you may have been told in primary school that you should never start a sentence with a conjunction like 'Because'. However, putting a conjunction at the beginning of a sentence is fine as long as it is joining two simple sentences. For example: Because Julia's team lost the football match, it has been relegated to a lower division.

TEXT 3 – ARTICLE: WHY DEEPFAKES ARE A NET POSITIVE FOR HUMANITY

This article by journalist and blogger Simon Chandler was published on the business website Forbes.com in 2020. The modern technological phenomenon of 'deepfakes', developed using artificial intelligence, allows video images to be manipulated by replacing a person with someone else's likeness. In response to widespread fears that the technology could be used to deceive, Chandler argues for its benefits.

Deepfakes are your friend. Yes, deepfake technology has understandably become notorious in the wake of deepfake porn videos and the threat deepfakes seemingly pose to politics. However, the ability to generate realistic simulations using artificial intelligence will, on the whole, be only a positive for humanity.

Increasingly, new uses are being found for deepfakes. Good uses. Whether recreating long-dead artists in museums or editing video without the need for a reshoot, deepfake technology will allow us to experience things that no longer exist, or that have never existed. And aside from having numerous applications in entertainment and education, it's being increasingly used in medicine and other areas.

In short, deepfakes work via the use of deep generative modelling. Basically, neural networks of algorithms learn how to create realistic looking images and videos of real (or fictitious) people after processing a database of example images. From being trained on images of a real person, they can then synthesise realistic videos of that person. Ultimately, the same technology can also be used to synthesise the same person's voice, which has led to fears that we're not far from fake yet entirely believable videos of politicians and celebrities doing or saying outrageous things.

But this is the worst-case scenario. Much more realistically, deepfake technology will play an increasingly constructive role in recreating the past and in envisioning future possibilities. This is already being borne out by an expanding range of examples.

Most recently, Reuters collaborated with AI startup Synthesia to create the world's first synthesised, presenter-led news reports, using the same basic deepfakes technology to create new video reports out of pre-recorded clips of a news presenter. What was most novel about this is that, by using deepfake technology, you can automatically generate video reports personalised for each individual news viewer.

Aside from TV, deepfakes also have considerable potential in the art world. Last year, researchers at Samsung's AI lab in Moscow were able to transform Da Vinci's famed Mona Lisa into video, using deep learning to show the subject of the painting moving her eyes, head and mouth.

Likewise, Dalí Museum in St. Petersburg, Florida used deepfake technology last year as part of a new exhibition. Named Dalí Lives, it displayed a life-sized deepfake of the surrealist artist that had been created via 1,000 hours of machine learning of the artist's old interviews. This deepfake recreation delivered a variety of quotes which Dalí had actually spoken or written over the course of his career.

Dali's words were spoken by an actor, but a Scottish company, CereProc, was able to train its own deepfake algorithms on audio recordings of former president John F. Kennedy. By training its deepfake technology in this way, the company was able to create 'lost' audio of the speech JFK was due to give in Dallas on November 22, 1963, the day he was assassinated.

The examples above show how deepfakes can serve to help bring history and art 'alive' for a wider audience. And if this helps to get thousands or millions of people interested in art and history, then the world can only benefit.

Other positive uses are emerging in education and entertainment. A UK-based health charity used deepfake technology to have David Beckham delivering an anti-malaria message in nine languages last year. Meanwhile, the likes of Nvidia [is] working on using AI-based deepfakes technology to create the graphics for video games.

And moving beyond image-based media, the underlying machine learning technology of deepfakes will have beneficial impacts on other areas. In medicine, for instance, UCL AI professor Geraint Rees predicts that 'the development of deep generative models raises new possibilities in healthcare.' One such possibility is the use of deep learning to synthesise realistic data that will help researchers to develop new ways of treating diseases without [using] actual patient data.

Work in this area has already been carried out by Nvidia, the Mayo Clinic and the MGH & BWH Center for Clinical Data Science, which in 2018 collaborated on using generative adversarial networks to create 'fake' brain MRI scans. The researchers found that, by training algorithms on these medical images and on 10% real images, these algorithms became just as good at spotting tumours as an algorithm trained only on real images.

Such applications are likely only the beginning of deep learning's role in medicine, while synthesized data is currently being used in other sectors in order to protect privacy. For now, of course, deepfakes will continue to have a bad reputation, given that they're most well-known for (potentially) threatening democracy. Still, if we can educate ourselves to trust only videos delivered by reputable sources (in the same way we trust only certain sources of text-based news), we'll soon find that the good of deepfakes will more than outweigh the bad.

QUESTION A – 50 Marks

(i) Based on your reading of TEXT 3, what, in your opinion, are the three most important benefits to humanity of deepfake technology? Give reasons for your choices. (15)

(ii) TEXT 3 is an example of an article written by a journalist who specialises in emerging technology. Suggest why articles like TEXT 3 appeal to a particular audience. (15)

(iii) Based on your reading of TEXT 3, would you agree that Simon Chandler develops a compelling and persuasive argument? Support your response with reference to the article. (20)

Exam Mechanics

QUESTION A (iii)

6S Simplify

The key words in this question are 'compelling' and 'persuasive'.
- Compelling = fascinating, engrossing, entertaining, etc.
- Persuasive = convincing, plausible, reliable, etc.

6S Select

Select the evidence from the text that you will use to address the question. Note that you have been asked whether you agree that these two words are appropriate to describe the writer's style. You are free to disagree. If you find evidence in the text that the writer's style is not compelling/persuasive, it will shape your answer.

6S Sort

Sort the evidence you are going to use. You will most likely find more evidence in the text than you need, so you must choose the three most important/useful examples. The most pertinent evidence may be the first you come across, but it is just as likely to be the last. It is a good idea to lead with your strongest point (i.e. put that one first in your answer).

6S State, support and spell out

State your answer. You may entirely agree or disagree with the assessment of the writer's style, or you may partially agree and partially disagree. Whichever option you choose (based on your careful selection of the evidence), state it clearly in your opening line.

Having read TEXT 3, I agree that Simon Chandler's argument is both fascinating and convincing.

You will then need at least four pieces of evidence to support your statement. You must deal with both key words. You can give two examples of compelling writing and two examples of persuasive writing, or you could use three of one and one of the other. For each piece of evidence you discuss, follow these three steps:

1. **State** your main point.

   One reason I found Chandler's article compelling was his use of succinct and pithy sentences.

2. **Support** your point with evidence from the text.

   'Deepfakes are your friend' is a strong opening sentence.

3. **Spell out** exactly why your chosen example is compelling/persuasive.

   The way it addresses the reader instantly grabbed my attention. Deepfake technology is often thought of as being suspect, so the bold claim that deepfakes are a 'friend' both surprised and intrigued me.

QUESTION B – 50 Marks

In TEXT 3, Simon Chandler argues that despite many people's concerns about it, the benefits to humankind of the new technology called 'deepfakes' actually outweigh the dangers. Write a **blog post** in which you explore whether modern technology (other than deepfakes) is more beneficial than harmful. Your discussion should identify a specific technology (or technologies) about which people may be concerned, outline the potential negatives associated with it and evaluate whether the benefits outweigh the dangers.

Sample Answer

QUESTION B

Fictitious blog page title.	Generation Z – Tech
Heading for the particular post.	Is AI All Bad News?
Date of posting.	7/07/22

Thanks to everyone who got in touch after my last post: Online Learning – It's the Way Forward (read here). I'd like to mention @JayStockxxx24, who had this to say:

> In the long run it's going to be technology that poses the biggest danger to humankind. Never mind whether gadgets are making kids lazy – it's only a matter of time until AI wipes us out altogether.

Introduction makes the genre clear. Blogs have followers and can be interactive. They can be updated and may mention previous posts.

You raise an interesting point, Jay. So that's where I want to focus today, by asking: Is artificial intelligence (AI) all bad news?

Using the evidence supplied (here, in TEXT 2) is encouraged.

Jay isn't the only one worried about AI. Elon Musk, the world-famous founder, CEO and chief engineer at SpaceX, is also very concerned about the evolution of super-intelligent AI. He can be seen on numerous platforms explaining how he feels that the risk of unrestrained AI could, in fact, be the end of humanity itself. 'It scares the hell out of me,' he tells his audience. 'It's capable of vastly more than almost anyone knows, and the rate of improvement is exponential.' (To watch, click here.)

Includes hyperlinks – an expected feature of a blog post.

Uses a made-up statistic to support argument.

Obviously, this is not something we can ignore. In a recent YouGov poll, 43% of British respondents believed that self-sustaining AI would pose an existential threat to humanity. Musk has famously compared the development of rogue AI to the world being colonised by super-intelligent aliens; humanity simply won't stand a chance. Those who are not wiped out will be enslaved – imagine the worst aspects of *The Matrix* and the *Terminator* films combined!

Intended audience will appreciate references to popular culture.

Uses language of argument to emphasise point.

However, we should also remember that all technology, going back to the first stone axe, has been developed by humans to make our lives better. Nuclear fission is a technology that offers us almost unlimited energy. Yet because of it, people have been living under the cloud of possible annihilation since the end of the Second World War. But it hasn't happened. Why? Because the use of this technology is tightly regulated. The same will have to be done with AI.

Gives specific examples of advantages of AI.

The benefits to mankind of AI cannot be overstated. In essence, AI is an amazingly advanced problem-solving tool. AI has the ability to leverage truly enormous volumes of data for analysis. Its applications can be found at the cutting edge of a staggering number of exciting advances that will, no doubt, raise the net value of human happiness over the next century. For example, in modern medicine, AI is used to analyse possible variations of molecular structures when fabricating new medicines and vaccines. AI can be used in modelling trials with innovative new treatments for diseases from arthritis to Alzheimer's. Imagine a world where people can be vaccinated against cancer and can enjoy a high quality of life into their nineties and beyond.

Then there is the exciting future of driverless vehicles, an advancement in human transportation that will rival the invention of the internal combustion engine itself. This technology, which relies heavily on AI, will result in far safer roads all over the world.

Uses facts and statistics to support argument.

Currently, the number of road deaths in Ireland in any given year is between 150 and 200. In the UK, it's nearly 2,000. For every death, you can predict a further eight injuries, many of which will be life-altering. Now extrapolate those numbers to every country in the world! All that human misery and suffering will be avoided when human error is taken off our roads. AI will make that possible.

Returns to opening point – a good way to conclude.

So yes, as Jay says, there are undoubtedly dangers associated with the development of AI. However, using technology is an inevitable part of being human. We will continue to innovate. Knowing the possible dangers will help us mitigate against them. The future with AI could be a bright one indeed!

Encourages readers' comments, in keeping with the one used at the start of the post.

Is AI a blessing or a curse? Have your say – post your comments below.

Thanks to you, I'm nearly at half-a-million followers! If you're new here, remember to subscribe.

A-Z Grammar Guide

Nouns

A word is classified according to the function it performs in the sentence. In the following extract from TEXT 3, the word 'deepfake' has two functions: it is used first as a noun and then as an adjective:

> 'Deepfakes are your friend. Yes, deepfake technology has understandably become notorious …'

For information about adjectives, see page 15.

Nouns are names. Any 'thing' you can think of, if it exists, has a name that is a noun. There are four types of noun:

1. **Common nouns** are the names of physical objects. For example: the *chair* you are sitting on, this *book*, the *clouds* above.

2. **Proper nouns** are the names of specific people, places, etc. They are written with initial capital letters. Unlike the generic common noun 'girl', the proper noun *Mary* refers to a specific girl. The same applies to 'day' and *Sunday*, 'month' and *May*, 'city' and *Paris*, etc. All titles of books, films and plays are proper nouns and should be capitalised.

> **Hint**
>
> Remember:
> • If you can put an article (a/an or the) in front of it, it is a noun.
> • If you can put 's or s' after it to show possession, it is a noun.

3. **Collective nouns** are the names given to groups of things. For example: a *herd* of cows, a *packet* of crisps, a *bouquet* of roses. Some of the more remarkable collective nouns include: a *smack* of jellyfish, a *flamboyance* of flamingos, a *murder* of crows. They should be treated as singular when used in a sentence. Take the example of a *team* of football players: there are eleven people in the team, but there is only one team. So, the grammatically correct usage is:
   The team is travelling to Galway for the cup final. ✓
   Not: The team are travelling to Galway for the cup final. ✗

4. **Abstract nouns** are the names given to things that exist but have no physical form. For example: *honesty, justice, revenge, love, hate, fear*.

Some nouns are often incorrectly capitalised. 'Mum', 'dad' or 'uncle', etc. are capitalised only when the word is being used as a person's name.

• Can we go now please, Mum? – 'Mum' is capitalised here because it is used as a name.
• Can I go and ask my mum? – 'mum' is not capitalised here because it is being used generically.

Likewise, the cardinal points of the compass and the seasons of the year do not get capitalised unless they are used as part of a specific name (proper noun).

• You need to travel west in order to visit West Virginia.
• I go skiing every winter and I love the Winter Olympics.

When writing a descriptive passage, include as many different noun types as you can. Name people and places as well as the common objects. Try to be precise: why say 'dog' when you can say 'Chihuahua' and create a more specific image? Use abstract nouns to describe concepts, emotions and ideas. Inventing an original collective noun can elevate a piece of writing: a giggle of schoolgirls or a sulk of teenagers.

SECTION II COMPOSING (100 marks)

Write a composition on **any one** of the assignments that appear in **bold print** below.

Each composition carries 100 marks.

The composition assignments are intended to reflect language study in the areas of information, argument, persuasion, narration, and the aesthetic use of language.

1. In TEXT 1, Klara, the robot with artificial intelligence, is described as having 'unique qualities', particularly her 'appetite for observing and learning'.

   Write a personal essay in which you reflect on your own appetite for observing and learning.

2. In TEXT 2, Elon Musk expresses his concern that the development of artificial intelligence, if it is not carefully regulated, may represent a danger to the public.

   Write a feature article, suitable for publication in a popular magazine, in which you discuss the issue (or issues) that you think currently pose the most danger to the public. Your article may be serious, or humorous, or both.

3. In TEXT 3, Simon Chandler discusses a technology that can alter recordings of someone's voice and manipulate video images to exploit people's identities.

   Write a short story in which a deception about someone's identity is central to the plot.

4. In TEXT 2, Elon Musk describes a future in which many jobs have become automated and identifies a significant challenge for people who may no longer be able to derive 'meaning' from their employment.

   Write a discursive essay about how people nowadays find meaning in their lives from their work/employment.

5. The illustration that accompanies TEXT 3 shows how deepfake technology can be used to make a famous painting, the *Mona Lisa*, appear alive.

   Write a short story in which the subject of a famous work of art, or a famous fictitious character from film or literature, is actually brought to life.

6. In TEXT 2, Elon Musk envisages a future in which everybody receives a 'universal basic income'.

   Write a speech in which you argue for or against the motion: *Ireland should introduce a universal basic income.*

7. In TEXT 3, we learn how 'deepfakes can serve to help bring history and art "alive" for a wider audience'.

   Write a personal essay in which you celebrate your own love of art and/or history and reflect on how your engagement with art and/or history has influenced you. You may interpret 'art' to refer to any of the visual, musical or theatrical arts.

Theme 3
Street Art

We turn our attention to the world of public visual art in this theme. Artwork created and/or displayed in a public space can be called 'street art'. It often divides opinion. Whether you consider spray-painted walls the work of vandals or artists will depend on your personal perspective. Civic sculpture can also be fraught with controversy.

The paragraphs below are taken from the three texts we will be exploring over the course of this theme. Take a look at the three samples and discuss the following questions:

Discuss

1. Of which genre of writing is each text an example?
2. What features or styles of writing helped you to identify the genre of each of these samples?
3. Where would you be likely to encounter each of these genres?

Sample 1 – Text 1

Alongside much-loved works, this is a country riddled with bad public sculptures, neglected public sculptures and even artist-disowned public sculptures, owing to a lack of adherence to their original vision. Division over public art is not new, but suspicion and confusion are also a relic of what Kennedy describes in her book.

Sample 2 – Text 2

I shove a dreadlock away from my face and pull down the handkerchief mask I've been breathing through. The thin material hangs lightly around my neck as if it's still holding my breath for me.

I take a few steps back from the wall and consider my work.

In the circle of my lantern's light, a ferocious blue lion roars in my direction. Streaks of teal and turquoise slice through his mane in an exhilarating way, but I'm not loving the flatness in his yellow eyes.

I'm startled by the growl of a car approaching, and the underpass I'm standing in lights up from headlights rounding the distant bend. *Shit.*

Sample 3 – Text 3

Pest Control, the tongue-in-cheek-titled organization set up by the artist to authenticate the real Banksy artwork, also protects him from prying outsiders. Hiding behind a paper bag, or, more commonly, e-mail, Banksy relentlessly controls his own narrative. His last face-to-face interview took place in 2003.

SECTION I   COMPREHENDING   (100 marks)

TEXT 1 – THE PÚCA OF ENNISTYMON

TEXT 1 has two components. The first is an opinion piece written by Cristín Leach for *The Sunday Times Ireland*, which appeared in *Culture* magazine in May 2021. The author is responding to a controversy surrounding a proposed piece of public art for Ennistymon, County Clare. The second is a photograph of the proposed sculpture and its creator, Aidan Harte.

In 1922 the Irish Free State dropped drawing as a compulsory subject in primary schools. It was not returned to the curriculum until 1971. Until free secondary education was introduced in 1967, Irish teenagers could study art only in private, faith-run schools. In her recent book, *Art and the Nation State*, Róisín Kennedy argued: 'This education system, in which only the privileged had access to art, encouraged an elitist engagement with visual art in Ireland.'

Thomas Bodkin's 1949 *Report on the Arts in Ireland* stated: 'No other country of Western Europe cared less, or gave less, for the cultivation of the arts.' A group of Scandinavian designers visiting Ireland in 1961 said: 'Without some reasonably developed form of art education in the various levels of schools in Ireland, it will be impossible to produce the informed and appreciative public so necessary as a background to the creative artist.' Bodkin believed the absence of art in education had pervaded the entire nation's attitude to it. This legacy has been multigenerational.

This month a divisive hoo-ha about an on-street sculpture destined for the town of Ennistymon in Co. Clare hit the public consciousness. Clare County Council had opted to pause plans to install [Aidan] Harte's *Púca of Ennistymon* 'to enable a broader public engagement process to take place'. This was in response to local objections to the piece. Harte's planned *Púca* (sculpted in clay but not yet cast), is a 2m tall bronze with an outsized horse's head and the distended, exaggerated body of a man. Irish writers, actors, artists, art historians and comedians took to social media to praise it.

Harte posted a photograph of himself posing alongside the clay *Púca*. The comments rolled in, varying from delight to dismissal, and some honest backtracking from locals: 'I didn't like it at first, but I changed my mind … Pity others don't value the folklore and mythology behind it.' One sentiment loomed large: a decision about how the town appears was made for them, rather than by them or with them.

The council's omission, from its announcement, not only of the artist's name but the names of those on the selection panel did not help: 'An adjudication panel comprising a community representative, an independent artist, the project manager for the Ennistymon scheme and Clare County Council's arts office selected the winning entry in accordance with the General National Guidelines on Public Art commissions.' It's remarkable that in a town with about a thousand people that the name of the community representative is not common knowledge. If a feeling of secrecy is the problem, this is not the way to address it.

Harte's remit was to draw attention to the town. He has also drawn attention to this issue. Some locals are now actively arguing for the *Púca*. There are as many people commenting that they want it in their town as there are Ennistymon people saying they would prefer not to have it there.

Alongside much-loved works, this is a country riddled with bad public sculptures, neglected public sculptures and even artist-disowned public sculptures, owing to a lack of adherence to their original vision. Division over public art is not new, but suspicion and confusion are also a relic of what Kennedy describes in her book.

A local priest's labelling of the sculpture 'pagan' and 'sinister' garnered good headlines, but there have also been calls for schoolchildren in Co. Clare to tell their teachers if they want the *Púca* installed.

These children have the benefit of huge improvements in Irish arts education in recent decades. This is a sculpture for the next generation too. Let's ask them what they think.

Aidan Harte with his clay model of the Púca

Footnote on Opinion Pieces

An opinion piece is written in order to convince. It uses the **language of argument** and the **language of persuasion**.

In TEXT 1, Cristín Leach uses some typical techniques of argumentative and persuasive language, including:

- **Triads:** lists of three such as 'bad public sculptures, neglected public sculptures and even artist-disowned public sculptures' – the repetition here creates a sense of urgency and adds weight to her argument.

- **References to experts/published opinions:** quotes from academics in the field of art education strengthen her overall contention.

- **Imagery:** conveys complex concepts in a simple form; for example, 'this is a country riddled with bad public sculptures' personifies Ireland as being marred by poor examples of public sculpture – 'riddled' literally means perforated with holes, but someone can also be 'riddled' with disease, which conveys Leach's loathing for this situation.

- **Strident tone:** her opinions are expressed strongly and confidently and are presented as indisputable. She does not use qualified phrases such as 'I think that …'.

QUESTION A – 50 Marks

(i) Based on your reading of TEXT 1, explain three insights you gained into the extent to which Ireland's relationship with the visual arts has changed over the last century. (15)

(ii) In the fourth paragraph, the author quotes an online comment: 'Pity others don't value the folklore and mythology behind [the *Púca* statue].' What is your personal opinion about the value of folklore and mythology? (15)

(iii) Identify four features of the language of argument and/or the language of persuasion used in TEXT 1, and discuss how effectively these features are employed by Cristín Leach to develop an astute and thought-provoking argument. Support your response with reference to the text. (20)

Exam Mechanics

QUESTION A (i)

6S Simplify

Simplify the question by identifying the key words.

> Based on your reading of TEXT 1, explain three insights you gained into the extent to which Ireland's relationship with the visual arts has changed over the last century.

You are likely to come across the words 'insights' and 'extent' fairly regularly in exam questions.

- Insights = understanding, wisdom or new knowledge.
- Extent = amount, degree or range. It invites you to make a value judgement about your findings.

Question A (i) is asking you to identify three examples of *new knowledge* you gained from reading TEXT 1. This new knowledge should relate to how much Ireland's relationship with the visual arts has changed over the last one hundred years. Has it

Hint

Do not waste time giving your opinion about the insights you gained; Question A (i) is about comprehension only.

changed a lot? Or not very much? When we want to know the extent to which something has changed, we look at how it is now and compare it with how it was. The *degree of difference* allows us to gauge how much it has changed.

6S Select

Read through the text and highlight any information that addresses this question. Brief notes to yourself in the margin will help you to sort out the evidence you find. Here are two examples:

> Curriculum change in 1922 (a good point to start 100-year period).

> Art back in schools in 1971 = change.

> Art's status in schools in the first half of the century.

In 1922 the Irish Free State dropped drawing as a compulsory subject in primary schools. It was not returned to the curriculum until 1971. Until free secondary education was introduced in 1967, Irish teenagers could study art only in private, faith-run schools. In her recent book, *Art and the Nation State*, Róisín Kennedy argued: 'This education system, in which only the privileged had access to art, encouraged an elitist engagement with visual art in Ireland.'

Theme 3: Street Art

Art's status in 1949.

Art's status in 1961.

Thomas Bodkin's 1949 *Report on the Arts in Ireland* stated: 'No other country of Western Europe cared less, or gave less, for the cultivation of the arts.' A group of Scandinavian designers visiting Ireland in 1961 said: 'Without some reasonably developed form of art education in the various levels of schools in Ireland, it will be impossible to produce the informed and appreciative public so necessary as a background to the creative artist.' Bodkin believed the absence of art in education had pervaded the entire nation's attitude to it. This legacy has been multigenerational.

Ireland's current relationship with visual arts – changed from 1922?

Ireland's changing relationship with arts/art education.

Alongside much-loved works, this is a country riddled with bad public sculptures, neglected public sculptures and even artist-disowned public sculptures, owing to a lack of adherence to their original vision. Division over public art is not new, but suspicion and confusion are also a relic of what Kennedy describes in her book.

A local priest's labelling of the sculpture 'pagan' and 'sinister' garnered good headlines, but there have also been calls for schoolchildren in Co. Clare to tell their teachers if they want the *Púca* installed. These children have the benefit of huge improvements in Irish arts education in recent decades. This is a sculpture for the next generation too. Let's ask them what they think.

6S Sort

You now have a selection of suitable quotations, but you will not need all of them in your answer. For example, in the first extract above, 1922 is an important start date, but the points made about the arts in 1949 and 1961 are quite similar. Decide which information you are going to use.

The evidence in the second extract relates to the author's view of the current situation. You want to show how the relationship has changed, so you could start by stating how things were and then look at how things are, or you could do it the other way around. Sort the information into the order you prefer.

6S State, support and spell out

The body of your answer for Question A (i) should contain three paragraphs. Each paragraph should:

1. **State** an insight you gained into the extent to which Ireland's relationship with the visual arts has changed over the last century.

   For a long time Irish people thought that art was only for high-brow or rich people.

2. **Support** your choice with evidence from TEXT 1. You can use direct quotations or paraphrase evidence from the text.

> The Irish Free State removed drawing from primary schools in 1922 and did not reinstate it as a subject until 1971. Only teenagers whose families could afford private schooling had the chance to study art in secondary school. According to the author, this 'encouraged an elitist engagement with visual art in Ireland'.

3. **Spell out** exactly what this evidence told you about the extent to which Ireland's relationship with the visual arts has changed.

> This told me that Ireland's early policymakers did not value the visual arts, but opinions evolved and led to a change in policy in the 1970s.

Follow this process for each of the three parts of your answer.

QUESTION B – 50 Marks

Imagine that your local county council has proposed a public discussion about erecting the *Púca* statue (pictured on page 46) in your town. Write a **letter to the editor** of your local newspaper in which you support the council's proposal. In your letter you should clearly explain your feelings about the subject matter of the sculpture, discuss your assessment of its visual impact on the observer and suggest, with reasons, the best possible site for the statue to be located.

Exam Mechanics

QUESTION B

Read the question and highlight the main task. This task will inform your entire answer. It will indicate what **genre** you will be writing in, what your **purpose** is and what **layout/ structure** to use. Identify the type of **audience** you will be writing for, which will determine the appropriate **style and register** to use. **Number the points you need to cover** to make sure that your answer addresses all aspects of the question.

> Imagine that your local county council has proposed a public discussion about erecting the *Púca* statue (pictured on page 46) in your town. Write a **letter to the editor** of your local newspaper in which you support the council's proposal. In your letter you should clearly explain your feelings about the subject matter of the sculpture **(1)**, discuss your assessment of its visual impact on the observer **(2)** and suggest, with reasons, the best possible site for the statue to be located **(3)**.

Genre: a letter to the editor.

Purpose: to support the proposal to erect the *Púca* statue in your town and to argue for the statue to be placed in a particular location.

Layout/structure: letters to the editor follow certain conventions. See the guidance below for details on how to structure your letter. The three specific tasks in this question should each have their own paragraph(s). Therefore, including an introduction and a conclusion, you will write at least five paragraphs.

Audience: one error some students make when writing a letter to the editor is to assume that the audience is the editor alone.

Hint

The best way to learn how to write a letter to the editor is to do it for real. Why not give it a try? Apart from getting good practice, you may well see yourself published. Newspaper editors are always looking for interesting opinions on current issues, especially those expressed by young people. What issue do you feel strongly about? Start by reading some letters that have been printed in recent editions. Many newspapers also have an online archive of letters submitted.

Most newspapers have guidelines on how to write a letter that is likely to be published. Check out the specific newspaper's website to access these rules.

Although it is addressed to the editor, the reason for writing the letter is to have it published in the newspaper. Therefore, your audience is all the readers of that newspaper.

Style and register: a letter to the editor is a formal communication. Your language needs to be clear and concise and your tone should be confident and self-assured. Avoid using 'I think' or 'in my opinion' – just state your opinion.

(1) Explain your feelings about the subject matter – the *Púca* statue itself and/or Irish mythology generally.

(2) Discuss your assessment of the visual impact of this specific artwork.

(3) Suggest where the statue should be placed in your town and give at least two reasons for your choice of location.

Letter to the editor guidance

Greeting: start with either 'Sir – ' or 'Madam – '; it is not the convention to put 'Dear' in front. Do not use 'Sir/Madam' as it is assumed you know the correct term.

Opening paragraph: identify the issue you are raising. Remember that not all readers will be entirely up to speed on the topic, so you need to make what you are discussing clear. If the issue is something you first read about in the newspaper you are writing to, your opening paragraph should include the headline of the article you are referring to and the date of publication. If you know it, you could also include the author's name. For example: 'I would like to applaud our county council's decision to consult the public about its proposal to erect the *Púca* statue in our town ('Is the *Púca* coming to town?', Bill Bailey, 20 June).' If you are responding to a letter from the letters' page, you do exactly the same thing.

Following paragraphs: get straight to the point, making your arguments clearly but concisely. Use the language of argument and the language of persuasion to convince as many readers as possible to agree with your point of view. Avoid long-winded or complicated sentences.

Conclusion: make it strong and succinct.

Sign-off: the standard sign-off for letters to the editor is 'Yours, etc.' followed by your name. Do not use your own name in the exam – invent one instead.

TEXT 2 – RORY

TEXT 2 is the opening chapter of the novel *Love and Vandalism* by Laurie Boyle Crompton, an author of young adult fiction. The novel tells the story of Rory, the daughter of the town's new police sergeant. Rory has been keeping a secret from her father.

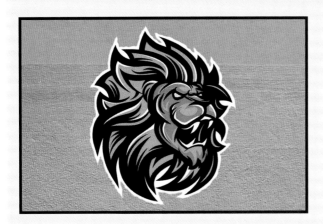

My can of spray paint rips into the gentle night, releasing a loud *psssht* into an open mouth of fangs.

I shove a dreadlock away from my face and pull down the handkerchief mask I've been breathing through. The thin material hangs lightly around my neck as if it's still holding my breath for me.

I take a few steps back from the wall and consider my work.

In the circle of my lantern's light, a ferocious blue lion roars in my direction. Streaks of teal and turquoise slice through his mane in an exhilarating way, but I'm not loving the flatness in his yellow eyes.

I'm startled by the growl of a car approaching, and the underpass I'm standing in lights up from headlights rounding the distant bend. *Shit.*

I fling a long, black tarp over all my supplies and hiss, '*Rory's sorry*,' to the cans that clatter and clink together in response.

The car's high beams grow steadily brighter as I run from the scene. The second I reach the end of the cement wall, I recklessly launch myself headfirst into the bushes beside the road.

I hear the car slow to a crawl as I lie facedown in the underbrush and pray to whatever graffiti gods are within earshot, *Please don't be a police cruiser. Or my dad. Or I'm-begging-you-oh-pleasepleaseplease, not my dad driving his police cruiser.*

The car lingers. My lion has been spotted. I lift my head and see a mild-mannered Jeep Wrangler stopped just inside the underpass. The top is down, but the thing is on spring lifts, and from my position on the ground I can't see over the Jeep's massive tires.

I will the driver to leave my cans and pull away. Maybe I should've joined Kat at her weird Jedi Mind Trick training workshop after all. I'm not really clear on what she and her Star Wars groupies do together, but I think it has something to do with trying to channel The Force to make shit happen with their minds. Also, they like to wave around flashlight lightsabers while dressed in bathrobes.

Desperately, I whisper at the driver, 'Move-your-vehicle's-ass-you-need-to-go-go-go-far-away-now-please-thanks.'

A camera's flash lights up the underpass for an instant before the Jeep jumps forward and roars away.

So I guess that's how Jedi Mind Tricks work. I sigh with relief. The driver just wanted a photo of the newest lion in New Paltz. Probably didn't even realize the paint's still wet.

It was a fluke that anyone came down this deserted road in the first place, but I stay on the ground a few minutes, breathing hard as I imagine all the horrible ways the scenario could've gone.

The local police department is on a campaign to rid the town of graffiti art, and according to an article in *The New Paltz Times*, the police sergeant was quoted as saying he considers each new lion painting a 'personal offense.'

The New Paltz police sergeant also happens to be my dad, but of course, he has no idea the paintings are mine––or that his being *personally* offended makes them so much more fun for me to paint.

I fling the tarp back off my supplies, and my spray cans rattle with relief.

The lantern illuminates the wall, and I lock eyes with the newest member of the carousing graffiti pride I've created throughout our rural upstate town.

So far, I've been painting my lions in out-of-the-way places, but I hope to change that very soon.

Everybody is going to notice the lion I'm planning next.

I used one of my custom stencils on this one's body, so it shares the same stance as all the others, but with my special spray techniques, I've made his face one of a kind.

I'm convinced the only way to capture each lion's unique rage-y-ness is by going freehand.

The rough texture of the wall gives this particular fellow a snarly quality, and the idea of his roar echoing through the underpass makes me smile.

Somewhat satisfied, I pack my workspace into a long, plastic crate, shove the rolled-up tarp on top, and drag the clinking heap through the weeds to where my hatchback waits.

With a grunt, I toss everything in the back, jump into the driver's seat, and, after a churn and a shift, I'm zipping down the road.

I notice a splotch of blue paint on my wrist and lick my finger to rub at it. The dashboard's weak glow shows the blue spot spreading ominously as I speed through the winding woods, leaving my lion to say …

everything I can't.

QUESTION A – 50 Marks

(i) Based on your reading of TEXT 2, explain three insights you gained into the character of Rory. Support your answer with reference to the text. (15)

(ii) TEXT 2 ends with the words: 'I speed through the winding woods, leaving my lion to say … everything I can't.' In your opinion, which medium of visual art 'speaks' an artist's message most clearly to the viewer: graffiti, film or sculpture? Give reasons for your answer. (15)

(iii) Identify four features of the language of narration evident in the above text, and discuss how effectively these features are employed by Laurie Boyle Crompton to write a captivating and dramatic opening to her novel. Support your response with reference to the text. (20)

Exam Mechanics

QUESTION A (i)

6S Simplify

The question states exactly what you need to find, so highlight the key words.

> Based on your reading of TEXT 2, explain three insights you gained into the character of Rory. Support your answer with reference to the text.

Before you start reading the text, you already know to look for information about the type of person Rory is and to pay attention to how she looks and behaves, what she says and how others react to her.

6S Select

As you read the text, highlight any references to Rory's appearance, personality or behaviour and make brief notes for yourself. For example:

> Is mask for disguise or to protect from paint fumes? Or both?

I shove a dreadlock away from my face and pull down the handkerchief mask I've been breathing through. The thin material hangs lightly around my neck as if it's still holding my breath for me.

> Speaks to paint cans (personifying them) – seems very attached to her art.

I fling a long, black tarp over all my supplies and hiss, *'Rory's sorry,'* to the cans that clatter and clink together in response.

6S Sort

Highlighting something does not mean you have to use it. You will probably have identified more than three ideas from the text, so choose the strongest points you can make. In the examples above, the attachment Rory feels for her cans of spray paint is a much stronger point to select than the simple fact that she is wearing a mask.

6S State, support and spell out

As you have been asked for three insights, your examiner will expect you to write three paragraphs. Each paragraph should:

1. **State** the aspect of Rory's character you have chosen to discuss.

> A significant insight I gained into Rory's character is how passionate she is about her artwork, and her dedication to being a graffiti artist.

2. **Support** your idea with a quote or reference.

> The first clue we are given to show us Rory's devotion to her art is the way she personifies her cans of spray paint. She flings a black tarp over her paint supplies to hide them from the approaching vehicle and whispers 'Rory's sorry' to them.

3. **Spell out** how your quote supports your idea and the insight you gained from this aspect of Rory's character.

> Clearly, she feels an almost maternal concern for her paints and supplies. She speaks in the third person, calling herself 'Rory', as someone does when speaking to a small child. It is as though she is abandoning them and feels guilty about it. Her concern shows how important these objects are to her and, by extension, how utterly devoted she is to her art.

Follow this process for each of the three insights you discuss in your answer.

Theme 3: Street Art

QUESTION B – 50 Marks

▶ Imagine that the appearance of Rory's images of a lion have come to the attention of the local media as well as the police. Write the text of a **news report** on this story, to be delivered on a local radio station. The report should communicate the facts of the case, describe the police department's official response and discuss the public reaction to the images.

Sample Answer ▶

QUESTION B

Ted:	Welcome back to News Hour here at New Paltz FM, the best station for regional and local updates. Now, to some local news. Have you seen what many are calling the New Paltz Blue Lion? Community leaders are demanding police action after a number of these images appeared on walls around town in recent weeks. We sent roving reporter Sandra Martinez to bring you this report.
	[Cut to Sandra – sound of traffic]
Sandra [S]:	Thanks, Ted. I'm here at the junction of Main and Fifth Avenue and can see the usual rush-hour traffic as the citizens of New Paltz travel home from work. However, there's something new about the overpass this evening. Next to me is the image of a ferocious blue lion, at least seven feet tall, roaring out at commuters. Some of our listeners may have seen similar images around town, but this is the largest and most public example so far. I'm joined now by Sergeant Maguire of the New Paltz Police Department, who has agreed to come on air to tell us more about this. Good evening, Sergeant Maguire.
Maguire [M]:	Hello. Good to talk with you, Sandra.
S:	Thanks for coming on. So, what is your opinion of this image that people are calling the New Paltz Blue Lion? It's actually quite artistic, isn't it?
M:	No, Sandra, I do not believe so. I believe it is a criminal act of vandalism.
S:	Many of the citizens of New Paltz disagree with you. Let me play you a vox pop we recorded earlier.

Annotations:

- Script format is appropriate for a radio transcript.
- Establishes context using a suitable style.
- Uses evidence from TEXT 2.
- Typical wording for news report – adds authenticity.
- Typical instruction.
- Made-up location using common US street names.
- Imitates sensational language of a tabloid-style radio broadcast.
- Live on-air interviews are a typical feature of radio reports.
- Made-up surname for Rory's father to add authenticity.
- Reporters tend to ask deliberately challenging questions.
- Short for *vox populi* (Latin for 'the voice of the people'), a technique used by radio stations to get a 'snapshot' of public opinion about something.

[Cut to vox pop]

Voice 1:	Yeah, I think they're very cool. Just what this old town needs.
Voice 2:	I like the lion. Make it the New Paltz town mascot!
Voice 3:	I love the colours. It really brightens up the place.

[Cut back]

S: What do you make of that, Sergeant? People seem to be impressed.

M: I believe that the vast majority of citizens are as concerned by this senseless and illegal act as I am.

S: In an interview with *The New Paltz Times* recently, you said you considered each new lion painting as a personal offence. Do you stand by that?

M: Yes, I stand by what I said. I love my town and I am personally offended by this defacement of public property. The whole police department is in complete accord on this issue. We will bring the perpetrator to justice.

S: Could it be someone from out of town doing it? Perhaps that anonymous graffiti artist from England?

M: Banksy?

S: Yes! I can see you've been doing your research, Sergeant.

M: Well, I guess we've learned a lot over the past few weeks.

S: Perhaps these works could one day be worth money?

M: [laughing] No, this image is painted freehand. Banksy uses stencils. This is not worth the time it will take for Freeway Maintenance to clean it off. At taxpayers' expense, I might add.

S: So, have you any leads on who is behind these images? And are they the work of just one person?

Annotations:

- Slang/colloquialisms are acceptable when used knowingly and in the right context.
- Direct reference to the information contained in TEXT 2.
- Mimics the typical diction of a police sergeant.
- Refers to information from TEXT 3 – not necessary, but examiner would notice it!
- Uses evidence from TEXT 2.

M:	I can tell you that we are following a definite line of inquiry. The person behind this is probably something of a misfit, with unhappy family relationships. This is a cry for help, and I would like to take this opportunity to appeal to this person to hand themselves in. There must be listeners who know who this person is. Is it someone living with you? Watch for suspicious activity. Where are they buying their paints? Where are they keeping their equipment? Do you know where your teenagers are going at night? Parents: be vigilant! Any information you can give us will help. You can contact the department at 555 2162.
S:	Thank you, Sergeant Maguire. That number again?
M:	555 2162.
S:	Thanks again.
M:	My pleasure.
S:	So there you have it, folks. Whether you love the Blue Lion or hate him, the artist seems to be one step ahead of the law for now. Back to you, Ted.
	[cut back to studio]
Ted:	Thanks, Sandra. Now, from a blue lion in New York to the Cubs in Chicago. Let's go to Bernadette with all of today's sports news.

Example of dramatic irony.

More dramatic irony.

Segue from one item to the next.

A-Z Grammar Guide

Verbs, tenses and participles

Verbs are essential grammatical components of sentences. There are few hard rules in English grammar that cannot be broken, but here are two on which you can rely:

1. Every sentence must have a verb.
2. Every verb must have a tense.

You were probably taught that verbs are 'doing' words, but this is true only to a certain extent. Some verbs are indeed clear physical actions. For example: 'I shove a dreadlock away from my face and pull down the handkerchief mask'. These verbs are written in the present simple tense because we understand the actions to be occurring concurrently with the narration. However, look at this sentence: 'Please don't be a police cruiser.' In this case, be is a verb, but it is not exactly an action. The verb here is conveying a state of being rather than doing; other examples include: I am, you are, she is, we were.

Next look at this full sentence:

> I shove a dreadlock away from my face and pull down the handkerchief mask I've been breathing through.

The highlighted words also denote an action. In this case, the action was already being performed: Rory has been breathing through the handkerchief since some time before the narration began. 'I've been breathing' is an example of a verb written in the **present perfect tense**.

Perhaps the first thing you notice about this tense is that the verb is not just one word, it is three words. It is important to remember that verbs often are a combination of words. Why is this? Look again at rule 2 above: *all verbs must have a tense*. In the example, the words 'have been' give the word 'breathing' its tense. The word 'breathing' on its own has no tense.

Consider the sentence 'Breathing is very important.' 'Breathing' is not a verb here because it has no tense on its own. It is a **present participle**. Present participles always end in –*ing*. The verb in this example is 'is'. If we replace 'Breathing' with 'Water' – 'Water is very important.' – there is no confusion because we do not usually think of the word 'water' as a verb. Examples of verbs formed with present participles from TEXT 2 include: 'I'm not loving the flatness in his yellow eyes' and 'as if it's still holding my breath for me'.

Look at the following sentence: 'Holding on for dear life, the climber waited for rescue.' The verb here is 'waited' because that word is clearly in the past simple tense. Another way to look at it would be to change the sentence into the present simple or the future continuous:

• Holding on for dear life, the climber waits for rescue.
• Holding on for dear life, the climber will be waiting for rescue.

The participle 'Holding' does not change, regardless of the tense, so it cannot be the verb in this sentence.

Remember rule 1: *all sentences must have a verb*. So the phrase 'Holding on for dear life' cannot be a sentence on its own because *holding* is a participle here and not a verb. 'Holding' is connected to the noun in the sentence (it gives us more information about the climber).

When people use a participle but forget to connect it to a noun, or connect it to the wrong noun, it is known as a **dangling participle**. Consider this example: 'Driving around the corner, the house looked magnificent.' It sounds like the house is driving around the corner, which makes no sense. To avoid being ambiguous or misleading, the writer should have written something like: 'Driving around the corner, I noticed that the house looked magnificent.'

Correct the following dangling participle errors:

1. Having finished my essay, the teacher collected my test paper.
2. Looking quite dried out and withered, Sarah took the pot plants out to the garden.
3. Walking through the supermarket, the fruit looked delicious.
4. Flying low over the sea, Dublin came into view.

TEXT 3 – GRAFFITI

TEXT 3 is composed of two elements. The first is an edited extract from an informative article published in the *Smithsonian* magazine in 2013 about the English street artist known as 'Banksy'. The second element is made up of two examples of works created by Banksy, both of which make use of written text.

On his way to becoming an international icon, the subversive and secretive street artist turned the art world upside-down

When *Time* magazine selected the British artist Banksy—graffiti master, painter, activist, filmmaker and all-purpose *provocateur*—for its list of the world's 100 most influential people in 2010, he found himself in the company of Barack Obama, Steve Jobs and Lady Gaga. He supplied a picture of himself with a paper bag (recyclable, naturally) over his head. Most of his fans don't really want to know who he is (and have loudly protested Fleet Street attempts to unmask him). But they do want to follow his upward trajectory from the outlaw spraying—or, as the argot* has it, 'bombing'—walls in Bristol, England, during the 1990s to the artist whose work commands hundreds of thousands of dollars in the auction houses of Britain and America. Today, he has bombed cities from Vienna to San Francisco, Barcelona to Paris and Detroit. And he has moved from graffiti on gritty urban walls to paint on canvas, conceptual sculpture and even film, with the guileful documentary *Exit Through the Gift Shop*, which was nominated for an Academy Award.

Pest Control, the tongue-in-cheek-titled organization set up by the artist to authenticate the real Banksy artwork, also protects him from prying outsiders. Hiding behind a paper bag, or, more commonly, e-mail, Banksy relentlessly controls his own narrative. His last face-to-face interview took place in 2003.

While he may shelter behind a concealed identity, he advocates a direct connection between an artist and his constituency. 'There's a whole new audience out there, and it's never been easier to sell [one's art],' Banksy has maintained. 'You don't have to go to college, drag 'round a portfolio, mail off transparencies to snooty galleries or sleep with someone powerful, all you need now is a few ideas and a broadband connection. This is the first time the essentially bourgeois** world of art has belonged to the people. We need to make it count.'

* Argot means the jargon or slang used by a particular group of people.

** The bourgeois world Banksy is referring to is the world of rich people who own art galleries and/or buy art.

Image 1

Image 2

Footnote on Visual Texts

When approaching a visual text, the first question to ask yourself is: what type of image is it? Is it a painting? Is it computer-generated? A pencil drawing? A photograph? An advertisement? A poster? Essentially, who is communicating the image to you? If it is a pencil drawing, someone drew it. If it is an advert, someone is advertising something. Someone created the thing you are looking at. Next ask yourself: *why?*

Both images in TEXT 3 are photographs of original works that appeared in public spaces. Remember that you are looking at not only what the artist chose to produce, but also what the photographer chose to show you. Another photograph could show the same thing from a different perspective. What does the photograph focus on? Why? What angle is the photograph taken from? What time of day is it? Such issues will affect your interpretation of a photograph.

Here is another photograph of a Banksy image. Our interpretation of this artwork depends a great deal upon the position from which the photograph has been taken. The photographer chose to take this picture from a particular spot. While it shows us both sides of the Banksy image, the photographer has chosen to focus slightly more on the boy than on the fire. If the photograph had been taken from a position further to the left, the opposite would be true. Someone else might have chosen to show only one side of the image. How would these decisions affect your interpretation of the artwork?

Once you have considered the influence of the creator of the image, you can look more closely at the image itself. Start by describing exactly what you see. Take your time, and try to make out the details. For example, look closely at TEXT 3, Image 1.

- Why has the artist chosen to paint the lettering in red? Is it just to make the words stand out, or are we supposed to be reminded of blood?

- What is the relationship between the lettering and the rat? It has a red paw, and it seems to have 'signed' the message on the wall with a paw print. Can we assume that the rat is the supposed 'author' of the message?

- Why is the rat posed in that particular position? Is it looking over its shoulder because it is nervous about being caught? Or is its expression supposed to convey confidence, defiance or pride in its work?

- Why has Banksy chosen a rat to be the 'speaker' of this message? (Note: rats are something of a **motif** or recurring image for Banksy.) What do rats symbolise? Has it something to do with the way authorities might view graffiti artists?

- Then think about the message itself. The artist is clearly using irony, since graffiti is illegal in most jurisdictions. Is the artist's message that graffiti really can change things? Is that why it is illegal?

Discuss

Read through the discussion on irony and sarcasm on pages xxii–xxiii. Then, work with a partner to discuss how irony is used in Image 2.

QUESTION A – 50 Marks

(i) Based on your reading of the written element of TEXT 3, explain three insights you gained into the street artist called Banksy. (15)

(ii) The Irish online news website TheJournal.ie recently conducted a poll to discover people's opinions about street art. Most respondents answered that 'some [graffiti] is art – but most isn't'. Give your personal response to this issue. (15)

(iii) Based on your interpretation of the two images by Banksy in TEXT 3, discuss how each uses a combination of text and illustration in order to amplify the impact of the artist's message on the viewer. In your answer, make detailed reference to the textual and visual elements of the images. (20)

Sample Answer

QUESTION A (ii)

Brief introduction states personal opinion.

I agree with the majority of the respondents to TheJournal.ie's poll. Some graffiti is art but most is not.

Refers to evidence contained in the paper – not obligatory, but a sensible approach to take if you can.

The images of graffiti included in this exam paper are good examples of the aesthetically pleasing variety of graffiti. The picture of the blue lion that accompanies TEXT 2 is dramatic and vibrant, and I would have no objection to seeing it painted in a public space near where I live.

Linking word demonstrates that an argument is being built.

Similarly, if all graffiti was of the same quality as the variety produced by Banksy, I would argue that it is art. The Banksy images reproduced in this paper are ingenious, ironic and thought-provoking. They can also be humorous and, at times, poignant. Banksy's work addresses important themes, and has been presented all over the world.

Linking word indicates a shift in approach.

However, most of the graffiti I see in my day-to-day life is not the

Offers evidence not contained in the paper.

kind of graffiti shown here. On the bus shelters and the streets in the area where I live, people spray-paint their 'tags'. I do not accept that

First example to support opinion.

this is art. Someone inventing a 'cool' moniker for themselves to display on any available public space is unsightly. There is no artistry in this.

Evidence explained.

Furthermore, there is graffiti at my school that definitely could not be called 'art'. Some people like to write crude or indecent messages;

Second example.

others just vandalise the desks and other school equipment.

Further explanation.

Graffiti can indeed be a visual medium through which talented artists engage with challenging issues facing society. Some street artists, such as Banksy, do so with great humour and insight. Some graffiti

Conclusion sums up the main argument.

artists produce visually stunning works that would enhance any locality. However, in my own experience, the vast majority of graffiti is not of this type.

QUESTION B – 50 Marks

Your Leaving Certificate class has decided to enter your school's graffiti art competition. The winning entry will be permitted to spray-paint their proposed design wherever in the school they specify. The inspiration for the winning design must be drawn from your class's study of literature currently prescribed for Higher Level Leaving Certificate English. Write the text of your **competition entry** in which you describe the image you propose, explain your choice of image by referring to the literature you have studied and nominate, with at least one reason, the site of the proposed image.

Exam Mechanics

QUESTION B

Read the question and highlight the main task. This task will inform your entire answer. It will indicate what **genre** you will be writing in, what your **purpose** is and what **layout/ structure** to use. Identify the type of **audience** you will be writing for, which will determine the appropriate **style and register** to use. **Number the points you need to cover** to make sure that your answer addresses all aspects of the question.

> Your Leaving Certificate class has decided to enter your school's graffiti art competition. The winning entry will be permitted to spray-paint their proposed design wherever in the school they specify. The inspiration for the winning design must be drawn from your class's study of literature currently prescribed for Higher Level Leaving Certificate English. Write the text of your **competition entry** in which you describe the image you propose **(1)**, explain your choice of image by referring to the literature you have studied **(2)** and nominate, with at least one reason, the site of the proposed image **(3)**.

Genre: a competition entry.

Purpose: a little like a sales pitch, you want to win over your audience and ensure that your ideas are judged to be the best of all the entries.

Layout/structure: there is no specific layout for a competition entry and examiners are told to expect a variety of approaches. Many students decide to use a letter format.

Audience: who would judge such a competition at your school: the principal; a panel of senior staff; the board of management; the art teacher? Address your chosen audience in your opening and demonstrate awareness of them throughout your entry by making references to the school's history/culture/achievements, etc.

Style and register: use the most appropriate register for your chosen audience. If your entry is aimed at a panel of judges, the default register is to write formally. Use aesthetic language as well as the language of argument and the language of persuasion.

(1) Describe the proposed image. Remember that graffiti can be an image, text or both. Convince the judge(s) that your image is the best choice with aesthetic language: rich descriptions, emotive words, lots of colour and vibrancy.

(2) Explain the inspiration for your choice of image. Which studied text does it come from and why? Does it illustrate a key moment? Does it represent a general theme? Whatever the ideas behind your image are, why are they relevant to your school context? Use the language of argument to develop a strong case for your choice of image.

(3) Where exactly in your school should it be displayed? Why? Do not be afraid to go into specifics; that is what you would do in a real entry of this sort.

SECTION II COMPOSING (100 marks)

Write a composition on **any one** of the assignments that appear in **bold print** below.

Each composition carries 100 marks.

The composition assignments are intended to reflect language study in the areas of information, argument, persuasion, narration, and the aesthetic use of language.

1. All three texts on this paper are concerned with the visual arts.

    Write a personal essay in which you reflect on your experience of, and the value you place upon, visual art.

2. Rory, the central character in TEXT 2, has a complicated relationship with her father.

    Write a discursive essay in which you consider the importance of intergenerational relationships.

3. In TEXT 1, we read about a sculpture of the Púca, a shape-changing supernatural entity from Irish mythology. We also see the artist Aidan Harte's interpretation of what the Púca might look like.

    Write a short story, suitable for inclusion in a collection of supernatural fiction, in which the Púca is central to the plot.

4. In Image 2 of TEXT 3, Banksy makes use of the following quotation from Marcus Aurelius, a Roman emperor: 'What we do in life echoes in eternity.'

    Write a personal essay in which you reflect on the meaning of this quotation in your life.

5. The signature image used by Rory, the graffiti artist we read about in TEXT 2, is a blue lion.

    Write a short story in which a lion and a bathrobe are central to the plot.

6. In TEXT 1, Cristín Leach argues that children should be consulted for their opinions on public issues.

    Write an article, for publication in a national newspaper, in which you argue either for or against the proposition: *Young people should have a far more meaningful role in local and national decision-making.*

7. In TEXT 3, we learn that Banksy was included in *Time* magazine's list of the World's 100 Most Influential People.

    Write the text of a speech to be delivered at an international public-speaking competition on the theme: *The Five Most Influential People in the World Today.*

Theme 4
Ghosts

The supernatural has fascinated writers and readers alike for centuries. From *Hamlet* to *The Lord of the Rings*, *A Christmas Carol* to *Harry Potter*, ghosts and hauntings can be found in some of the best-loved stories ever written.

The paragraphs below are taken from the three texts we will be exploring over the course of this theme. Take a look at the three samples and discuss the following questions:

Discuss

1. Of which genre of writing is each text an example?
2. What features or styles of writing helped you to identify the genre of each of these samples?
3. Where would you be likely to encounter each of these genres?

Sample 1 – TEXT 1

My walk home would take me past the old Victorian house where the great writer John Synge and his widowed mother had endured their last years, a house that appears several times in *Ghost Light*. As a child, I passed it often, was faintly afraid of it, often wondered about the stories it had seen. On a wintry night it could be forbidding as the Bates Motel, or as Wuthering Heights in a rainstorm. But on a moonlit summer evening in that coast-town of seagulls and steeples, a strange beauty seemed to glitter from its windows.

Sample 2 – TEXT 2

… the townspeople are asleep.

Except for Judith. She is coming along the street, wrapped in a cloak, the hood covering her head. She goes past the school, where the fox was until a moment ago; she doesn't see it but it sees her, from its hiding place in an alleyway. It watches her with widened pupils, alarmed by this unexpected creature sharing its nocturnal world, taking in her mantle, her quick-stepping feet, the hurry in her gait.

Sample 3 – TEXT 3

One of Ireland's most well-known haunted hotels is the Cabra Castle hotel in Kingscourt, Co. Cavan. It was once declared the second scariest hotel in the world by Tripadvisor. Legends about the hotel have been circulating for generations. It was the third stop on my ghost busters tour. I stayed in the most haunted room, but the ghosts were a no show.

SECTION I   COMPREHENDING   (100 marks)

TEXT 1 – GHOST LIGHT

Award-winning Irish author Joseph O'Connor explains what inspired him to write his 2019 novel *Ghost Light* in this preface to the book.

On a Saturday night, when I was a teenager in 1970s Ireland, my pals and I would go to the school-kids' disco at the Presentation College, Glasthule. 'Prez', as it was known, was fairly grimy at the time, but fantastically exciting, too. [...] The climax of the evening was always Led Zeppelin's 'Stairway to Heaven', and if you hadn't persuaded someone to slow-dance with you before that song sped up, the consensus was that you were going home alone. And most Saturday nights, that's what happened to me. Tongue-tied, nervous, I faced the long road home. But, still, there was a love story in Glasthule.

My walk home would take me past the old Victorian house where the great writer John Synge and his widowed mother had endured their last years, a house that appears several times in *Ghost Light*. As a child, I passed it often, was faintly afraid of it, often wondered about the stories it had seen. On a wintry night it could be forbidding as the Bates Motel, or as Wuthering Heights in a rainstorm. But on a moonlit summer evening in that coast-town of seagulls and steeples, a strange beauty seemed to glitter from its windows.

My late mother, a great reader, had often told me the strangest story of all: how in the last years of Synge's life, this reticent, broken genius, the son of a Protestant land-owning family, had fallen tempestuously in love with a Catholic girl from the inner city of Dublin, a young actress called Molly Allgood. [...]

A couple of years ago, I began writing this novel inspired by Molly Allgood and Synge. I started with the uncertainty most novelists have at the outset. You don't know if your story is going to work at all. What tense should it be written in? Who should be the

narrator? Every book needs to have a style, its own unique voice, and to find it can be gruellingly frustrating. But somehow, over time, through dozens of drafts, I came to see that this story needed to be simple, focused closely on Molly. She began to loom up at me from the phantoms of dead drafts, as funny and flirtatious as I had imagined her in my teens. I suppose I learnt to stand out of her way, to let her lead me into the story of *Ghost Light*. I follow her through a day in the 1950s in London, when the past comes back to an elderly Irish actress who was once the beautiful muse of a genius.

To write fiction based on real people and those they loved is a morally ambiguous enterprise, to say the least. *Ghost Light* is a work of the imagination, frequently taking immense liberties with fact. The experiences and personalities of the real Molly and Synge differed from those of my characters in numerous ways. Yeats and Lady Gregory and Sean O'Casey appear in the book too, no doubt in forms some biographers won't like. Then again, these giants often said they had fanned their fictions from the sparks of real life, renaming the people who had inspired their stories. The practice was sometimes a camouflage, sometimes a claim of authenticity. It was an option I considered carefully but decided against in the end, and so I dare to ask the forgiveness of these noble ghosts of world literature for not changing the names of the innocent.

Theme 4: Ghosts

65

To finish a book is an ambiguous feeling too. You have worked so long and hard on it, you know its every line and comma. In the final stages of editing, you dream about it. And then suddenly, the day is coming when it must go out into the world. You won't be there to hold its hand, to reason away its deficiencies, to explain it to those who will encounter it. There is a kind of joy in finishing, but there is fear and apprehensiveness too. You want the book to find friends who will meet it halfway. Perhaps it's similar to what a parent feels when a child leaves the house. This day was always coming; it's what everything was building towards; but there is anxiety in the mix, a sense of encroaching realities, and if I am honest, there is even a touch of sadness. You come to know your characters so well; everything about them. Things you'll never know about your spouse or your closest friend, you know about a person you have created. To see her walk away, into the great, wide world, is to watch a little piece of your self take its chances. But that's what a novel is for: to offer itself to the reader. I hope you find something in it that speaks to you.

– Joseph O'Connor

Footnote on Front Matter

The writing at the very start of a book is known as 'front matter'. There are various kinds of front matter, including:

- **Prologue:** found in a work of fiction, it is part of the story and can be dramatic to whet the reader's appetite.
- **Foreword:** found in fiction and non-fiction, it is a type of essay written by someone other than the author. A new edition of a novel, for example, may include another author's praise for the book.
- **Preface:** found in fiction and non-fiction, it is a type of essay by the author explaining their interest in the subject of the book or describing how and why they wrote it. TEXT 1 is an example of a preface.
- **Introduction:** found in all types of publications, it acquaints readers with information that will aid them in understanding the rest of the book. It outlines the book's major themes and prepares readers for what they can expect. It may discuss the origins of the book or the process by which its contents were assembled. The author may thank people or organisations for their help in compiling the book. The editor of a collection of essays, poetry, photography, recipes, etc. will often write an introduction. The style and tone will be determined by the intended audience and, of course, the topic of the book itself.

Hint

You might think that since the introduction appears first, it is written first. However, the introduction is the *last* part of the book to be written. Whoever writes the introduction needs to have a detailed knowledge of whatever the rest of the book contains.

Of these four types of front matter, you are most likely to be asked to compose an introduction.

QUESTION A – 50 Marks

(i) Based on your reading of TEXT 1, explain three insights you gained from Joseph O'Connor about the challenges involved in writing works of fiction. (15)

(ii) Joseph O'Connor tells us that he hopes his reader finds something in his novel *Ghost Light* that 'speaks' to them. From the texts you have studied for your Leaving Certificate course*, identify a moment that 'spoke' to you. Explain in detail what it was about this moment that had such an effect upon you as a reader. (15)

* Texts specified for study for Leaving Certificate English, including poetry, single texts and texts (including films) prescribed for comparative study.

(iii) Based on your reading of TEXT 1, would you be interested in reading the novel *Ghost Light*? Discuss the elements of Joseph O'Connor's writing in this preface that might make you want to read his novel. (20)

Sample Answer

QUESTION A (i)

> **Provides an overview of the answer – demonstrates purposefulness. The points and support will follow in the remaining paragraphs.**

From reading TEXT 1, I learned about how beginning a novel can be difficult and uncertain. I also learned about some key choices involved when writing historical fiction and about the emotional challenges of finishing a novel.

> **Use either the author's full name or surname – never use only their first name.**

> **Includes short quotations within sentences to maintain the flow of the writing.**

> **Sums up why this is an insight. Links back to the question.**

O'Connor tells us that when he started writing *Ghost Light*, he felt the same uncertainty that 'most novelists have at the outset'. He had to make decisions about what tense to write in and who his narrator would be. He tells us that this process can be 'gruellingly frustrating' and he had to write 'dozens of drafts' before he slowly came to realise that his story 'needed to be simple' and should be 'focused closely on Molly'. Before reading this, I had not understood that the work of a novelist was so exhausting.

> **Linking phrase introduces second insight.**

I also discovered that a novel written about real people poses its own challenges. The author describes the decisions involved as 'morally ambiguous' because he had to take 'immense liberties with fact'. In this novel, real people such as W. B. Yeats and Lady Gregory are characters, and O'Connor may have felt hesitant about having them speak or act in particular ways. He had the option of renaming these characters, which he did consider 'carefully' before deciding 'against it in the end'. All he could do then was hope that 'these noble ghosts of world literature' would forgive

> **Refers to the 'challenges' of the question.**

him for the liberties he has taken with them. These are difficult decisions that I had not considered prior to reading the extract.

Theme 4: Ghosts

> **Introduces third point using a key word from the question.**

A third insight I gained into the difficulties facing novelists is in the emotional uncertainty they may feel when it comes to finishing the book and sending it out into the world. O'Connor says that novelists know 'every line and comma' of their books because they have worked so hard on them. They also come to know their characters better than their 'spouse' or 'closest friend'. That is why there is 'a touch of sadness' about saying goodbye and letting go. He describes this as watching 'a little piece of your self take its chances' in the 'great, wide world'. Before reading this preface, I had not realised a novelist

> **Links back to the question.**

became quite so attached to their characters, or that ending a novel can be, in its own way, as challenging as starting one.

QUESTION B – 50 Marks

In TEXT 1, the author Joseph O'Connor tells us about when he was younger and would walk past an old Victorian home in Glasthule that was once owned by the famous Irish playwright John Synge. O'Connor says that he 'often wondered about the stories it had seen'.

Your Transition Year class has decided to publish a collection of memoirs and stories as told by the older people in your locality. As the editor of this collection, write the text of the **introduction** for the publication. In it, you should explain the purpose of the book by discussing the importance of local history, look forward to some of the content the reader can expect and thank all those who took part in the project.

Exam Mechanics

QUESTION B

Read the question and highlight the main task. This task will inform your entire answer. It will indicate what **genre** you will be writing in, what your **purpose** is and what **layout/structure** to use. Identify the type of **audience** you will be writing for, which will determine the appropriate **style and register** to use. **Number the points you need to cover** to make sure that your answer addresses all aspects of the question.

Your Transition Year class has decided to publish a collection of memoirs and stories as told by the older people in your locality. As the editor of this collection, write the text of the **introduction** for the publication. In it, you should explain the purpose of the book by discussing the importance of local history **(1)**, look forward to some of the content the reader can expect **(2)** and thank all those who took part in the project **(3)**.

Genre: introduction to a collection of texts (for more information, see page 66).

Purpose: to introduce your readers to the themes and topics included in the collection; to give them an overview of the origins of the project as well as letting them know what to expect. As part of this discussion, you will be explaining the importance of local history. Since you are trying to preserve your locality's history by collecting the memoirs of local people, this is obviously a topic about which you are passionate, and that passion should come through in your writing.

Layout/structure: normal prose structure; optional heading of 'Introduction'.

Audience: the readers are likely to be locals interested in local stories and history, the contributors themselves, the parents of all the students involved and the staff at your school. Show you are keeping your audience in mind by referring to them directly and making lots of references to local features: places, personalities, the school, sports teams, etc. For example:

 Hint

Anonymity is an integral part of the examination process. Do not forget to change the name of your school.

> The book you are now holding in your hand is the product of much hard work over the summer holidays.
>
> You can be sure that the cover price you paid for *Down Memory Lane, a Local History Project* was money well spent because for every euro raised, 75 cents will be going straight into Fr Tristin's fund to restore the old mill on Joseph Street.

Style and register: your writing will be enthusiastic, warm and friendly – not too formal.

(1) Discuss the importance of recording local history as a context for the inception of the collection. You could tie this in with the specific circumstances that sparked the idea to produce the book as well as details of the book's purpose.

(2) Make specific references to some of the content of the memoirs that are reproduced in the collection. As the editor, you would have proofread every word of these stories and would know the unique personalities, the tragic moments, etc. to highlight. You may choose to link these to the insights you gained into local history by working on this project. Obviously, you will need to make a great deal of this up.

(3) Thank everyone who took part, including the classmates who helped put the collection together and the people who contributed their stories. Does anyone in particular deserve a special mention?

A-Z Grammar Guide

Apostrophes

There are two types of apostrophe: the apostrophe of possession and the apostrophe of contraction.

Apostrophes of possession

If someone possesses something, an apostrophe is used to show this. Examples from TEXT 1 include:

- *Led Zeppelin's* 'Stairway to Heaven'
- the last years of *Synge's* life.

If the thing doing the possessing is plural, the apostrophe comes after the *s*. For example, *school-kids' disco* makes it clear that it is a disco for any schoolchildren who want to attend. If the posters advertising this event read *school-kid's disco*, it would mean that the disco is for one particular kid only.

Apostrophes of contraction

To *contract* means to make smaller; so, apostrophes of contraction are used to replace the letters that are removed when words are shortened. For example, in 'when *I'd* walk past that house', *I'd* is a contraction of *I would*. The letters in red have been removed and an apostrophe has been inserted in their place.

An interesting oddity appears in TEXT 1: 'in forms some biographers *won't* like'. Here, *won't* is a contraction of *will not*, but where did the 'o' come from? *Won't* is actually a contraction of *woll not* or *wonnot*, which are terms no one has used since the Middle Ages. *Won't* is still with us because it is easier to say than *willn't*, but it means exactly the same.

Common mistakes

An apostrophe is never used to show possession with a personal pronoun like *his*, *hers*, *theirs* or *ours*. The word *who's* does exist, but it is a contraction of *who is*. The correct possessive form of who is *whose*.

An apostrophe should not be placed before the *s* of a plural. The author of TEXT 1 writes: 'when I was a teenager in 1970s Ireland' and 'in the 1950s in London'. The *1970s* and *1950s* are plural terms, which is why they have an *s* at the end. As they are neither contractions nor indicators of possession, they do not require an apostrophe. People mistakenly put apostrophes in plurals so often that the error has been given a name: the grocer's apostrophe. Although it is often seen on signs in greengrocers' shops, this mistake is made all the time in a wide variety of settings.

An exception

An exception to the above rules is evident in these examples from TEXT 1:

- you know *its* every line and comma
- Perhaps *it's* similar to what a parent feels.
- You won't be there to hold *its* hand

In the case of *its* and *it's*, an apostrophe is used to indicate only a contraction and not possession. In other words, *it's* is short for *it is*. When you want to show that something belongs to *it*, you use *its* without an apostrophe.

TEXT 2 – JUDITH

This text is from the historical novel _Hamnet_ by Maggie O'Farrell, which imagines the domestic life of William Shakespeare, his family home in Stratford-upon-Avon and his wife and three children: twins Judith and Hamnet and their older sister Susanna. In this extract, Judith is hoping to catch a glimpse of the spirit of her deceased twin brother. O'Farrell's novel was nominated Best Book of 2020 by _The Guardian_ and _The Financial Times_.

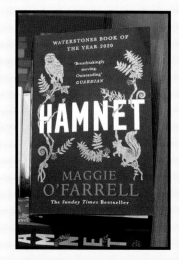

Night-time in the town. A deep, black silence lies over the streets, broken only by the hollow lilt of an owl, calling for its mate. A breeze slips invisibly, insistently through the streets, like a burglar seeking an entrance. It plays with the tops of the trees, tipping them one way, then the other. It shivers inside the church bell, making the brass vibrate with a single low note. It ruffles the feathers of the lonely owl, sitting on a rooftop near the church. It trembles a loose casement a few doors along, making the people inside turn over in their beds, their dreams intruded upon by images of shaking bones, of nearing footsteps, of drumming hoofs.

A fox darts out from behind an empty cart, moving sideways along the dark and deserted street. It pauses for a moment, one foot held off the ground, outside the Guildhall, near the school where Hamnet studied, and his father before him, as if it has heard something. Then it trots on, before swerving left and vanishing into a gap between two houses.

[...]

The town is quiet, its breath held. In an hour or so, the dark will begin to weaken, light will rise and people will wake in their beds, ready – or not – to face another day. Now, though, the townspeople are asleep.

Except for Judith. She is coming along the street, wrapped in a cloak, the hood covering her head. She goes past the school, where the fox was until a moment ago; she doesn't see it but it sees her, from its hiding place in an alleyway. It watches her with widened pupils, alarmed by this unexpected creature sharing its nocturnal world, taking in her mantle, her quick-stepping feet, the hurry in her gait.

She crosses the market square quickly, keeping close to the buildings, and turns into Henley Street.

A woman had come to see her mother in the autumn, seeking something for her swollen knuckles and painful wrists. She was, she told Judith when she opened the side gate to her, the midwife. Her mother seemed to know the woman; she gave her a long look, then a smile. She had taken the woman's hands in her own, turning them gently over. Her knuckles were lumpen, purple, disfigured. Agnes had wrapped comfrey leaves around them, binding them with cloth, then left the room, saying she would fetch some ointment.

The woman had placed her bandaged hands on her lap. She stared at them for a moment, then spoke, without looking up.

'Sometimes,' she had said, apparently to her hands, 'I have to walk through the town late at night. Babies come when they come, you see.'

Judith nodded politely.

The woman smiled at her. 'I remember when you came. We all thought you wouldn't live. But here you are.'

'Here I am,' Judith murmured.

'Many a time,' she continued, 'I've been coming along Henley Street, past the house where you were born, and I've seen something.'

Judith stared at her for a moment. She wanted to ask what, but also dreaded the answer. 'What have you seen?' she blurted out.

'Something, or perhaps I should say someone.'

'Who?' Judith asked, but she knew, she knew already.

'Running, he is.'

'Running?'

The old midwife nodded. 'From the door of the big house to the door of that dear little narrow one. As clear as anything. A figure, it is, running like the wind, as if the devil himself is at its back.'

Judith felt her heart speed up, as if she were the one condemned to run for eternity along Henley Street, not him.

'Always at night,' the woman was saying, passing one hand over the other. 'Never during the day.'

And so Judith has come, every night since, slipping out of the house in the dark hours, to stand here, waiting, watching. She has said nothing of this to her mother or Susanna. The midwife chose to tell her, and her only. It is her secret, her connection, her twin. There are mornings when she can feel her mother looking at her, observing her tired, drawn face, and she wonders if she knows. It wouldn't surprise her. But she doesn't want to speak to anyone else about it, in case it never comes true, in case she can't find him, in case he doesn't appear to her.

[...]

Please, is what she is thinking. Please come. Just once. Don't leave me here like this, alone, please. I know you took my place, but I am only half a person without you. Let me see you, even if only for the last time.

She cannot imagine how it might be, to see him again. He would be a child and she is now grown, almost a woman. What would he think? Would he recognise her now, if he were to pass her in the street, this boy who will for ever remain a boy?

Footnote on Historical Novels

A historical novel is a work of fiction that is **set during a particular period in history**. There is some debate about how far back in time a book's setting has to be in order for it to be considered historical fiction. However, it is generally accepted that the events of the novel should occur at least one generation (25 years or so) before it was written.

Relying on **research** rather than personal experience, the author of historical fiction attempts to capture the spirit of the age in which the novel is set: the social conditions, people's manners and customs, their speech patterns, their clothing, etc. An accurate portrayal of the details of the time period will create a convincing picture. Readers of historical fiction want to be **transported to a different time and place**.

Historical fiction is often written around **notable historical figures**; real people who actually existed. These are usually depicted alongside **fictional characters** made up by the author in order to service the plot. The plot itself can be driven by **real historical events** or by a **combination of history and fiction**. The novel *Hamnet* is an example of this. William Shakespeare really did have twin children called Hamnet and Judith, and Hamnet did die at an early age. However, the circumstances of his death and the way others react to it spring from O'Farrell's imagination. Many of the other characters in the novel are also inventions of the author.

QUESTION A – 50 Marks

(i) Based on your reading of TEXT 2, what do you learn about Judith's character? Refer to three aspects of Judith's character in your answer, supporting your response with reference to the text. (15)

(ii) In the above text, Maggie O'Farrell has created a place that grips the reader's imagination. From the texts you have studied for your English Leaving Certificate course*, identify a place that gripped your imagination. Explain in detail why this place gripped your imagination. (15)

* Texts specified for study for Leaving Certificate English, including poetry, single texts and texts (including films) prescribed for comparative study.

(iii) Based on your reading of TEXT 2, do you agree that Maggie O'Farrell displays superb narrative skills, including the effective use of aesthetic language, which enable her to craft an atmospheric story? Support your answer with reference to the text. (20)

Exam Mechanics

QUESTION A (ii)

As we have seen in previous themes, students are sometimes required to refer to their studied texts for Paper 2 while answering Paper 1. This is another such question.

6S Simplify

Highlight or underline the key ideas in the question. What is this question asking you to do?

In the above text, Maggie O'Farrell has created a place that grips the reader's imagination. From the texts you have studied for your English Leaving Certificate course, identify a place that gripped your imagination. Explain in detail why this place gripped your imagination.

6S Select

Now you have to search your knowledge of your studied texts and select an example of a gripping sense of place. You can refer to anything you studied as part of your English Leaving Certificate course, so mentally check through your poetry, your single text and your comparative texts (including the film if you studied one).

The extract in TEXT 2 grips the reader's imagination because it is spooky and atmospheric. That does not mean you have to find a similarly spooky or atmospheric scene from your texts. Your chosen scene could be beautiful, grim, exotic, exciting, charming, bizarre, etc. – as long as it grips (captivates, excites, fascinates, intrigues) your imagination.

6S Sort

Think about the examples of 'gripping' places from your texts that you have identified. Choose the one that you can best use to answer the question. To do this, you may want to consider the following questions:

- What does the place look/sound/feel like?
- Can I discuss three aspects that grip my imagination?
- Can I recall any relevant quotes about it (however short)?

Theme 4: Ghosts

- What happened there? Was the place a backdrop to an important scene? Did a key moment in the text occur there? Was it violent? Poignant? Humorous?
- Did the place grip my imagination because it is different from what I am used to or what I was expecting?
- Does the place reveal something about the social setting of the text? Is it somewhere exotic? Is it far back in history, or in the future? Do the people there have unusual customs?

6S   State, support and spell out

This question requires an introduction in which you identify which text you are using. It is important to include the title and the author (if you are discussing a film, the 'author' is the director). Quickly outline the place you have chosen so your reader is up to speed. Then briefly list three reasons why the particular place 'gripped your imagination' to give your answer purposefulness. Be careful not to summarise the events – focus on the setting.

The main body of your answer will comprise three paragraphs. Each paragraph will:

1. **State** a reason why your chosen place gripped your imagination.
2. **Support** your reason with text-based evidence.
3. **Spell out** in detail how your evidence supports your stated reason.

A conclusion is optional.

Sample Answer ▶

QUESTION A (iii)

Introduction states opinion and answers question without any supporting quotations or explanations.	I agree that Maggie O'Farrell displays superb narrative skills in TEXT 2. She uses aesthetic language, vivid imagery, precise and effective sentence structure and both dialogue and internal monologue to great effect in order to create a very atmospheric piece.
First stated answer.	The author uses some particularly striking personifications. The night breeze is personified as it 'slips invisibly, insistently through the streets'. We
Uses quotes to support answer.	hear how it 'plays with the tops of the trees', 'shivers inside the church bell' and 'ruffles the feathers of the lonely owl' on a rooftop. As we follow this breeze through the silent village, we are given an aerial view
Describes the effect of the first technique.	of the scene, like the establishing shot of a film. A playful, mischievous wind is a kind of ghostly presence from the start. I found this a highly effective way of
Returns to the question.	opening the scene and establishing an eerie atmosphere.

Second stated answer. Linking word 'also' connects to previous paragraph.

The author's meticulous sentence structure also displays her superb narrative skills. She employs pithy and succinct phrases for dramatic effect. She introduces her character with just the words: 'Except for Judith.' This sets the character apart from all those at home asleep and singles her out as being unique. The author also combines these pithy phrases into triads to enhance the rhythm of her sentences. 'It is her secret, her connection, her twin' and 'in case it never comes true, in case she can't find him, in case he doesn't appear to her' are both examples of this narrative technique. The rhythm and pace of these lines

Returns to the question, using key words.

demonstrate the author's narrative skill.

Third and fourth stated answers – phrase connects to the following paragraph, showing these concepts are closely related.

The author also makes effective use of dialogue and internal monologue to intensify the impact of the scene. The conversation with the midwife (in flashback) is conveyed through dialogue. This allows us to understand the importance of what the midwife says to Judith, as well as the reaction that this news elicits. The midwife spoke 'without looking up' because she was weighing her words carefully, knowing the impact they might have. When she heard about the apparition, 'Judith felt her heart speed up', demonstrating the effect the words have had on her.

The extract ends with questions that Judith is asking herself in the form of an internal monologue: 'What would he think?' The effect of this is that we fully understand her uncertainty and confusion, as well as the depth of her grief for her dead twin.

Phrase linking the two paragraphs.

The techniques of both dialogue and monologue greatly reinforce the empathy we feel for this character.

Conclusion sums up the argument.

The effective use of imagery, sentence structure, dialogue and monologue in this extract demonstrates Maggie O'Farrell's superb narrative skills.

QUESTION B – 50 Marks

In TEXT 2, Judith walks the streets of her village at the dead of night hoping to see the ghost of her dead brother. Imagine that the subject of the supernatural is one in which you have a particular interest and about which you regularly blog. Your blog posts are either sceptical about supernatural phenomena or accepting of them. Having read TEXT 2, write the text of your next **blog post**. In your post you should outline your opinion regarding supernatural phenomena, describe any personal experiences of the supernatural that you have experienced or heard about and attempt to persuade your readers that your view of the supernatural is the correct one.

Exam Mechanics

QUESTION B

Read the question and highlight the main task. This task will inform your entire answer. It will indicate what **genre** you will be writing in, what your **purpose** is and what **layout/ structure** to use. Identify the type of **audience** you will be writing for, which will determine the appropriate **style and register** to use. **Number the points you need to cover** to make sure that your answer addresses all aspects of the question.

> In TEXT 2, Judith walks the streets of her village at the dead of night hoping to see the ghost of her dead brother. Imagine that the subject of the supernatural is one in which you have a particular interest and about which you regularly blog. Your blog posts are either sceptical about supernatural phenomena or accepting of them. Having read TEXT 2, write the text of your next **blog post**. In your post you should outline your opinion regarding supernatural phenomena **(1)**, describe any personal experiences of the supernatural that you have experienced or heard about **(2)** and attempt to persuade your readers that your view of the supernatural is the correct one **(3)**.

Genre: a blog post. Bloggers regularly post content online on any particular theme. Each post is essentially a self-published article or essay.

Purpose: the theme of this series of blogs is the supernatural, and your purpose in today's post is to reinforce your stance on the concept of supernatural phenomena – whether you are a confirmed sceptic or a passionate believer, you want to convince your readers to agree with you. Using descriptive and/or narrative language, you also need to share personal experiences you have had or have heard about.

Layout/structure: blogs tend to have catchy titles – think of something appropriate that will attract potential readers to your blog. The post itself will need a heading specific to the topic. Many give a date and time as well, but these are not compulsory. A blog is a type of social media platform, so include features such as hyperlinks to videos or other pages. There may be comments posted by your followers, and you may want to convey the impression that this post is one of a series by referring to issues you have dealt with before.

Audience: your audience could be truly global, depending on your appeal. Some readers will share your views on the supernatural and some will be of completely the opposite view and are following you because they like to argue! Established bloggers will have built up a rapport with their regular readers.

Style and register: your readers will naturally be interested in the topic of ghosts and the unexplained, so you can expect them to be fairly knowledgeable in this area. There is no specific age bracket (if it were a talk to your class, for example, you would know exactly the age of your audience), so make sure your references are sufficiently accessible for a broad range of readers. The style of language to use will be argumentative and persuasive, as well as narrative and descriptive in parts. You are free to use humour if you wish.

(1) Outline your opinion about supernatural phenomena. Remember that as part of a series of posts, many (but not all) of your readers will know your viewpoint, so for them you are restating or reframing your opinion. For new readers, it will be a little like joining a television series in the middle of the season, so quickly help them catch up.

(2) Describe (and/or narrate) a personal experience. You will probably find yourself in one of the following scenarios:

- Believer in the supernatural
  - You have had a personal experience and are going to describe it.
  - You have not had a personal experience, but you will include ones that you heard from someone else or read about.
- Sceptical about the supernatural
  - You have had a personal experience that some might consider to be supernatural. However, you are not convinced and explain why.
  - You have not had a personal experience and will use the ones you have heard about to illustrate how these types of stories have natural explanations.
  - You have heard about experiences that you cannot explain, but you do not think they are sufficient to prove the existence of ghosts.

(3) Persuade your readers that your view of the supernatural is the correct one. This is not a stand-alone task; it will be an argument developed throughout the blog. Remember to drive home your opinion in your conclusion.

 Hint

A great way to end a piece of writing like an article, speech or blog is to come back to however you started. So, if you start with a striking image or a thought-provoking quote, return to it at the end.

A-Z Grammar Guide

Adverbs

Adverbs are **modifying** words. They give us more information. Consider the following sentence from TEXT 2:

> A breeze slips invisibly, insistently through the streets, like a burglar seeking an entrance.

The words highlighted here are examples of adverbs. They are telling us more about the verb 'slips'. How does the breeze slip? It slips *invisibly* and *insistently*.

Many adverbs end in –ly, as seen in the example above, but not all; and the role of many adverbs is to modify a verb, but this is not always the case.

Adverbs modify verbs by telling us:

1. **How** the action is performed. The above example includes this kind of adverb.
2. **When** and **where** the action is performed. In the example below, the words in blue are verbs, so the word 'Sometimes' is an adverb because it tells us *when* the midwife has to walk.

> 'Sometimes,' she had said, apparently to her hands, 'I have to walk through the town late at night. Babies come when they come, you see.'

When the work of an adverb is performed by more than one word, we call it an **adverbial phrase** or an **adverbial clause**. For example, the phrase 'through the town' tells us where the midwife has to walk and the phrase 'late at night' gives us more information about when she has to walk.

Discuss

Have another look at the sentence below describing the movement of the fox. Can you identify how many adverbial phrases and clauses the author has used to modify the verb 'pauses'?

> It pauses for a moment, one foot held off the ground, outside the Guildhall, near the school where Hamnet studied, and his father before him, as if it has heard something.

TEXT 3 – I WENT IN SEARCH OF IRELAND'S MOST TROUBLED GHOSTS

TEXT 3 contains two elements. The written element is an edited extract from a feature article by journalist Conor Pope that was published in *The Irish Times* at Halloween 2019. The visual element is a collection of three images.

Several years ago while channelling my inner Scooby Doo I went in search of some of Ireland's most troubled ghosts hoping to be scared witless. But apart from hearing a young girl screech murder in the dead of night in a 600-year-old castle [...] it was a pretty uneventful adventure really.

First I went to Ross Castle – a charming B&B on a placid lake in Meath, said to be one of the most haunted castles in Ireland. It was mid winter and I arrived armed with a ghost detector loaned to me by a professional spirit hunter who had warned me that it was not a toy despite the fact that it looked for all the world like just that. I was shown to the most haunted room in the castle, at the very top of a spiral staircase in the ancient tower.

It was Sabina's Room.

The plan was I would set up the not-a-toy box in the place where spirits roamed and simply let it scan the air around me for ghostly waves which it would convert into speech recognisable to a more alive human ear.

I was maybe a little sceptical as I climbed into my bed in the room where Sabina the heartbroken teenage girl died after her brother had possibly drowned her boyfriend.

Sabina was the daughter of Richard Nugent, known as the Black Baron because of his black heart. He was an unforgiving soul and less than pleased when Sabina decided that the only boy who could ever please her was Orwin, the son of a chieftain man.

So, in the best Romeo and Juliet tradition – although some years before it was a tradition – the star-crossed lovers eloped. Or tried to. They planned to take a boat across the nearby lake but the Black Baron and his son got wind of their plans and gave chase. Orwin drowned.

It was an accident. Or was it? Three days later Sabina died of a broken heart.

'To this day, Sabina haunts the castle's walls. Visitors and guests make frequent encounters with her spirit, still in search of her lover – and restless until the day she will be reunited with him,' the castle website says.

Stories of sightings among guests abound. One American psychic started sobbing the moment she was shown to her room because Sabina's presence was so strong. Another guest disappeared early one morning after being spooked by a ghost (most likely the Black Baron) who 'made love to me last night', as she wrote in the hotel guestbook.

While I was mildly concerned that the Black Baron might come after me too I was mostly untroubled by thoughts of dead people as I fell asleep that night. But then, shortly before 2am, the little black ghost detector crackled into life and alerted me to a presence in my room.

The reception wasn't amazing and brought me back to nights spent listening to Radio Luxembourg on a bad radio in the west of Ireland in the 1980s. Then a single word came from the box.

It was 'MURDER'.

Or was it 'murmur'? Or 'marbles'? 'Mother?'

I asked for clarification and spent ages tinkering with the box, willing it to speak more but after a few more crackles it died.

And I heard no more from Sabina. Although the box did come back to life in the car on the way home. And I am pretty sure it said 'murder'. Or 'marbles'. I am still not sure if that means Sabina came home with me.

After the castle came the gaol. Wicklow Gaol is another spot beloved of the ghost hunters and we can tell it's spooky because it still spells jail gaol. It has had a grim enough history since it first opened its heavy wooden doors to guests in the early part of the 18th Century. I visited twice – on one occasion a mystic held a seance and sought out prisoners to talk to. All I remember is a table shaking violently as a ghost called Willie tried to get in touch with us. 'Harder Willie, harder. Push it harder,' the mystic said excitedly. I sniggered like a schoolboy.

[...]

Despite all the evidence suggesting it's hokum, the ghost-hunting phenomenon is enduring and, according to the Haunted Hotel Guide, there are more than 450 haunted hotels and castles across Ireland offering haunted adventures. There are ghostly bus tours in Dublin and scores of pubs – including the Gravediggers in Glasnevin – that have capitalised on their ghostly regulars.

One of Ireland's most well-known haunted hotels is the Cabra Castle hotel in Kingscourt, Co. Cavan. It was once declared the second scariest hotel in the world by Tripadvisor. Legends about the hotel have been circulating for generations. It was the third stop on my ghost busters tour. I stayed in the most haunted room, but the ghosts were a no show.

[...]

Image 1

Image 2

Image 3

QUESTION A – 50 Marks

(i) Based on your reading of TEXT 3, explain three insights you gained into the personality of its author, Conor Pope. (15)

(ii) In the above text, Conor Pope describes how in one hotel he visited on his search for ghosts, an 'American psychic started sobbing ... because Sabina's presence was so strong'. From the texts you have studied for your Leaving Certificate English course*, identify a character whose presence in the text was particularly impressive or who left a lasting impression on you. Give reasons for your choice. (15)

* Texts specified for study for Leaving Certificate English, including poetry, single texts and texts (including films) prescribed for comparative study.

(iii) Based on your reading of TEXT 3, to what extent would you agree that Conor Pope's writing style is both informative and humorous? In your answer, make detailed reference to four aspects of the writing style used by the author and to the impact these had on the piece. (20)

Exam Mechanics

QUESTION A (iii)

6S Simplify

The question tells you exactly what you need to find, so highlight the key words.

> Based on your reading of TEXT 3, to what extent would you agree that Conor Pope's writing style is both informative and humorous? In your answer, make detailed reference to four aspects of the writing style used by the author and to the impact these had on the piece.

The phrase 'to what extent would you agree' invites you to make a judgement call. You are welcome to argue whichever way you wish. The word 'extent' means you can agree on a sliding scale from complete disagreement to partial agreement to full agreement.

The key words remaining in the question tell you that you must discuss 'four' aspects of 'writing style' that are (or are not) 'informative' and 'humorous'. What do the words 'informative and 'humorous' mean?
- Informative = useful, instructive, illuminating, etc.
- Humorous = funny, playful, amusing, etc.

6S Select

Look for any examples of Conor Pope's writing style that could be considered either funny/amusing or useful/illuminating. Highlight all the examples you can find in the text.

Obviously, if you do not agree with the statement, you will also need to find sufficient evidence to support that position.

6S Sort

You should have more examples highlighted in the text than you need for the answer, so now choose the best four. Remember that you do not have to deal with 'informative' and 'humorous' equally (two points each) if you do not want to: it is acceptable to make three points for one and one for the other.

6S State, support and spell out

1. **State** your position/opinion about the writer's style. Do you fully agree that it is both informative and humorous? Or is it just humorous and not informative? Or is it neither?

> I completely agree with the statement that Conor Pope's writing style is both funny and instructive. One way in which his humour manifests in the article is in the nonchalance with which he approaches the subject matter of ghosts and hauntings.

 Hint

In this sample introduction the key words 'informative' and 'humorous' have been replaced with 'instructive' and 'funny'. It is a good idea to demonstrate both a broad vocabulary and a clear understanding of the key concepts from the very start of your answer.

2. **Support** your idea with a quote or reference.

> 'Then a single word came from the box. It was "MURDER". Or was it "murmur"? Or "marbles"? "Mother?"'

3. **Spell out** how your quote supports your assessment of the author's writing style.

> Hearing the word 'MURDER' at two o'clock in the morning while sleeping in a haunted room would be considered by many as highly dramatic and possibly terrifying. The use of capital letters in 'MURDER' conveys an added sense of melodrama. However, Pope then deliberately subverts that sensational moment by questioning what he actually heard. The tension is broken with relief. And as 'marbles' would be a particularly ridiculous thing for a ghost to say, my response was to laugh.

Follow this process for each of the four parts of your answer. You may wish to conclude with a brief summary of your points.

 Hint

Introductions and conclusions are not compulsory. However, in a question like this one that asks whether you agree with something, and specifically *to what extent* you agree, the logical introduction will be to address this by stating your position clearly.

Theme 4: Ghosts

QUESTION B – 50 Marks

You have been asked to write the text for a **promotional article** to be published online by the editor of the *Haunted Hotel Guide* mentioned in TEXT 3. Your article should promote **one** of the sites illustrated in the three images that accompany the text. In your promotional article you should: advertise your chosen property as a desirable destination for ghost hunters, describe the kinds of ghostly experiences guests might encounter and offer some advice to readers about the best ways to ensure having a real, but safe, ghostly experience. The article may be humorous, or serious, or both.

Sample Answer

QUESTION B

Indicates image chosen.	(Image 1)
Gives castle a fictitious name (inspired by the novel *Dracula* by Bram Stoker). An article, promotional or otherwise, requires an appropriate heading.	**Bram Castle, Transylvania – Do you dare to visit?**

Bram Castle is a charming 800-year-old gothic castle situated beside a mist-shrouded lake in the very heart of Dracula country. It is also world-famous as the most haunted castle on the planet. So, if you want to feel the thrill of spine-tingling spookiness while also enjoying five-star luxury, Bram Castle is the ideal destination for you.

Uses details from Image 1.

Language of persuasion promotes the location – Task 1: 'advertise your chosen property'.

Paranormal investigation, both as a profession and as a hobby, has become phenomenally popular across the globe in the past decade, and Bram Castle has appeared on numerous dedicated websites as well as being featured on the well-known American documentary series *Ghost Hunters*. 'I've been to many, many haunted places in my time,' says Jason Hawes of the *Ghost Hunters* team. 'But there is definitely something special about Bram Castle. It's an atmosphere. You can feel the weight of its history. The hairs on the back of my neck stood up practically the whole time we were there.' Click here for the full episode.

Real documentary series creates an air of authenticity.

Uses fictitious quotation.

Demonstrates awareness of online audience.

Come and stay in Lucy's room, situated at the very top of the spiral staircase of the ancient East Tower. Lucy was the wife of Count von Black. Hers is a tragic tale, which begins way back in the twelfth century. Married off to von Black when still only 16, she could never love her much older husband. Instead, she fell for the chief steward's son Olaf. When the count learned of his young bride's betrayal, his fury was terrifying; his revenge, ruthless. Olaf and his whole family suffered the count's wrath, with the most unspeakable torments inflicted upon von Black's love rival. But perhaps the worst fate befell poor Lucy. She was locked in the East Tower and the count swore she would never see sunlight again. Lucy, heartbroken, died three days later.

Draws heavily from TEXT 3. Using the texts for inspiration is encouraged; changing details to suit your purpose shows flexibility and creativity.

Task 2: 'describe the kinds of ghostly experiences guests might encounter'.

To this very day, Lucy's grieving spirit haunts the castle. Guests and visitors frequently encounter her as she roams the tower, searching for her murdered lover. Or you may bump into Count von Black himself! His wicked heart and his brutal treatment of his poor bride seem to have doomed him to haunt the ancient tower as well. You may hear the clink of his spurs or the rattle of his sabre as he paces the corridors on quiet, moonless nights. People say you can see his malevolent black shadow as he strides across the yard between the tower and reception, just the way he is thought to have done when he learned of the affair.

These are two of the most famous ghosts said to haunt the ancient halls of Bram Castle, but these walls have seen war, famine and plague over the course of their long and bloody history. Countless other mysterious entities have been reported, from the Headless Knight to the shrieking spirit of the Drowned Hag. Bram Castle has earned the honour

Addresses Task 1.

of being 'The Most Haunted Hotel in the World'. It has to be the absolute go-to number one choice for a creepy weekend for any ghost hunter.

Task 3: 'offer some advice to readers about the best ways to ensure having a real, but safe, ghostly experience'.

The popularity of Bram Castle with ghost hunters has meant that all would-be paranormal investigators need to book well in advance to avoid disappointment. While the views from the tower of the rugged Transylvanian scenery are magnificent in summer, experts agree that the best time of year to catch sight of the ghostly residents is mid-winter. The nights are longer, the shadows somehow darker. As the

Addresses Task 2.

winter wind rushes off the lake, the moaning in the eaves can often sound like the grieving cries of a heartbroken teenage girl.

Addresses Task 3.

Make sure to pack the standard investigation equipment. You will need a reliable camera, and many ghost hunters will want a good voice-recording device too. Bring a notepad so you can jot down any experiences while they are fresh in your mind. Most importantly, make sure to travel with a friend. If you encounter something that you

Addresses Task 1.

cannot explain, they will be an extra set of eyes and ears and can help you make sense of it later. And both of you will get to enjoy the

Conclusion uses a question to challenge readers to visit this destination.

castle's luxurious accommodation and Michelin-starred restaurant.

The ancient towers of Bram Castle await your visit. Just one question remains: do you dare to meet the villainous Count von Black?

SECTION II   COMPOSING   (100 marks)

Write a composition on **any one** of the assignments that appear in **bold print** below.

Each composition carries 100 marks.

The composition assignments are intended to reflect language study in the areas of information, argument, persuasion, narration, and the aesthetic use of language.

1. In TEXT 1, Joseph O'Connor describes a house in Glasthule, the area in which he lived as a teenager. He remembers how 'on a moonlit summer evening in that coast-town of seagulls and steeples, a strange beauty seemed to glitter from its windows'.

   Write a descriptive essay in which you capture the 'strange beauty' of a place that you know.

2. In TEXT 2, Maggie O'Farrell's character of the midwife describes how she has seen 'A figure … running like the wind, as if the devil himself is at its back.'

   Write a short story, suitable for a science-fiction collection, in which a figure 'running like the wind, as if the devil himself is at its back' is central to the narrative.

3. In TEXT 3, Conor Pope describes Richard Nugent, the Black Baron, who was 'an unforgiving soul'.

   Write a personal essay in which you reflect on the importance of forgiveness.

4. In TEXT 1, Joseph O'Connor refers to Molly Allgood, the main character of his novel, as 'an elderly Irish actress who was once the beautiful muse of a genius'.

   Write a discursive essay in which you consider the subject of genius. In the course of your essay, you should identify people you believe to be geniuses and explain why.

5. In TEXT 1, Joseph O'Connor tells us that 'there was a love story in Glasthule'.

   Write a short story, for inclusion in a collection of romantic fiction, about characters who find love in an unexpected location.

6. In TEXT 2, Maggie O'Farrell writes an atmospheric description of a rural village at night, including glimpses of the natural landscape and wildlife.

   Write a personal essay in which you reflect on the value you place upon the natural world and your connection with nature.

7. In TEXT 1, we see a young Joseph O'Connor in the 1970s as he walks 'past the old Victorian house' that once belonged to 'the great writer John Synge'.

   You are competing in the final of a national public-speaking competition. The topic to be addressed is: *We can never escape the enduring legacy of history.* You are free to agree or disagree with the statement. Write the speech you would deliver.

Theme 5
Stranger in a Strange Land

A person who is far from home, who finds themselves in a foreign country or surrounded by an unfamiliar culture, might be said to be a 'stranger in a strange land'.

The paragraphs below are taken from the three texts we will be exploring over the course of this theme. Take a look at the three samples and discuss the following questions:

Discuss

1. Of which genre of writing is each text an example?
2. What features or styles of writing helped you to identify the genre of each of these samples?
3. Where would you be likely to encounter each of these genres?

Sample 1 – Text 1

I am going to the mountains, my native element, this afternoon. Send me the United Irishman, or the Nation.

So farewell, the dearest companion of my last years. I sigh to close our long-divided conversation. I shall think of you in my hours of melancholy.

Thomas Reilly

Sample 2 – TEXT 2

Alexander felt a clicking into place of things, a feeling that all the strange unexpected things that had happened to him had been moved into alignment by some benevolent all-knowing force, that this small stone building on the land of a rich man in the company of a poor man was exactly where he was meant to be, that his life was unfolding, slowly, strangely, exactly as it should.

Sample 3 – TEXT 3

I was reminded of what had happened in Sarajevo, all those years before. I had thought I might die then and had thought so during the shell attack on the safe house the previous evening. Maybe *this* was the moment it ended. And if it was, did I need to save myself? The answer, of course, was no.

SECTION I   COMPREHENDING   (100 marks)

TEXT 1 – THOMAS REILLY

This text is an edited version of a letter sent from New York in 1848 by recent Irish immigrant Thomas Reilly to his friend John Kelly in Dublin.

Albany,
New York
April 24th, 1848

Dear John,

[...]

I will now give way to some of my adventures. I left Dublin on the 19th Feb. I arrived in Liverpool on the 20th, took out my passage tickets the same day, did not sail for America until 1st March ...

Well, I set sail and our ship, the 'Patrick Henry', was resolved to bring us to the South Sea Islands instead of to New York. We had the two first days very fair and rounded the Irish coast like a seagull, the wind followed in our wake for three days on the Atlantic.

The fourth day the Monsters of the deep showed their heads, the Captain said we would have a storm, and truly Boreas[1] spent his rage on us that night. We were tumbled out of our berths, the hold was two feet full of water, a leak was gaining an inch a minute on us, our topsails were carried away, the most of male passengers were all night [relieving] each other at the pump and in the morning I left my hammock at seven o'clock to look at the terrible sea ...

How will I describe a gale on the Atlantic as follows ... At five o'clock p.m. all hands were tuned up close reef sail, not a stitch of canvass to be seen spread, six o'clock wind right ahead, the vessel lying to a rolling from side to side like a heavy log as she was, the passengers quaking with fear.

Ten o'clock, the scene below no light, the hatches nailed down, some praying, some crying some cursing and singing, the wife jawing the husband for bringing her into such danger, everything topsy-turvy, – barrels, boxes, cans, berths, children rolling about with the swaying vessel, now and again might be heard the groan of a dying creature, and continually the deep moaning of the tempest.

The scene above, bare poles, thunder and lightning, the ship almost capsized, lying on her beam, sheets of water drenching her decks, the sea swelling far above her masts, engulfing her around, and huge billows striking her bows and sides with the force and noise of a thousand sledgehammers upon so many anvils.

The ship receding with every wave, sometimes standing perpendicularly on her stern and shaking like a palsied man and then plunging decks and masts under water and raising to renew the same process. She would screech with every stroke of the waves, every bolt in her quaked, every timber writhed, the smallest nail had a cry of its own.

One o'clock in the morning, not a soul on the deck, standing upright, oh mercy one of our masts has gone over the side, bulwarks stoved in, 30 tons of water washing the decks from stem to stern. The Captain is panic struck. Tom Reilly is waiting on the quarter-deck to get into the lifeboat.

The captain speaks, carpenters cut away the broken spars, look out for the next spar, here it comes, The Mizen top[2] is carried away. The ship lurched on her side and lay in a state of distress until daylight.

We had 15 storms one greater than another.

26th day. Dear John,

[...]

We had severe weather in the Gulf, yet we were fortunate. An unfortunate vessel from New Orleans bound for Liverpool was struck by lightning. She was laden with cotton, it took fire. Oh, that was an awful sight. Our ship was far in the distance but the Margaret of Newry saved the crew of the burning craft, a great deal of property consumed.

She burned down to her coppers and resembled a pillar of fire all night. Was not that a poor sight on the wide sea. It shocks me even now. Several other affairs happened but how can I relate them here, with a heart bowed down by weight of care. After a voyage of five weeks, we landed in New York ...

I would advise no one I have regard for to emigrate unless the persons interested to come have friends before them, who will receive them and snatch them from all the evils of Society. You would hardly believe were I to tell you, all the trials, cheats, plots and chicanery of every kind which I had to overcome.

If a man has seven senses, it would take 500 senses largely developed to counteract the sharpers[3] of Liverpool and New York. It would be worth the teaching for a man to come here. The women (I mean the Irish) are great slaves in this country. Oh the profligacy[4] of some are awful.

[...]

Write and answer quickly – tell me the whole status of affairs and one request I ask of you is to show this letter to my mother ...

I have no intention to stop in Albany. The Irish volunteers expect to go to Canada to raise the standard of revolution. If they do I will go along with them ...

I am going to the mountains, my native element, this afternoon. Send me the United Irishman, or the Nation.[5]

So farewell, the dearest companion of my last years. I sigh to close our long-divided conversation. I shall think of you in my hours of melancholy.

Thomas Reilly

[1] Boreas is the Greek god of the north wind.

[2] Mizen (or mizzen) top is the platform at the top of the mizzen mast, situated towards the back end (stern) of a sailing ship.

[3] Profligacy means reckless extravagance; here, it implies sexual licentiousness.

[4] Sharpers are con artists.

[5] The United Irishman and the Nation were Irish nationalist newspapers.

Footnote on Personal Letters

Personal letters are usually written with an audience of one in mind and the writing style tends to be quite personal and intimate in nature. The tone depends entirely on the relationship between the author and the reader. In TEXT 1, the tone is wistful and melancholic in places. It is clear that Thomas is somewhat shell-shocked by the ordeals he has endured and that he misses the company of his friend John.

The author might ask the reader to carry out particular actions or to do small favours, such as passing on messages to mutual acquaintances back home. These requests are often for ordinary, everyday things: in TEXT 1, Thomas asks John to send him a newspaper from Ireland. Such appeals often feature **specific instructions** or **imperative verbs**. In the case of more demanding favours, **persuasion or argument** may be employed.

Letters from travellers or immigrants will typically be rich in **description** as they endeavour to relate the wonders or the difficulties they have experienced on their journey. The use of **aesthetic language** is also a common feature. They might include **advice** if the person they are writing to intends to follow in their footsteps, in which case you will also encounter the **language of information**. In TEXT 1, Thomas warns John about some of the dangers a traveller would need to be wary of, such as the 'sharpers' in Liverpool and New York.

Personal letters tend to include the author's **plans** for their immediate or their long-term future. In TEXT 1, Thomas speculates about whether he might join the Irish volunteers if they are sent into Canada.

QUESTION A – 50 Marks

(i) From your reading of TEXT 1, what do you think were the three most challenging hazards Thomas Reilly faced since leaving Ireland? (15)

(ii) In TEXT 1, Thomas Reilly tells his friend John that the mountains are his 'native element'. What natural element best resonates with you? Give reasons for your answer. (15)

(iii) 'Thomas Reilly uses aesthetic language in order to vividly convey extraordinary experiences.' Do you agree with this statement? Support your answer with reference to Reilly's use of aesthetic language. (20)

Exam Mechanics

QUESTION A (i)

6S Simplify

The question tells you exactly what you need to find, so highlight the key words.

> From your reading of TEXT 1, what do you think were the three most challenging hazards Thomas Reilly faced since leaving Ireland?

Before you even start reading the text, you know that you will be reading about someone called Thomas Reilly and that he made a journey and he faced dangers. You are being asked to make a judgement call: you have to choose what you think are the three most challenging hazards, which means you can expect to find more than three.

6S Select

As you read the text, highlight any references to dangers and difficulties faced during Thomas's journey (up to and including the moment he wrote the letter). Put your own brief notes in the margin to help you rank these dangers.

6S Sort

What are the most challenging hazards? What criteria will you use to judge them against each other? For example, would the risk of being cheated by con artists in New York be more or less likely than being drowned in a storm? Or is being swindled less dangerous because it is unlikely to be fatal?

State, support and spell out

Your examiner will expect you to answer Question A (i) with (at least) three paragraphs. You may opt to give a brief introduction listing the three hazards you have chosen. Each subsequent paragraph contains three parts.

1. **State** the hazard you have selected.

> One of the most dangerous hazards faced by Thomas Reilly on his journey was the threat of fire on a ship struck by lightning.

2. **Support** your idea with a quotation or reference.

> The sight of an 'unfortunate vessel' burning after being struck by lightning shocked him so much that he still feels appalled by it weeks after the event. He describes the burning ship as a 'pillar of fire' and says that it was 'an awful sight'. He and the rest of the passengers on the *Patrick Henry* watched as the ship 'burned down to her coppers'.

3. **Spell out** how your quote supports your idea and why the aspect you have chosen is one of the most challenging.

> They must all have been thinking how lucky they were that their ship had escaped the same fate. As fire can completely destroy a wooden ship, being struck by lightning must be one of the worst hazards he faced on his journey.

Follow this process for each of the three parts of your answer.

Sample Answer

QUESTION A (iii)

An (optional) introduction answers the question and states the main points of the argument.

I agree that Thomas Reilly makes use of striking aesthetic language to convey his extraordinary adventures. He describes his ordeal during the storm at sea with well-chosen similes and his sensuous diction captures the sights and sounds of the storm. He also carefully manages his punctuation and choice of tense to convey the chaos and panic on board the ship.

States first point. Ideas will be discussed in the order given in the introduction.

Reilly's use of imagery in the passage is especially evocative. He describes the movement of the ship with vivid similes. First, he describes

Supports point with quotations.

the vessel as it 'rounded the Irish coast like a seagull'. In this comparison we get the sense of the ship moving smoothly and swiftly. However, this is quickly juxtaposed with another image as the ship is caught in a storm and is 'rolling from side to side like a heavy log' and 'shaking like a palsied man'. The contrast between the ship gliding freely like a bird

Spells out how the quotes support the point.

and it moving like a heavy log or a man having a seizure emphasises the powerlessness the passengers must have felt when the boat was completely in the grip of the storm.

Linking phrase.

States second point.

Supporting quotations.

Spells out how the quotes support the point.

Apart from his use of similes, Reilly employs sensuous language to convey the extraordinary sounds he heard and the sights he saw. He describes the noises below deck during the storm. He heard people 'praying', 'crying', 'cursing', 'singing', 'jawing' and groaning against the continuous 'deep moaning' of the storm itself. The effect of this cacophony of sound is to transport the reader into the scene, so we can almost experience the confusion felt by Reilly and the other passengers.

Linking sentence states third point.

Supporting quotation.

Spells out how the quote supports the point.

Reilly also portrays the extraordinary sights he saw. He describes the scene with 'everything topsy-turvy, – barrels, boxes, cans, berths, children rolling about with the swaying vessel'. The effect of these images following on from each other in rapid succession is to convey the shocked disorientation Reilly felt as he stood trying to take in all these extraordinary events.

Linking sentence states fourth point.

Example from the text.

Sums up point.

Example and quotation.

Sums up point.

Finally, Reilly's grammar communicates the chaos and confusion of a storm at sea. In paragraphs three to nine, Reilly uses comma splices in order to join phrases and clauses to one another in long, tumultuous sentences that convey the panic and chaos he felt during the storm. He also changes into the present tense to express a sense of immediacy and danger: 'look out for the next spar, here it comes'. The use of the present tense involves the reader further because it seems like the events are happening in the present moment of his narration.

Short conclusion refers back to the question.

Therefore, I agree that Thomas Reilly uses aesthetic language to vividly convey the extraordinary experiences he had.

QUESTION B – 50 Marks

In TEXT 1, Thomas Reilly has emigrated from Ireland to America. Many young Irish people still leave Ireland every year seeking their fortunes and/or adventure overseas. Write the text of a **talk** to be delivered to your class in which you consider some of the positives and negatives associated with emigration. Through the course of your talk, you should make a clear argument for whether young Irish people should emigrate or remain in Ireland.

Exam Mechanics

QUESTION B

Read the question and highlight the main task. This task will inform your entire answer. It will indicate what **genre** you will be writing in, what your **purpose** is and what **layout/structure** to use. Identify the type of **audience** you will be writing for, which will determine the appropriate **style and register** to use. **Number the points you need to cover** to make sure that your answer addresses all aspects of the question.

> In TEXT 1, Thomas Reilly has emigrated from Ireland to America. Many young Irish people still leave Ireland every year seeking their fortunes and/or adventure overseas. Write the text of a **talk** to be delivered to your class in which you consider some of the positives and negatives associated with emigration **(1)**. Through the course of your talk, you should make a clear argument for whether young Irish people should emigrate or remain in Ireland **(2)**.

Genre: a talk.

Purpose: the purpose of a talk is usually to inform, persuade, instruct or entertain – all four could apply in this case.

Layout/structure: your structure could be loosely modelled on that of an argumentative or persuasive speech (see 'Seven steps to convince an audience' on pages 154 and 155).

Audience: your classmates and teacher. As well as greeting and thanking your audience, insert references to them throughout the talk.

Style and register: an informal register is acceptable here as you are speaking to your peer group. Demonstrate knowledge of audience with references to the things you have in common with them – the school, your local community, popular music, internet trends, etc. (remember to change key details if they could affect your anonymity). Your language style will be **discursive**, with elements of argumentative and persuasive styles.

(1) You need to discuss the positive aspects of emigration as well as the negatives. For example, a positive aspect might be the chance for emigrants to experience a new culture and broaden their minds. A negative might be the loss to Irish society generally when large numbers of young people leave. Illustrate your ideas with examples. This part of the talk could be written in an objective and detached style.

(2) You need to argue for either emigrating or staying. In this part of your talk you could begin using the language of argument and the language of persuasion. Another option would be to make your argument throughout the speech, so that when you are weighing up the positives and negatives it is already clear which side you are on.

 **Grammar Guide**

Comma splices

Have another look at the following sentence from the third paragraph of TEXT 1:

> The fourth day the Monsters of the deep showed their heads, the Captain said we would have a storm, and truly Boreas spent his rage on us that night.

This sentence contains three independent clauses:

1. The fourth day the Monsters of the deep showed their heads
2. the Captain said we would have a storm
3. truly Boreas spent his rage on us that night.

Clause 1 is joined to clause 2 with only a comma, which is an example of a comma splice. The two clauses are independent of each other and each could stand alone as its own sentence.

In the vast majority of cases, a comma is not a strong enough 'glue' to join two clauses and should be amended. There are three ways to fix a comma splice:

1. Keep the comma and add a conjunction (and, but, because, whether, etc.).
2. Replace the comma with a full stop to make two complete simple sentences.
3. Replace the comma with a semi-colon.

 Hint

A semi-colon joins two closely connected clauses; the words after the semi-colon develop the information given before it. For example: *The car wouldn't start; I think the battery was dead.* A colon introduces information: a quote, an explanation, an example or a list. For example: *I have an idea: let's borrow David's jump leads.*

The first two clauses in Reilly's sentence could be expressed as follows:

1. The fourth day the Monsters of the deep showed their heads, after the Captain said we would have a storm.
2. The fourth day the Monsters of the deep showed their heads. The Captain said we would have a storm.
3. The fourth day the Monsters of the deep showed their heads; the Captain said we would have a storm.

While comma splices are best avoided, like so many rules in English, this rule can be bent for literary effect. It could be argued that Reilly's use of commas conveys the sense of chaos on the ship. The loosely joined clauses topple one after the other and we are left with a clear impression of the confusion and panic on board.

The second sentence in Reilly's third paragraph contains six clauses:

1. We were tumbled out of our berths
2. the hold was two feet full of water
3. a leak was gaining an inch a minute on us
4. our topsails were carried away
5. the most of male passengers were all night [relieving] each other at the pump
6. in the morning I left my hammock at seven o'clock to look at the terrible sea.

Clauses 5 and 6 are joined with the conjunction 'and'. However, clauses 1 to 5 have been comma-spliced together. Rewrite these clauses using a combination of the three methods to fix comma splices.

TEXT 2 – ALEXANDER

This extract is taken from the 2020 novel *Strange Flowers* by Irish author Donal Ryan. It is the 1970s and Alexander, a Londoner from a Jamaican family, has moved to rural Ireland to be with his Irish wife, Moll. Alexander, his wife and child are living in the same cottage as Moll's parents, Paddy and Kit.

Moll's parents were shocked at their sudden grandparenthood, and embarrassed by the sudden presence in their house and in their lives of a tall black stranger. He could feel their discomfort thickening the air of the cottage. He resolved to say as little as possible, to allow them to adjust. He had nothing to say anyway. He'd brought his son so that he'd have a mother, and he was here to have a wife, to live with her as God intended. He wondered if his invocation of God's will would impress them and judged quickly that it wouldn't. He guessed that their faith was as fervent as his parents' but quieter: he didn't think that they'd shout Bible verses at one another in an argument, or that they'd have many arguments at all. Kit seemed always to be on the point of laughing; Paddy seemed always to be about to say something, and then deciding against it. They didn't seem able to sit in his presence, but moved around behind him arranging things, tidying things away or taking things down from the ancient-looking cupboards along the kitchen's far wall; stoking the huge open fire at the other end; making tea; making sandwiches; asking Moll was the child all right, was he asleep, what time would she have to feed him, would he need to be changed. He could see that Kit was smitten by the child, and that Paddy was no less

so, but was less inclined to fuss about him, because fussing, to a man like Paddy, was woman's work.

The greenness of the place. Everywhere greenness, trees heavy with it, hedgerows dappled light and dark and every shade of it, rolling fields of grass and green hills as far as his eye could see, and a lake below them in a silver line and, at the far side of it, below the blue and white and grey horizon, more greenness, more grassy hills and forests. Streams of flowers dazzling through the green along the roadsides and the lanes. Branches drooped with berries reaching out from hedgerows, everything blooming and buzzing and dripping with life. Even the rain had a shimmer of green to it. The dizzying inversion of the ratio of block and concrete to greenness and trees and flowers: it was almost too much. London had its islands of tidy and arranged greenness, compressed on all sides by stone. Here the whole world was a bed of yielding earth and greenness, dotted here and there with grey, laced thinly with winding roads on which cars moved slowly in single file and people walked, and old men in dark suits and white collars and knotted ties and flat caps pedalled creaking bicycles, regarding the world around them imperiously, exchanging in drawling voices the greetings of the day. And then, at night, the heart-lifting brightness of the stars.

Paddy and Kit asked nothing of him but he read Paddy's pause by the door and glance towards him before he left the cottage one morning in that first week as a silent request for him to follow. Good lad, Paddy said, the first time that Alexander rose to accompany him on his morning check of livestock and fences.

[...]

From then on he walked the fields with Paddy every morning and evening. It seemed to Alexander as though Paddy felt obliged to bring him on his twice-daily patrols, to teach him the art of stewardship. As though one day he were going to hand over the stewardship of the farm to him, Alexander, as some kind of appropriated birthright. He'd point at things and explain them to Alexander, and instruct him on the performance of tasks in the manner of a man passing down ancient wisdoms, and Alexander supposed that there was no other way for Paddy to frame this strange intercourse in his mind, this relationship he never thought he'd have. [...] Paddy was a small man and strong, full of talk about the weather and the news and the changing season and the flowers and trees and what was blooming and what was dying, and one cold clear night they helped a ewe to birth a breeched lamb and Paddy instructed Alexander to lean himself across the ewe's neck and shoulder where she lay on a bed of straw so that she wouldn't try to get up. The ewe was shorn pink and she raised her neck and turned her eyes to Alexander, and it looked for a moment as though she was crying and then as though she was smiling, and all he could do was say, Shush now, easy now, and as Paddy pushed his hand into the sheep's body and pulled the lamb pink and white and glistening wet by its hind legs into the world, Alexander felt a clicking into place of things, a feeling that all the strange unexpected things that had happened to him had been moved into alignment by some benevolent all-knowing force, that this small stone building on the land of a rich man in the company of a poor man was exactly where he was meant to be, that his life was unfolding, slowly, strangely, exactly as it should.

Footnote on Literary Fiction

Literary fiction (as opposed to genre fiction or popular fiction) tends to be character-driven instead of plot-driven. The author's focus on **developing characters** allows readers to establish a **deep understanding and empathy** with those characters. Character development is given a higher priority than creating fast-paced action or dramatic cliffhangers. Settings tend to be **realistic and down to earth**, unlike those found in other types of fiction such as sci-fi, horror or fantasy. However, literary fiction should not be thought of as slow or overly intellectual. The plot may progress at a more leisurely pace, but it still advances an intriguing story.

There is a sub-genre of literary fiction called the **family saga**. Novels in this tradition follow the exploits and adventures of characters over two or more generations. The measured pace of the writing allows readers to become closely involved with the changing fortunes of these characters over a significant number of years. The novel *Strange Flowers* by Donal Ryan, from which TEXT 2 is taken, is an example of this genre.

QUESTION A – 50 Marks

(i) From your reading of TEXT 2, what are three impressions formed by Alexander of the new place in which he finds himself and of the people by whom he is surrounded? (15)

(ii) In TEXT 2, Paddy instructs Alexander 'in the manner of a man passing down ancient wisdoms'. In your opinion, what are the three most important things that one generation should teach the next? Give reasons for your answers. (15)

(iii) 'Donal Ryan conveys a vivid sense of both character and place in his writing.' Do you agree with this statement? Support your answer with reference to Donal Ryan's writing style and language in TEXT 2. (20)

Sample Answer

QUESTION A (i)

Introduction states all three points that will be discussed in the answer.	The impression that Alexander forms of the place he finds himself is that Ireland's landscape is lush and green when compared with the city he came from. The way he views the people he came to live with is that they felt awkward around him at first, but then Paddy found a way to accept him into their lives.
First stated point.	The impression that Alexander forms of rural Ireland is that, unlike London, it is lush and full of growth: 'Everywhere greenness', 'rolling fields of grass and green hills as far as his eye could see'. He has lived all his life in the city of London, which has only 'islands of tidy and arranged greenness' surrounded by 'block and concrete'. However, in Ireland he sees that everything is 'blooming and buzzing and dripping with life', and the whole world is 'a bed of yielding earth and greenness'.
Quotations and explanation combined.	
Second stated point. Quotes support this idea.	At first, when Alexander moved in with his parents-in-law, he noticed that their 'discomfort' was 'thickening the air of the cottage'. He knew that Moll's parents felt uncomfortable having 'a tall black stranger' live with them. He observed that they 'didn't seem to be able to sit in his presence'; they kept moving around because they could not relax.
Linking phrase introduces third stated point.	However, Paddy seems to discover a way to relate to Alexander when he silently invites his son-in-law to accompany him as he inspects the farm every morning and evening. He begins teaching him 'the art of stewardship' as if he is thinking about how he will one day hand down the responsibility of looking after the farm to Alexander as 'some kind of appropriated birthright'. Alexander realises that for Paddy there was 'no other way … to frame this strange intercourse in his mind'. So, Alexander understands that his father-in-law has come to accept him in these terms.
Supporting quotations.	
Spells out the third point.	

Theme 5: Stranger in a Strange Land

Exam Mechanics

QUESTION A (ii)

6S **Simplify**

Highlight or underline the key ideas in the question. What is this question asking you to do?

> In TEXT 2, Paddy instructs Alexander 'in the manner of a man passing down ancient wisdoms'. In your opinion, what are the three most important things that one generation should teach the next? Give reasons for your answers.

This question can be answered fully without making any reference to TEXT 2. Instead, you need to:

- identify the three most important things that one generation should teach the next
- explain and justify your choices.

6S **Select**

You now need to jot down some ideas and then perform a little mental selection. In an exam, you can use any page in your answer booklet for rough work. You might find it helpful to make a spider diagram. For example:

Self-respect/care for the self

A knowledge of the past/history

Kindness and generosity

Important for older generation to teach younger

Tolerance of others/respect for different views/cultures

Stewardship/care for the environment/care for living creatures

Select three ideas to develop into your answer.

6S **Sort**

Decide in which order you want to discuss your selected ideas. Which is the most important? Will you start with this, or will you work up to it?

State, support and spell out

The examiner will expect you to answer Question A (ii) with three paragraphs (four if you want to give a brief introduction). Each of the three main paragraphs will:

1. **State** one of the ideas you have selected to discuss.

> The most important idea that an older generation can pass down to a younger generation is the crucial concept of humanity's role as stewards of planet Earth.

2. **Support** your choice with evidence or examples.

> Our news feeds are constantly filled with reports of extreme weather events; floods, wildfires, droughts and hurricanes are increasingly common. The devastation caused by climate change is in evidence all around us. Even though many people have a vested interest in denying the reality of a warming planet, and humanity's role in causing it, we can see with our own eyes the terrible losses resulting from a lack of effective stewardship.

3. **Spell out** exactly why you chose this idea.

> Looking after the environment in which we live is the most important responsibility bestowed upon each and every generation. If the next generation does not learn this crucial lesson from the current one, we may one day find that we have made the planet uninhabitable. Clearly, learning to look after our environment is the most important lesson of all.

Follow this process for the three parts of your answer.

QUESTION B – 50 Marks

In TEXT 2, Alexander, a man born in London to Jamaican parents, has moved to rural Tipperary. Imagine that Tourism Ireland has appealed to young Irish people to write an **open letter** intended for people from other cultures who are interested in visiting Ireland. In your letter, offer recommendations about where they should visit, describe what you consider to be a quintessentially Irish experience and explain at least one aspect of Irish society that might seem quaint or unusual to a newcomer.

> **! Hint**
>
> An open letter is a letter intended for a wide audience. They are often published online or in the print media.

Sample Answer

QUESTION B

Suitable salutation for an open letter.

Dear Fellow Global Citizens,

Phonetic spelling for non-Irish-speaking audience.

Céad mile fáilte! (ke-ad mee-la fall-cha)

Triad (list of three).

That means 'a hundred thousand welcomes' as Gaeilge (in Irish), and on behalf of everyone here in the land of Tayto crisps, rain and rich green landscapes, let me extend to you the warmest of Irish greetings!

Addresses audience with appropriately warm tone.

Factual evidence – language of argument.

Over nine million tourists visit Ireland each year. That's nearly double our population! Our guests hail from every corner of the globe. Wandering around the cobbled streets of Temple Bar in Dublin, you will hear excited chit-chat in every vernacular imaginable: Mandarin, Spanish, Afrikaans, Zulu, Russian ... So what is the enduring allure of the Emerald Isle, and what delights await you upon your arrival?

Vivid imagery.

Rhetorical question – language of persuasion.

Task 1 – offer recommended destinations.

Your first stop is likely to be Dublin. Why not linger in the capital city for a couple of days before exploring the rest of the island? Take a boat cruise on the River Liffey or visit the Guinness Storehouse. If you're fortunate to be here in mid-March, you could not do better than to attend the annual St Patrick's Day parade.

Less than an hour from Dublin city is Newgrange. This world-famous Neolithic monument is older than Stonehenge. The visitor centre is open seven days a week and no pre-booking is necessary. Continuing north will bring you to Belfast, where you can visit the Titanic Quarter or take a tour of the compelling murals of the Falls and Shankill roads. Travelling south you can visit Blarney Castle in County Cork, kiss the Blarney stone and be blessed with the 'gift of the gab'. And be sure to take in the stunning scenery as you drive the Ring of Kerry or cycle through Killarney National Park. The beauty of holidaying on a relatively small island is that nowhere is out of reach!

Emotive language – persuasive.

Wherever you go, you will experience the reason so many people make Ireland their number-one holiday destination. There is a genuineness behind every Irish greeting, and a warmth behind each smile that you won't get anywhere else. Perhaps it's just a shared pot of tea and a slice of soda bread with slatherings of butter. Or having the craic (banter) with strangers who treat you like an old friend. You will find that Ireland is the home of saints, scholars and social gatherings.

Triad employs alliteration for rhythm.

Task 2 – describe a quintessential Irish experience.

Whatever else you do while here, make sure you soak up some Irish trad music at a ceili (Irish for a 'visit' or an impromptu party). You will find many traditional Irish pubs throughout the country, and when you do, you can be assured of a casual and friendly atmosphere, hearty food and engaging conversation. Someone will take out a flute or a fiddle. Someone else will play the accordion or the banjo. Or perhaps you will hear the ancient art of the Irish storyteller. The ceili is such a quintessentially Irish pursuit that the traditional Irish pub has been exported all over the world, but nowhere can quite capture the ambiance like right here in Ireland.

Task 3 – explain aspects visitors might find quaint/unusual.

When first meeting a native Irish person, do not expect them to say 'Top of the mornin'' or to interject their sentences with 'Begorrah!' because no one here actually says these things! They are much more likely to say: 'What's the craic?', which is simply their way of asking how you are doing. The correct response to this is to say that you are 'grand'. The word 'grand' is a particularly useful one to remember. It describes a general well-being: 'I'm grand', as well as casual optimism: 'Ah, it'll be grand', or sometimes sarcasm: 'Oh, grand!', or even sadness; 'Ah, grand.' Another thing to keep in mind is the Irish custom of 'slagging'. Irish people tend to demonstrate the affection they feel for each other with good-humoured insults, so if the person you are chatting to begins to 'slag' you, this is just their way of being friendly.

Conclusion makes final appeal for tourists to visit.

Whether you're marvelling at the haunting symmetry of the Giant's Causeway in County Antrim, soaking up the majestic grandeur of the Cliffs of Moher in County Clare or simply browsing through the multitude of goods on display in Cork's English Market, be assured that the welcoming Irish smile you see is genuine, because we don't just want you to visit, we want you to re-visit next year!

Translation for non-Irish-speaking audience.

Mise le meas (Yours sincerely),

Mary O'Connor (17), for Tourism Ireland

TEXT 3 – WAR DOCTOR

TEXT 3 is an extract taken from a memoir, *War Doctor*, written by David Nott, a doctor who has worked with the International Committee of the Red Cross (ICRC) in some of the world's most dangerous places.

The security manager began shouting at Mauro and me. 'You have to go! Now! Right now!'

By this time, the little girl was asleep, and on the ventilator. She was a pitiful sight, her bowel hanging out of a hole in her abdominal wall and fragmentation wounds in her chest, arm and abdomen. I looked at her blood pressure monitor, which read around 60 systolic. We would be leaving her in the theatre uncovered, getting cold, and still bleeding internally. The time she had left to live could be counted in minutes, not hours, whether there was an airstrike or not.

By now everybody else had left the operating theatre. Even the security manager had gone to clear the other rooms. Lots of things went through my mind. The most burning thought was that I could not leave this little girl to die on her own, having suffered the most extreme injuries. She was an innocent child and did not deserve such a fate. She had to be protected from this dreadful violence, not be part of it.

I was reminded of what had happened in Sarajevo, all those years before. I had thought I might die then and had thought so during the shell attack on the safe house the previous evening. Maybe *this* was the moment it ended. And if it was, did I need to save myself? The answer, of course, was no.

I was on my own in the world, with no parents, no siblings, no wife, no children and no dependants. In the grand scheme of things, it didn't much matter whether I lived or died; at least I would be doing something

that I loved, and I might even save this girl in the process. I made a conscious decision to stay.

The patient was now fully anaesthetized and the ventilator was working.

I turned to Mauro and said, 'You can go, you don't need to stay.'

'Are you staying?'

'I'm staying.'

'Then I'll stay with you.'

I brought my operating set to the table, and looked again at Mauro. Our eyes locked. It was a look that conveyed so much: part fear, part trepidation; a mixture of regret, respect and farewell.

'You should go,' I said again.

'No, David, I will stay with you.'

He, too, was a veteran of many missions, also unmarried with no dependants. I suppose we had both been thinking the same thing.

So we stayed with the little girl, waiting for the bomb to drop or the missile to strike, or whatever it might be. I wondered what it would be like. But I calmly prepared the girl's abdomen with iodine, picked up the green drapes and clipped them into position. [...]

I made an incision the full length of her abdomen, from just below the breastbone to the pubic area. Inside was a large piece of shrapnel that had caused mayhem. It had entered into the right iliac fossa, around the hip bone, and the hole it had made had allowed the small bowel to escape. It had cut a hole in her bladder and in some parts of her small and large bowel, and had also gone directly into the spleen, which was bleeding profusely. I strained to hear any sound of incoming rockets. Nothing. The hospital was silent. I looked at Mauro, who raised his eyebrows back at me.

The scrub nurse had left a lot of unopened swabs on the side and I asked Mauro to open them all up for me so I could pack her abdomen. The familiar process took my mind off the situation we were in, and by the time I'd removed her spleen and started mobilizing various parts of her bowel, Mauro told me twenty minutes had passed since we'd begun. Still no attack. There was nothing to do but carry on. We completed the operation, repairing the holes in her small bowel and colon, and making her abdomen look normal again. I then turned my attention to her left arm and repaired the artery damaged by another piece of shrapnel.

Two hours later, the theatre floor was still deserted. We decided to wake her up in the operating theatre. As we were doing this, people started to drift back in, amazed to see us still there. Clearly, there was to be no attack.

I am not sure where the information had come from but I was told that it was a credible source – the ICRC were embedded with both sides – and that's why everybody had panicked and left. Nor do I know how many patients died in other operating theatres, or what happened to them. I only knew that our little girl was alive, and kept my fingers crossed that she would recover. I went to see her every day after that, and got to know her family very well. Her name is Aysha and the photograph I have of me standing by her hospital bed, both of us smiling, says it all.

Footnote on Memoirs

Although memoirs are similar to autobiographies, they should not be confused with them. An autobiography tends to tell the author's complete life story, whereas a memoir has a specific focus on a **particular period or experience**. Like biographies and autobiographies, memoirs are classified as **non-fiction** and **relate real events**.

A memoir is written from a **highly personal perspective**, and so the reader will develop a close understanding of the author, their opinions, personality and outlook.

Memoirs can share certain writing features with fiction: they often include **characterisation**, **dialogue** and **aesthetic language** as the author describes particular places they have been to, people they have encountered and conversations in which they participated. The fundamental difference from fiction is that a memoir contains the author's memory of things that actually happened in real life.

Of course, anyone's memory of events can become clouded, but we read memoirs, not necessarily for a historically accurate record of events, but in order to better understand the author's perspective on them.

QUESTION A – 50 Marks

(i) From your reading of TEXT 3, what is your impression of its author, David Nott? (15)

(ii) In TEXT 3, the author describes a photograph he has of himself and the little girl, Aysha, and he claims that it 'says it all'. In your opinion, which medium conveys a message better: a photograph or a written passage? Give reasons for your answer. (15)

(iii) 'David Nott's writing style vividly captures the tension and drama faced by medical staff working in a warzone.' Do you agree with this statement? Support your answer with reference to Nott's use of language in TEXT 3 to capture the tension and drama faced by medical staff working in a warzone. (20)

Exam Mechanics

QUESTION A (iii)

6S Simplify

The question states exactly what you need to find, so start by highlighting the key words.

> 'David Nott's writing style vividly captures the tension and drama faced by medical staff working in a warzone.' Do you agree with this statement? Support your answer with reference to Nott's use of language in TEXT 3 to capture the tension and drama faced by medical staff working in a warzone.

Take 30 seconds to write down synonyms (words that mean the same) for the key words 'tension' and 'drama'.

- Tension = pressure, suspense, strain, anxiousness.
- Drama = spectacle, action, sensation, vividness.

Now ask yourself: Does Nott's writing style reflect either of these two ideas?

6S Select

Read the text to find examples of where Nott uses language that conveys tension and/or drama. Highlight/underline and annotate them when you find them.

Direct speech, shouting – dramatic; conveys immediate threat – tension.	The security manager began shouting at Mauro and me. 'You have to go! Now! Right now!'
Reader likely to feel sympathy for a child – tension.	By this time, the little girl was asleep, and on the ventilator. She was a pitiful sight, her bowel hanging out of a hole in her abdominal wall and fragmentation wounds in her chest, arm and abdomen. I looked at her blood pressure monitor, which read around 60 systolic. We would be leaving her in the theatre uncovered, getting cold, and still bleeding internally. The time she had left to live could be counted in minutes, not hours, whether there was an airstrike or not.
Emotive language; vivid description – dramatic.	
Urgency of the moment – tension.	

What other examples can you find of the writing conveying the stress the doctors were under, or capturing the vivid spectacle of the scene?

6S Sort

Choose the four strongest examples from the text and decide which order to address them in for your answer. You do not need to follow the order in which they appear in the text.

6S State, support and spell out

Your examiner will expect you to answer Question A (iii) with four paragraphs (or five if you include an introduction). Each paragraph will:

1. **State** what you found dramatic/tense.

> Tension is created early in the text when Nott establishes the imminent danger of an airstrike and balances it against the amount of time he judges is available to save the girl's life.

2. **Support** your observation with quotations/examples.

> He tells us that the 'time she had left to live could be counted in minutes, not hours, whether there was an airstrike or not'.

3. **Spell out** what makes your chosen example dramatic/tense.

> The atmosphere in the operating theatre is tense because the only two remaining doctors expect to be killed by bombs at any moment. Added to this is the stress of their race against time to attempt to save the little girl who is extremely close to death.

Follow this process for each of the four parts of your answer.

Theme 5: Stranger in a Strange Land

QUESTION B – 50 Marks

Write a **proposal** to be submitted to a national council chaired by the President of Ireland suggesting one person you believe should be commemorated as a hero. The person may or may not be a public figure, and they may be living or deceased. Explain why you feel this person should be commemorated and suggest what form this commemoration might take.

Exam Mechanics

QUESTION B

Read the question and highlight the main task. This task will inform your entire answer. It will indicate what **genre** you will be writing in, what your **purpose** is and what **layout/structure** to use. Identify the type of **audience** you will be writing for, which will determine the appropriate **style and register** to use. **Number the points you need to cover** to make sure that your answer addresses all aspects of the question.

> Write a **proposal** to be submitted to a national council chaired by the President of Ireland suggesting one person you believe should be commemorated as a hero **(1)**. The person may or may not be a public figure, and they may be living or deceased. Explain why you feel this person should be commemorated **(2)** and suggest what form this commemoration might take **(3)**.

Genre: a proposal.

Purpose: to inform and persuade. Inform your audience about your chosen candidate, convince them that this person deserves the honour of being commemorated and persuade them as to how best to do so.

Layout/structure: examiners are told to allow for a variety of approaches. Many students choose to structure their answer similarly to a formal letter. Begin with an introduction in which you identify your nominee. Use the main body of your text to address all parts of the question. End with a strong conclusion before signing off.

Audience: a national council chaired by the President of Ireland. This council will probably be made up of notable personages such as leaders in business, politicians, celebrities or public figures from all walks of life.

Style and register: the language in your answer should be formal, dignified and respectful at all times. Use the language of information to convey the relevant qualities/acts that make your chosen candidate suitable for recognition. Use the language of argument and the language of persuasion to convince your audience. You can show an awareness of your audience by referencing a national context: other Irish heroes, Irish culture, Irish history, etc.

(1) Identify the person you think deserves national recognition as a hero. This person can be someone who is already known nationally, or they could be a hidden hero, perhaps someone from your own locality or family. They may be living or deceased. You can select someone from Irish history; however, personalities like Michael Collins or Patrick Pearse have already been recognised and honoured in numerous ways, so they might not be the best choice for this task.

(2) Use argument and persuasion in order to make your case. What does the word 'hero' mean to you? Does your candidate inspire others? Has this person committed a single act of bravery, or shown heroic qualities on a continual basis?

(3) How your candidate for commemoration should be honoured will depend on what it is they are being honoured for. Possibilities include: naming a new wing of a children's hospital after them in a ceremony officiated by the president; renaming the main road of your town in their honour; making a documentary on their life and airing it to the nation; setting up a bursary scheme in their name to assist deserving students to enter third-level education; erecting a statue of them – where would it go and what would it look like?

A-Z Grammar Guide

Using 'I' or 'me' in a sentence

TEXT 3 starts with the following sentence: 'The security manager began shouting at Mauro and me.' To some people, Nott's choice of words might appear incorrect. Surely it is supposed to be 'Mauro and I'? However, the author has it right; in this instance, 'me' is correct.

How do you know when to use 'me' and when to use 'I' when these words are listed with other people in a sentence?

First, you need to know the difference between the subject and the **object** of a sentence. To establish this, find the verb. In the opening sentence of TEXT 3, the verb is 'began shouting'.

The security manager began shouting at **Mauro and me.**

The subject (the thing doing the action in the sentence) is the security manager: he is the person who began shouting. The object (the thing(s) being acted upon) is Mauro and me: they are the ones the security manager began shouting at.

The rule of thumb for when to use 'I' or 'me' is:
- If it is part of the **object** of the sentence, use 'me'.
- If it is part of the subject of the sentence, use 'I'.

If the situation had been the other way around, it would have been written: 'Mauro and I began shouting at **the security manager.**'

A simple way to figure out whether to use 'me' or 'I' is to take the other people listed with you out of the sentence and hear how it sounds. Consider the following sentence:

Father came home with presents for **Taegan, Tabitha and me.**

Removing the other people listed (Taegan and Tabitha) would give:
- Father came home with presents for I. ✘
- Father came home with presents for me. ✔

Identify the correct term (me/I) to use in the following sentences:

1. Lauren and _____ decided we would go for a swim in the lake.

2. The invitation was only for Michelle and _____.

3. My friend and _____ spent many evenings talking by the fireside.

4. The driver of the car had to swerve at the last minute because he clearly didn't see Molly and _____.

SECTION II   COMPOSING   (100 marks)

Write a composition on **any one** of the assignments that appear in **bold print** below.

Each composition carries 100 marks.

The composition assignments are intended to reflect language study in the areas of information, argument, persuasion, narration, and the aesthetic use of language.

1. Thomas Reilly, who wrote the letter which features as TEXT 1, makes this observation: 'I would advise no one I have regard for to emigrate unless the persons interested to come have friends before them, who will receive them and snatch them from all the evils of Society.'

   Write a discursive essay in which you explore the importance of friends and friendship.

2. In TEXT 2, Donal Ryan describes a rural scene with the words 'the whole world was a bed of yielding earth and greenness'.

   Write a descriptive essay in which you take your reader on a journey inspired by your perceptions of nature.

3. In TEXT 3, David Nott experiences first-hand some of the horrific consequences of armed conflict.

   Write a speech, to be delivered to a World Youth Conference, in which you appeal for peaceful rather than military resolutions in cases of conflict around the world.

4. We read in TEXT 1 about a frightening storm at sea.

   Write a short story in which a storm plays a significant part in the narrative.

5. The theme linking the three texts on this paper is 'Stranger in a Strange Land'.

   Imagine that you are an alien from a distant world. You have recently spent time on Earth and have now returned to your own planet. Write a dialogue, in dramatic form, in which you try to explain to your fellow beings some human rituals, artefacts and behaviours you have witnessed. Your drama may be humorous, serious, or both.

6. In TEXT 2, the character Alexander experiences a 'clicking into place of things' and feels that his life is unfolding 'exactly as it should'.

   Write a personal essay in which you reflect on a moment (or moments) when things 'clicked into place' for you.

7. TEXT 3 features a doctor trying to save lives in the middle of a violent conflict.

   Write an article for a serious publication in which you consider whether medicine or war has had the greater impact on human history.

Theme 6
Fragile Planet

Sometimes the world may feel like a big and stable place. But against the infinite blackness of the universe, we are little more than an inconspicuous speck in the corner of an otherwise unremarkable galaxy. On that tiny pinprick of light, all of human history has played out. The very few humans who have viewed it from space all tend to remark on how precious it is, and how delicate seems life's foothold upon it. In this final theme, we consider some of the perils that may beset our home.

Discuss

1. Of which genre of writing is each text an example?
2. What features or styles of writing helped you to identify the genre of each of these samples?
3. Where would you be likely to encounter each of these genres?

Sample 1 – TEXT 1

The G7, as an example, is spending billions more on fossil fuels and fossil fuel infrastructure than on clean energy. This you compensate with beautiful words and promises that someone in the future will somehow undo your actions and make them net zero. And when your empty words are not enough, when the protests grow too loud, you respond by making the protests illegal.

Sample 2 – TEXT 2

How hard an impactor hits depends on a lot of variables – angle of entry, velocity and trajectory, whether the collision is head-on or from the side, and the mass and density of the impacting object, among much else – none of which we can know so many millions of years after the fact. But what scientists can do – and Anderson and Witzke have done – is measure the impact site and calculate the amount of energy released. From that they can work out plausible scenarios of what it must have been like – or, more chillingly, would be like if it happened now.

Sample 3 – TEXT 3

And Blue Origin's long-term goals have a strong environmental component, Bezos has stressed. Over the long haul, the company wants to help establish a bustling off-Earth economy, with millions of people living and working in space. Indeed, Blue Origin intends to help move most resource extraction and heavy industry off the planet, so that we don't further strip the planet and foul its soil, air and waters.

SECTION I   COMPREHENDING   (100 marks)

TEXT 1 – THE SHOW IS OVER

Greta Thunberg, world-famous Swedish campaigner for action on climate change, delivered this speech at the Austrian World Summit in 2021.

Thank you for having me.

Tomorrow, 150 weeks will have passed since we started the school strike for the climate. And during this time, more and more people around the world have woken up to the climate and ecological crisis, putting more and more pressure on you: the people in power. Eventually the public pressure was too much, and you had the world's eyes on you, so you started to act. Not acting as in taking climate action but acting as in role-playing. Playing politics, playing with words and playing with our future. Pretending to take responsibility, acting as saviours as you try to convince us that things are being taken care of. Meanwhile, the gap between your rhetoric and reality keeps growing wider and wider. And since the level of awareness is so low you almost get away with it.

But let's be clear. What you are doing is not about climate action or responding to an emergency – it never was. This is communication tactics dressed as politics. Disguised as politics. You, especially leaders from high-income nations, are pretending to change and listen to the young people

while you continue pretty much exactly like before. Pretending to take science seriously by saying 'science is back' while holding climate summits without even inviting one single climate scientist as speaker. Pretending to wage war against fossil fuels while opening up brand new coal mines, oil fields and pipelines. You don't only continue business as usual as before – in many cases, you're even speeding up and scaling up the process. Pretending to have the most ambitious climate policies while granting new oil licences, exploring future oil fields. Bragging about your so-called ambitious climate commitments – which, if you look holistically, are vastly insufficient – and then get caught not even trying to reach those targets. Pretending to care about nature and biodiversity while the world is cutting down a forest area the size of a football field every second. Pretending to be a climate leader while locking in a future common agricultural policy that will make the Paris Agreement impossible to reach. Pretending that you will 'build back better' after the pandemic, even though astronomical sums of money have already been locked in – and not in green projects, whatever 'green' means.

The G7, as an example, is spending billions more on fossil fuels and fossil fuel infrastructure than on clean energy. This you compensate with beautiful words and promises that someone in the future will somehow undo your actions and make them net zero. And when your empty words are not enough, when the protests grow too loud, you respond by making the protests illegal. [...]

But as your acts continue, more and more of us are seeing through your manuscripts and your role-playing. The gap between your actions and words is becoming more impossible to ignore while more and more extreme weather events are raging all around us. And as a result, young people all over this planet are no longer falling for your lies. You are distancing yourself further and further away from us and from reality. Some years ago, you could still claim that we're moving in the right direction. Today, that is no longer possible. 2021 is currently forecasted to be the year with the second highest emission rise, ever. You say we need to move slowly to bring the public along; however, how do you honestly expect to bring the people along if you don't treat this crisis like a crisis?

If [there] is one thing the pandemic has proven once and for all it is that the climate and ecological emergencies have never once been treated as emergencies. The climate crisis is today, at best, being treated only as a business opportunity to create new green jobs, new green businesses and technologies. As the pandemic unfolded, you did not say this will benefit the face-mask manufacturing industry or this will create new jobs in health care and hospitals. Taking bold climate action will naturally bring many advantages and benefits. Yet, needless to say, we will not be able to solve a crisis we do not treat as a crisis and that we do not understand the magnitude of.

Perhaps playing a role helps you sleep at night – saying things just for the sake of it because the words are in your scripts. But while you are busy working the stage, you seem to forget that the climate crisis is not something distant in the future. It is already taking so much from the most affected people in the most affected areas. This might just be a game to you – a game to win votes, popularity, points on the stock market or your next high-paid position in a company or lobbying firm. The ones who focus on the packaging rather than on the actual content and the ones with the most beautiful features and the most short-sighted, likeable policies [win]. You can, and will, of course, choose to continue to play your parts, say your lines and wear your costumes. You can, and will, continue to pretend.

But, nature and physics will not fall for it. Nature and physics are not entertained nor distracted by your theatre. The audience has grown weary. The show is over.

Thank you.

Theme 6: Fragile Planet

QUESTION A – 50 Marks

(i) Outline, in your own words, three of the main criticisms Greta Thunberg directs towards world leaders in her speech to the Austrian World Summit. (15)

(ii) Give your personal response to any three observations made by Greta Thunberg in TEXT 1 that made an impression on you. (15)

(iii) Do you agree that elements of the language of argument and the language of persuasion are used effectively in TEXT 1 in order to deliver a forceful speech? Give reasons for your answer, supporting your views with reference to the elements of argumentative and persuasive language evident in the text. (20)

Exam Mechanics

QUESTION A (ii)

6S Simplify

The question tells you exactly what you need to find, so highlight the key words.

> Give your personal response to any three observations made by Greta Thunberg in TEXT 1 that made an impression on you.

Before you even start reading the text, you know you will be reading ideas from Greta Thunberg. If you already know who she is, you will have a good idea about the topic(s) she will be addressing. You are looking for three observations made by her that made an impression on you.

You are likely to come across the words 'observations' and 'impression' fairly regularly in exam questions.

- Observations = opinions, findings, reflections, conclusions. Similar to an insight, an observation will probably contain knowledge that is new to you.
- Impression = impact, effect, influence, something that caused a reaction. An impression is literally the mark left behind on something when it comes into contact with something else.

When you are asked to discuss the impression someone's observation left on you, ask yourself what new idea you gained and how that has affected you. Did it make you feel shocked, anxious, amused or something else?

6S Select

As you read the text, highlight any interesting (possibly new) ideas you come across. Add a brief note in the margin with a key word or two describing your reaction to or thoughts about these ideas.

6S Sort

If you have highlighted more than three ideas, select which ones you want to discuss. Choose the three that had the greatest impact on you. Which ideas were the most surprising, concerning or alarming?

65 State, support and spell out

The examiner will expect you to answer Question A (ii) with three paragraphs (or four/five if you choose to do an introduction/conclusion – this is not compulsory but does show purposefulness). Each of the three main paragraphs will:

1. **State** an observation that made an impression on you.

> One of Greta Thunberg's observations that struck a chord with me is the terrifying speed with which the world is being deforested.

2. **Support** your statement with a quote or reference.

> She accuses world leaders of pretending to care about nature 'while the world is cutting down a forest area the size of a football field every second'.

3. **Spell out** the impact the observation had on you. Why did you choose to discuss the particular observation?

> Although I was aware that deforestation is a serious concern for environmentalists, I did not realise how quickly it is happening. Thunberg's 'football field' image is astonishing because it is so easily visualised. The idea of that much forest disappearing 'every second' horrifies me and makes me wonder when we will run out of forest. As we know how important the rainforests are to the health of our planet, the prospect of soon having little or no forest left is chilling.

Follow this process for the three parts of your answer.

Sample Answer

QUESTION A (iii)

> Opening statement answers the question without supporting evidence. Here, only part of the question's premise is agreed with.

I agree that Greta Thunberg delivers a forceful speech and uses the language of persuasion effectively. However, Thunberg's use of argumentative language is not so effective, and, as a result, I found her contentions less convincing than they could have been.

> First statement links the three paragraphs that will deal with persuasive techniques used.

Throughout her speech, Thunberg employs some very persuasive techniques. She establishes her main theme with

> First point stated.

a clever pun when she says that world leaders 'started to act. Not acting as in taking climate action but acting

> Supporting quotation.

as in role-playing.' Here she sets up the central image she returns to again and again: world leaders are playing a part and pretending to care with their 'manuscripts' and their

> Spells out effectiveness.

'role-playing'. This compelling technique portrays these world leaders in the minds of the audience as absurdly hypocritical.

Second point stated.

Thunberg uses apostrophe as an effective rhetorical device. She constantly refers to world leaders (who are not present) directly in the second person: 'And when your empty words are not enough … you respond by making the protests illegal.'

Supporting quotation. Ellipsis indicates omitted text.

Spells out effectiveness.

This technique adds to the bitter tone of the entire speech. She presents herself as fighting a faceless but powerful enemy, which will elicit empathy for her cause.

Linking word.

Thunberg also uses repetition, triads and pithy, strident language. She repeats the word 'pretending' to hammer home her message about leaders' hypocrisy. An example of a triad appears early on: 'Playing politics, playing with words and playing with our future.' Her rhythm is relentless and unforgiving. She employs short forceful sentences to great effect: 'The audience has grown weary. The show is over.' These rhetorical techniques combine to make Thunberg's speech emotionally charged and powerful.

Techniques that can be dealt with together as the third point.

Supporting quotation.

Spells out effectiveness.

Indicates change in direction – here the answer disagrees with the question's premise.

However, there is a marked absence in her speech of solid evidence that might have made it more effective. She does make specific references to issues like the Paris Agreement, and she does criticise current agricultural policy, but she does not develop or examine these topics further. She speaks about governments 'granting new oil licences' and 'exploring future oil fields' without presenting explicit details. She addresses world leaders as a homogenous group, as if all are equally to blame for inaction, without singling out any particular government or policy. She mentions the G7 and the billions those countries spend on fossil fuels, but she does not supply factual or statistical evidence to support this claim. Without solid evidence, facts and statistics, this speech relies mostly on raw emotion rather than reasoned argument.

Stated answer.

Examples and quotations to support answer.

Spells out reason for disagreement.

Conclusion sums up the argument.

Therefore, I agree that Thunberg's speech is forceful and persuasive, but, since it lacks much supporting evidence, I do not agree that it uses the language of argument effectively.

QUESTION B – 50 Marks

In TEXT 1, Greta Thunberg refers to the global movement she began in 2018 known as the 'school strike for climate'. Imagine that a collection of essays on climate change has been written by young activists from across the globe. As the editor of this collection, write the text of your **introduction** to be published with them online for an international audience. In it, you should inform your reader about the purpose of the collection, offer your recommendations for actions that can be taken by both individuals and governments to counter global warming, and discuss some of the content the reader can expect to encounter in the collection of essays.

Sample Answer

QUESTION B

Title and subtitle of the fictitious collection.

ACT NOW

'Deeds not Words'

Addresses reader directly; inclusive language establishes a personal connection.

Thank you for choosing our online anthology ACT NOW. Perhaps, like us, you are an activist. In this collection you will find plenty of voices just like your own, from all over the world; all just as outraged as you are about our governments' inaction in the face of the climate crisis.

Real movements add authenticity.

Use of Thunberg's first name implies the writer is on friendly terms with her, which could be the case in this context.

Perhaps you are yet to join our ranks. Perhaps you have heard about the Youth For Climate or the Fridays For Future (FFF) movements and are curious to know more. Then congratulations! By coming here, you have already taken your first steps in what may be the most important journey you will ever make.

Real date (taken from the question) and original Swedish-language title add authenticity. Links are a feature of online publications.

Since our movement began with Greta's brave solo stand outside the Swedish parliament buildings in 2018 (see Skolstrejk för klimatet for more information), there has been an unprecedented groundswell in youth activism. Never before has a single issue so united young people from all nations, all cultures and all creeds. Never before has the establishment been so openly challenged by a sector it had traditionally been able to ignore: children.

Repetition – rhetorical/persuasive device.

Acknowledgements are a common feature of introductions. By giving a link to another page, the feature is implied without having to write a list.

When a pandemic forced us off the streets, it also forced us to adapt and begin the Digital Strike. This anthology is the result of months of online activity and hard work from many activists who gave freely of their time. There are too many thoroughly deserving people to thank by name here, but please take a moment to read the Acknowledgements.

Theme 6: Fragile Planet

Task 3 – discuss some of the content the reader can expect. Note: the tasks do not have to be attempted in the order they appear in the question.

It is easy to feel overwhelmed by the number, size and complexity of the issues of climate change. So, the essays contained in this collection each focus on a different facet of the theme. For example, taking on the topic of rising sea levels are Angela Chuenglin of the Philippines and Maumoon Zakhi of the Maldives; both countries that are likely to suffer the worst effects of coastal flooding. There are essays from the deserts of Australia and Namibia, from the Mekong Delta and the slopes of the Andes. You can work your way through the contributions in order, or you can dip in and out; however suits you best.

Task 1 – explain the purpose of the collection.

Our aspiration in compiling this collection is to inform, to empower and to encourage. I hope, with you, we achieve these goals.

Task 1 continued.

The realities of our planet's plight are stark indeed. But our purpose is not to generate despair; far from it. In these essays you will find much about hope.

Task 3 continued.

Lucas Mbabmtwana, writing from his home in Soweto, expands on exactly that: hope. It is from his essay that we take the title of the collection: he urges us to Act Now. We do not need to feel helpless.

Link to task 2 – recommendations.

So, what can we do? Probably the most effective thing all of us can do – especially those in the western world – is eat less meat. Meat means cattle; cattle mean methane emissions and the burning of forests in order to make pasture. Other vital actions include cutting out food waste, taking up slow fashion, reducing or phasing out altogether our reliance on single-use plastics.

Task 2 (a) – what individuals could do.

Links two parts of task 2.

Remember what we have learned since 2018. We have a voice. People listen. So, contact your political representatives. Let them know what you expect of them. And what can governments do? First and foremost, they have to accept climate change as a fact and act upon that knowledge as if all our lives depend on it – because they do. Then, they need to loosen the stranglehold that the fossil fuel industry has over public policy. No matter how fast we reduce emissions now, there will still be climate impacts, which means we have to prepare. Governments have to adapt. We all have to change. There can be no going back to the way things were.

Task 2 (b) – what governments could do.

Returns to the subtitle for a sense of closure.

Our motto, and the subtitle of our anthology, is taken from the suffragette movement of the early 20th century. We, who clearly understand we are in a desperate struggle for our very future, and the future of the Earth, know that now is most certainly the time for 'Deeds not Words'.

As this is an online collection, a link is included to the essays.

Thank you for choosing this collection of essays. For a full list of contents, please click here.

Fictitious name of author and date of writing introduction.

Theresa McMahon,

31 August 2023

A-Z Grammar Guide

Conjunctions and sentence fragments

Conjunctions

Conjunctions join together words, phrases, clauses and sentences. Some examples of commonly used conjunctions are:

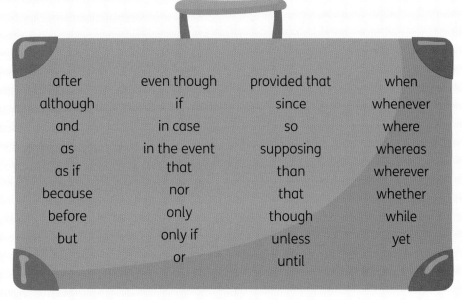

after	even though	provided that	when
although	if	since	whenever
and	in case	so	where
as	in the event	supposing	whereas
as if	that	than	wherever
because	nor	that	whether
before	only	though	while
but	only if	unless	yet
	or	until	

There are two **conjunctions** in the following sentence from TEXT 1:

> Eventually the public pressure was too much, **and** you had the world's eyes on you, **so** you started to act.

The two conjunctions make a compound sentence out of three simple sentences:

1. Eventually the public pressure was too much.
2. You had the world's eyes on you.
3. You started to act.

Instead of writing these ideas as short, choppy sentences, Thunberg combines them into a more elegant compound sentence with the use of conjunctions.

Good writing blends short, simple sentences with longer flowing ones. Too many short sentences will make your writing seem childish. Too many complex/compound sentences can become tedious. Varying your tempo has the effect of allowing your prose to flow. Thunberg not only uses compound and complex sentences, but she also includes plenty of pithy sentences and even some sentence fragments in her speech.

The rule about not starting a sentence with a conjunction is a myth. Most conjunctions can perform their role perfectly well, whether they come at the start of the sentence or are placed between the combined clauses. For example: 'Whether they come at the start of the sentence, or are placed between the combined clauses, most conjunctions can perform their role perfectly well.'

Theme 6: Fragile Planet

117

In TEXT 1, Thunberg begins a number of sentences with conjunctions without using them to actually join anything. For example:

- **And** during this time, more and more people around the world have woken up to the climate and ecological crisis, putting more and more pressure on you: the people in power.
- **And** since the level of awareness is so low you almost get away with it.
- **But** let's be clear.
- **But** as your acts continue, more and more of us are seeing through your manuscripts and your role-playing.

In these examples, the conjunction at the beginning is not being used in its normal grammatical role. You could remove the conjunction without altering the meaning or the grammar of the remaining sentence. Thunberg starts these sentences with conjunctions for rhetorical effect. Many speakers and writers use this technique to add a certain intensity and forcefulness to their words. You might imagine someone during a heated disagreement wading in with 'And another thing … !'

Sentence fragments

Another grammar 'rule' Thunberg breaks is her use of sentence fragments. For example:

- Disguised as politics.
- Playing politics, playing with words and playing with our future.

As we saw on page 36, all sentences must have a finite verb. Since neither of these examples have a finite verb ('playing' is a participle), they are not grammatically complete sentences.

Thunberg uses quite a wide variety of sentence types in her speech. She does this for rhetorical effect: to maximise the impact her words have on her audience.

TEXT 2 – FIRE FROM THE SKY

This extract is taken from the popular science (non-fiction) book *A Short History of Nearly Everything* by Bill Bryson. Bryson has travelled to Manson, Iowa in the USA to speak to geologists Ray Anderson and Brian Witzke. Manson is the site of a giant impact crater where an asteroid or comet hit the Earth 74 million years ago.

I asked them how much warning we would receive if a similar hunk of rock were coming towards us today.

'Oh, probably none,' said Anderson breezily. 'It wouldn't be visible to the naked eye until it warmed up and that wouldn't happen until it hit the atmosphere, which would be about one second before it hit the Earth. You're talking about something moving many tens of times faster than the fastest bullet. Unless it had been seen by someone with a telescope, and that's by no means a certainty, it would take us completely by surprise.'

How hard an impactor hits depends on a lot of variables – angle of entry, velocity and trajectory, whether the collision is head-on or from the side, and the mass and density of the impacting object, among much else – none of which we can know so many millions of years after the fact. But what scientists can do – and Anderson and Witzke have done – is measure the impact site and calculate the amount of energy released. From that they can work out plausible scenarios of what it must have been like – or, more chillingly, would be like if it happened now.

An asteroid or comet travelling at cosmic velocities would enter the Earth's atmosphere at such a speed that the air beneath it couldn't get out of the way and would be compressed, as in a bicycle pump. As anyone who has used such a pump knows, compressed air grows swiftly hot, and the temperature below it would rise to some 60,000 Kelvin, or ten times the surface temperature of the Sun. In this instant of its arrival in our atmosphere, everything in the meteor's path – people, houses, factories, cars – would crinkle and vanish like cellophane in a flame.

One second after entering the atmosphere, the meteorite would slam into the Earth's surface where the people of Manson had a moment before been going about their business. The meteorite itself would vaporize instantly, but the blast would blow out 1,000 cubic kilometres of rock, earth and superheated gases. Every living thing within 250 kilometres that hadn't been killed by the heat of entry would now be killed by the blast. Radiating outwards at almost the speed of light would be the initial shock wave, sweeping everything before it.

For those outside the zone of immediate devastation, the first inkling of catastrophe would be a flash of blinding light – the brightest ever seen by human eyes – followed an instant to a minute or two later by an apocalyptic sight of unimaginable grandeur: a roiling wall of darkness reaching high into the heavens, filling one entire field of view and travelling at thousands of kilometres an hour. Its approach would be eerily silent since it would be moving far beyond the speed of sound. Anyone in a tall building in Omaha or Des Moines, say, who chanced to look in the right direction would see a bewildering veil of turmoil followed by instantaneous oblivion.

Theme 6: Fragile Planet

Within minutes, over an area stretching from Denver to Detroit and encompassing what had once been Chicago, St Louis, Kansas City, the Twin Cities – the whole of the Midwest, in short – nearly every standing thing would be flattened or on fire, and nearly every living thing would be dead. People up to 1,500 kilometres away would be knocked off their feet and sliced or clobbered by a blizzard of flying projectiles. Beyond 1,500 kilometres the devastation from the blast would gradually diminish.

But that's just the initial shock wave. No-one can do more than guess what the associated damage would be, other than that it would be brisk and global. The impact would almost certainly set off a chain of devastating earthquakes. Volcanoes across the globe would begin to rumble and spew. Tsunamis would rise up and head devastatingly for distant shores. Within an hour, a cloud of blackness would cover the Earth and burning rock and other debris would be pelting down everywhere, setting much of the planet ablaze. It has been estimated that at least a billion and a half people would be dead by the end of the first day. The massive disturbances to the ionosphere would knock out communications systems everywhere, so survivors would have no idea what was happening elsewhere or where to turn. It would hardly matter. As one commentator has put it, fleeing would mean 'selecting a slow death over a quick one. The death toll would be very little affected by any plausible relocation effort, since Earth's ability to support life would be universally diminished.'

The amount of soot and floating ash from the impact and following fires would blot out the sun certainly for months, possibly for years, disrupting growing cycles. In 2001 researchers at the California Institute of Technology analysed helium isotopes from sediments left from the later KT impact and concluded that it affected the Earth's climate for about ten thousand years. This was actually used as evidence to support the notion that the extinction of dinosaurs was swift and emphatic – and so it was, in geological terms. We can only guess how well, or whether, humanity would cope with such an event.

And in all likelihood, remember, this would come without warning, out of a clear sky.

Footnote on Non-fiction

Non-fiction is **prose writing** that is **informative** and **based on fact**. The subject matter covered by non-fiction writing is vast: from cooking to home-improvement, travel writing, memoirs, arts and crafts, DIY, dictionaries and encyclopaedias.

TEXT 2 is taken from a genre of non-fiction writing called **popular science**. In this genre, you normally find a qualified scientist trying to make difficult scientific concepts accessible to the public. Some examples are *Cosmos* and *Pale Blue Dot* by Carl Sagan, *A Brief History of Time* by Stephen Hawking and *The Selfish Gene* by Richard Dawkins. The subjects they deal with are (respectively) astronomy, theoretical cosmology and genetic evolution. They make these challenging topics approachable.

Bill Bryson (the author of TEXT 2) takes on the history of science itself in *A Short History of Nearly Everything*. You might have noticed how he writes from a subjective viewpoint and relates an interview using direct speech. His language is both informative and entertaining to read. He also uses very striking aesthetic language in his vivid (but imagined) descriptions of the effects of a meteor strike.

QUESTION A – 50 Marks

(i) Outline, in your own words, the consequences of a meteor strike on Earth as described by Bill Bryson in TEXT 2. (15)

(ii) From your reading of TEXT 2, what are the likely long-term (years/decades/centuries) and planet-wide repercussions of such a meteor strike on Earth? Give reasons for your answer. (15)

(iii) Do you agree that elements of informative and aesthetic language are used effectively to engage the reader in TEXT 2? Give reasons for your answer, supporting your views with reference to the elements of informative and aesthetic language evident in the text. (20)

Sample Answer

QUESTION A (i)

Sums up the three main points without using supporting evidence.

The immediate major effect of a meteor strike on Earth like the one described by Bryson would be felt at the impact zone. Secondly, the shock wave would affect people over a very wide area, and thirdly, the after-effects would be felt worldwide.

Paraphrases the text to state the first consequence.

Supporting quotation.

The first area to suffer would be the place where the impact occurs. Superheated air compressed by the comet would incinerate everything in its path. Then a millisecond later, every remaining 'living thing within 250 kilometres' would be killed instantly by the blast. This explosion would be unimaginably powerful because it would propel '1,000 cubic kilometres of rock' up and outwards in a circular shock wave.

Linking phrase.

Supporting quotation.

Paraphrases text to illustrate point

The second zone of destruction would cover a much wider area. Everywhere within a circle with a diameter of '1,500 kilometres' from Manson would be knocked flat by the shock wave racing outwards at 'thousands of kilometres an hour'. Nobody would be able to hear this shock wave coming because it would be travelling much faster than the speed of sound. Bryson reports that an estimated billion and a half people would die within the first day.

Linking phrase.

Supporting quotation.

Paraphrases text to illustrate point.

The third consequence, and probably the most devastating, would be felt on a global scale. The shock of the impact at Manson would travel through the Earth's core, causing 'Volcanoes across the globe' to erupt and tsunamis to flood coastal areas around the planet. The sky would go dark and communications would be knocked out because of all the debris in the atmosphere. Much of the planet would be 'ablaze'. The effects of this cloud of darkness might be felt for years afterwards. It would disrupt 'growing cycles', causing crops to fail and affecting everyone, no matter how far away from the impact zone they live.

Theme 6: Fragile Planet

121

Exam Mechanics

QUESTION A (iii)

6S Simplify

Highlight or underline the key ideas in the question. What is this question asking you to do?

> Do you agree that elements of informative and aesthetic language are used effectively to engage the reader in TEXT 2? Give reasons for your answer, supporting your views with reference to the elements of informative and aesthetic language evident in the text.

You must look for examples of language that is:

- Informative = instructive, enlightening, explanatory, revealing.
- Aesthetic = descriptive, poetic, vivid, striking.

6S Select

As you read the text, highlight potential evidence and write brief annotations on how you might use it.

Simile to illustrate point – aesthetic language.	An asteroid or comet travelling at cosmic velocities would enter the Earth's atmosphere at such a speed that the air beneath it couldn't get out of the way and would be compressed, as in a bicycle pump. As anyone who has used such a pump knows, compressed air grows swiftly hot, and the temperature below it would rise to some 60,000 Kelvin, or ten times the surface temperature of the Sun. In this instant of its arrival in our atmosphere, everything in the meteor's path – people, houses, factories, cars – would crinkle and vanish like cellophane in a flame.
Contextual example – instructive.	
Factual information – instructive.	
Simile – aesthetic language.	

6S Sort

Remember that you are looking for the four best examples of informative and aesthetic elements of the text – two of each, or three of one and one of the other. You will have found more than four, so choose the ones you feel most confident explaining and discussing.

6S State, support and spell out

You may entirely agree or disagree with the given assessment of Bryson's style, or you may partially agree and partially disagree. Whichever option you choose (based on your careful selection of the evidence), state it clearly in your opening line.

> Having read TEXT 2, I agree that Bill Bryson uses both aesthetic and informative language to great effect in order to engage the reader.

The body of your answer should be four paragraphs. For each piece of evidence you discuss, follow these steps:

1. **State** your main point.

> Bill Bryson makes effective use of imagery to explain abstract or challenging concepts in a way that is both vivid and instructive.

2. **Support** your point with evidence from the text.

> The tremendous forces and velocities involved in a meteor strike are succinctly illustrated by means of a simile. To convey the process by which the air beneath the meteor becomes superheated, Bryson references a common phenomenon that most readers would have experienced: 'the air beneath it … would be compressed, as in a bicycle pump', resulting in heat that is 'ten times the surface temperature of the Sun'.

Hint

This simile also illustrates the author's use of aesthetic language. However, it is best to be clear about which element of the question you are dealing with in each paragraph, and not to try to address both together. Instead, you could make a separate point using the second simile ('like cellophane') from the example paragraph opposite to explain and discuss the aesthetic language used.

3. **Spell out** exactly why your chosen example is informative/aesthetic.

> Anyone who has used a bicycle pump and felt it get hotter would immediately grasp the physical processes at work. Furthermore, '60,000 Kelvin' would probably be a meaningless number without Bryson's description of that temperature being ten times hotter than the sun. Thus, a complicated natural phenomenon is elegantly and skilfully explained through the author's use of informative language.

Follow this process for the four parts of your answer.

Theme 6: Fragile Planet

QUESTION B – 50 Marks

Imagine that the catastrophic event described in TEXT 2 has occurred. With civilisation on the brink of collapse, you, as one of the few survivors, have decided to write a **reflective journal entry** to be buried in a time capsule. In it, you should share your impressions of human civilisation as you perceived it before it was all but destroyed, chronicle your recent experiences and describe the type of society you would like to see rebuilt.

Exam Mechanics

QUESTION B

Read the question and highlight the main task. This task will inform your entire answer. It will indicate what **genre** you will be writing in, what your **purpose** is and what **layout/ structure** to use. Identify the type of **audience** you will be writing for, which will determine the appropriate **style and register** to use. **Number the points you need to cover** to make sure that your answer addresses all aspects of the question.

> Imagine that the catastrophic event described in TEXT 2 has occurred. With civilisation on the brink of collapse, you, as one of the few survivors, have decided to write a **reflective journal entry** to be buried in a time capsule. In it, you should share your impressions of human civilisation as you perceived it before it was all but destroyed **(1)**, chronicle your recent experiences **(2)** and describe the type of society you would like to see rebuilt **(3)**.

Genre: a reflective journal entry – like a diary entry but, in this case, written with an audience other than yourself in mind.

Purpose: to reflect on and describe the present situation and how it came about; to inform and instruct a reader who may find your journal many years hence.

Layout/structure: a journal entry would usually include the date when, and sometimes the place where, it was written. Since this entry is written with an intended audience in mind, it could be structured similarly to a letter.

Audience: you do not know exactly who your audience will be, or how long your journal will remain in the time capsule before being found (if it ever is). You do not know the kind of world your reader will be living in; you can only guess. Assume that you are addressing an audience of one, even though your message might be intended for humankind generally.

Style and register: you are writing this journal entry after experiencing unimaginably catastrophic events – you may be living through the end of the world itself – and your style should reflect the gravity of the situation. You will also feel a natural urgency to record your thoughts and your message(s) for the future. Depending on your personality type, your mindset may be resolute, dismayed, stoic, despairing, etc. Remember that the word 'reflective' means you also need to show that you have thought deeply about things.

(1) Share your impressions of human society before it was all but destroyed. As your audience may well have no knowledge of the world before the meteor strike, this is your opportunity to describe it for them. What things about our society do they need to know about? What is – or is not – good about it?

(2) Chronicle (recount or record) your recent experiences. You should use narrative and aesthetic language and can draw heavily on the text here. If this meteor strike happened in the USA, what would your experience of it be like here in Ireland?

(3) Describe the type of society you would like to see rebuilt. Your tone would probably become more hopeful here. If humankind is to survive, it will have to rebuild. Perhaps you will be one of the people who can help to do that. How should we do things differently? Describe the world you want to see rise from the ashes. Give reasons for your ideas.

A-Z Grammar Guide

Dashes and hyphens

TEXT 2 features both the dash and the hyphen. What is the difference between these punctuation marks? How are they supposed to be used? Have a look at these three examples from the text:

Example 1

For those outside the zone of immediate devastation, the first inkling of catastrophe would be a flash of blinding light – the brightest ever seen by human eyes – followed an instant to a minute or two later by an apocalyptic sight of unimaginable grandeur …

Example 2

But what scientists can do – and Anderson and Witzke have done – is measure the impact site and calculate the amount of energy released.

Example 3

How hard an impactor hits depends on a lot of variables – angle of entry, velocity and trajectory, whether the collision is head-on or from the side, and the mass and density of the impacting object, among much else – none of which we can know so many millions of years after the fact.

- The punctuation marks highlighted in yellow are examples of dashes.
- The punctuation mark highlighted in blue is a hyphen.

Dashes are longer than hyphens, but can you also see how the two types of punctuation mark are performing different jobs in these examples? The essential difference is that dashes separate words while hyphens join them.

The dash

The word 'parenthesis' is used to describe a unit of words that has been inserted into a sentence as extra information. The words in parenthesis can be taken out of the sentence and it will still be grammatically complete. In this way, dashes (always two of them, each side of the parenthesis) can be used just like brackets. If you exchange the brackets in the previous sentence for dashes, you will see that they work in the same way.

The dash can add information, as we see in Examples 2 and 3 on page 125. In Example 2, the dashes insert a deft afterthought. In Example 3, the dash after the word 'variables' indicates that what follows are examples of those variables. Since Bryson then returns to the original sentence after the parenthesis, he has used dashes here instead of a single colon.

The dash can add a certain drama to a sentence. Look at Example 1 again. When you read the parenthesis using a dash, the pause is slightly longer than it would be if the author had used brackets. If Bryson had used brackets, the meaning would have lost some of its pizzazz.

A dash can be used on its own as well – unlike a bracket. Since the pause is that little bit longer, we understand the dash to be slightly stronger than a comma, but not as firm and final as a full stop. The dash is neither as emphatic nor as formal as the colon.

A dash can be used in dialogue to indicate that someone's speech has been cut short – perhaps for dramatic effect. For example: 'Come quickly! He's climbing in the window! He's –' but I heard no more because the phone was dead.

The hyphen

Example 3 includes an example of a **compound modifier** (double-worded adjective) describing the type of collision as 'head-on'. Here, the hyphen takes two words and makes them into a single unit that acts as an adjective. Other examples include:

- That life-giving shell of air ...
- Computer-generated imagery ....
- A self-made billionaire ...

Compound modifiers can contain more than three components. For example:

- That horse is the ten-to-one, odds-on favourite to win.

They can be interrupted (or suspended). For example:

- That's a six- or seven-metre shark!

Remember that all numbers between 21 and 99, when written out, should be hyphenated: twenty-one, ninety-nine, etc.

Adding a hyphen can completely alter your meaning. For example:

- The beautiful costume-wearing actor ...
- The beautiful-costume-wearing actor ...

In the first example, the actor is beautiful. In the second, it is the costume that is beautiful.

Hyphens help to prevent ambiguity. If you said that you had invited 30-odd people to your party, it is understood that you are giving a rough estimate of the number of guests. Remove the hyphen, however, and you could be hosting a very unusual evening indeed!

TEXT 3 – THE OVERVIEW EFFECT

This text has both visual and written elements. The written text is a news article published shortly after Jeff Bezos' historic first suborbital passenger spaceflight in July 2021. The two images that follow the written text have an environmental theme.

Jeff Bezos says his launch to space gave him greater appreciation of Earth's fragility

By Mike Wall 21/07/21

Bezos experienced the 'Overview Effect'.

LAUNCH SITE ONE, West Texas – Seeing Earth from space apparently made a big impact on the planet's richest resident.

Billionaire Jeff Bezos flew to suborbital space with three other people Tuesday (July 20) on the first crewed mission ever launched by his spaceflight company, Blue Origin. He said he greatly enjoyed the rocket ride and microgravity flips but was most struck, as astronauts tend to be, by the thought-provoking view.

'The most profound piece of it, for me, was looking out at the Earth, and looking at the Earth's atmosphere,' he said during a post-flight news conference Tuesday.

That life-giving shell of air seems sizable from the ground. 'But when you get up above it, what you see is it's actually incredibly thin. It's this tiny little fragile thing, and as we move about the planet, we're damaging it,' Bezos said, referring to greenhouse-gas pollution. 'It's one thing to recognize that intellectually. It's another thing to actually see with your own eyes how fragile it really is.'

Bezos has taken some steps to help protect that fragile shell and the rest of our beleaguered planet. Last year, for example, he announced the creation of the Bezos Earth Fund, which is dedicated to fighting climate change and boosting sustainability, and pledged $10 billion to get it up and running. And he now aims to start devoting more of his time to that project – time that was recently freed up after he stepped down as CEO of Amazon.

'I'm going to split my time between Blue Origin and the Bezos Earth Fund,' Bezos said during today's news conference. 'And there's going to be a third thing, and maybe a fourth thing, but I don't know what those are yet. I'm not very good at doing [only] one thing.'

And Blue Origin's long-term goals have a strong environmental component, Bezos has stressed. Over the long haul, the company wants to help establish a bustling off-Earth economy, with millions of people living and working in space. Indeed, Blue Origin intends to help move most resource extraction and heavy industry off the planet, so that we don't further strip the planet and foul its soil, air and waters.

Turning such bold dreams into reality starts with relatively small steps, Bezos said – like today's first-ever crewed launch of New Shepard, the company's suborbital space tourism vehicle.

'We're going to build a road to space so that our kids and their kids can build the future. And we need to do that. We need to do that to solve the problems here on Earth. It's not about escaping,' Bezos said.

'This is the only good planet in the solar system,' he said. 'We've sent robotic probes to all of them. This is the only good one, I promise you. So we have to take care of it. And when you go into space and see how fragile it is, you want to take care of it even more. And that's what this is about.'

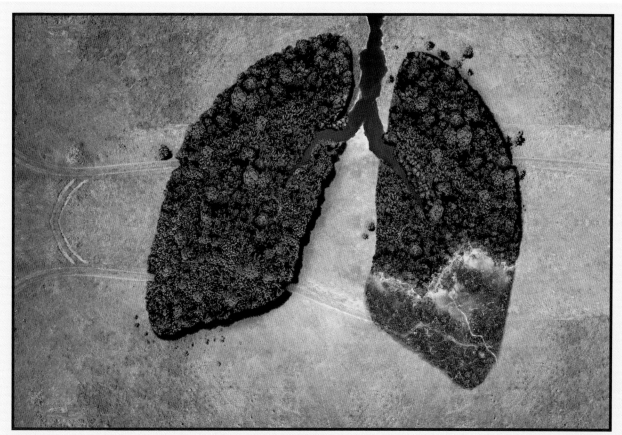

Image 1

Image 2

Footnote on Newspaper Reports

The defining purpose of a news report is to inform its readers about a particularly newsworthy story. The events in the report would typically have taken place very recently, which is why it is classified as 'news'. The writing style will depend on the type of newspaper.

- **Broadsheet newspapers** (*The Irish Times*, *Irish Independent*, etc.) focus on national and international news stories; there will be depth and research evident in the texts. The subjects covered tend to be 'serious' political and economic issues, world affairs, etc. The most important news stories are found on the front page. These publications also include feature articles (see page 3), but you normally find those on later pages.
- **Tabloid newspapers** (*Irish Sun*, *Irish Daily Star*, etc.) tend to focus on celebrity gossip and scandal. They are known for their attention-grabbing headlines (often using amusing puns) and sensational language. They are called 'red tops' because of the design of their front pages.
- **Regional newspapers** (*Connacht Tribune*, *Wexford People*, etc.) focus on local issues. They may take either a broadsheet or a tabloid-like format.

The structure of a typical news report can be visualised as an inverted triangle. A **headline** will suggest the main thrust of the story. The **lead paragraph** is typically one sentence long, sums up the main information and tries to answer these questions:

- Who did this happen to?
- When did this happen?
- Where did it happen?
- How did it happen?

The rest of the article develops on those questions by filling in the details. The **language of information** is used. The opinions of the writer should not be expressed. Instead, the writer will quote the statements and opinions of those involved. While writers of news reports are ostensibly objective in presenting the facts, they can still be biased in the statements and opinions they choose to include. For example, Mike Wall, the author of the written element of TEXT 3, has portrayed Jeff Bezos in quite a favourable light. Other journalists reporting on this spaceflight chose different perspectives to write it from.

Theme 6: Fragile Planet

QUESTION A – 50 Marks

(i) From your reading of the written element of TEXT 3, outline, in your own words, Jeff Bezos' plans for the future and how he was affected by his flight aboard the rocket ship New Shepard. (15)

(ii) In your opinion, which of the two images in TEXT 3 is more effective in conveying its message? Give reasons for your answer. (15)

(iii) Based on your reading of the written element of TEXT 3, discuss four stylistic features that make the article both an engaging and an informative piece of writing. Support your response with reference to the text. (20)

Exam Mechanics

QUESTION A (i)

6S Simplify

Simplify the question by identifying the key words.

> From your reading of the written element of TEXT 3, outline, in your own words, Jeff Bezos' plans for the future and how he was affected by his flight aboard the rocket ship New Shepard.

- Outline = summarise, sketch out.

6S Select

Read through the text and highlight any information that could be used to answer the question. Brief notes to yourself in the margin will help you to organise the evidence you have found. For example:

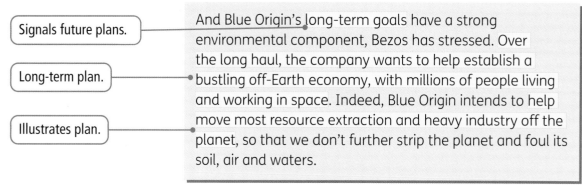

Signals future plans.

Long-term plan.

Illustrates plan.

And Blue Origin's long-term goals have a strong environmental component, Bezos has stressed. Over the long haul, the company wants to help establish a bustling off-Earth economy, with millions of people living and working in space. Indeed, Blue Origin intends to help move most resource extraction and heavy industry off the planet, so that we don't further strip the planet and foul its soil, air and waters.

6S Sort

Once you have found the relevant information, decide what order to present it in. This question is a straightforward information-retrieval task. Be careful, however, because the phrase 'in your own words' makes it clear that while quotations should still be used, your explanation of them needs to be very clear.

6S State, support and spell out

The body of your answer should contain three paragraphs (four/five if you want to include an introduction/conclusion). Each of the three main paragraphs should:

1. **State** one of his plans for the future or how the spaceflight affected him.

   One of the long-term plans of Jeff Bezos' company Blue Origin is to move their operations off the Earth altogether and to make money by exploiting the resources to be found in space.

2. **Support** your choice with evidence from the text.

   The company aspires to 'establish a bustling off-Earth economy' in space in which 'millions of people' will live and work. They also want to 'move most resource extraction and heavy industry' from Earth to space.

3. **Spell out** exactly what this told you about his plans/spaceflight experience.

   Blue Origin proposes to take mining for resources off the Earth altogether. Bezos expects that there will be plenty of opportunities for companies like his to generate financial returns by finding resources on other planets. If so, the Earth's overexploited natural resources can be spared any further depletion. As this industry moves off-planet, the company envisages that millions of workers will go along with it.

Follow this process for the three parts of your answer.

Sample Answer

QUESTION A (ii)

Introduction answers main question.	While both images communicate their messages powerfully, in my opinion, Image 1 conveys its point more effectively.
Describes image – demonstrates visual literacy.	Image 1 depicts a very stark warning indeed. Areas of forest are presented in the form of a pair of human lungs. The trachea and bronchi leading to the lungs from the top of the image are represented by a forking river. The symbolism of this is clear:
Interprets image; analyses meaning being conveyed.	the rivers and the forests of our planet represent the very air that we breathe. Trees provide the planet with oxygen; without oxygen, most life on Earth is not possible. In Image 1, our very
Sums up main message.	existence is under threat from the burning of the forests.
Linking statement.	Image 2 also conveys a powerful message. In it, we see a scene that is – mostly – very familiar to us. There is a sandy
Describes image.	beach, but it is marred by litter; particularly prominent in the foreground is a single-use plastic cup that someone has discarded. What is unusual, however, is the miniature figure of a man, who is smaller than the cup. He seems to be trying to push the cup away. Clearly, the message is that the issue of plastic litter is
Interprets image.	disproportionately large for one person to address; without a concerted effort, the problem is just too big for us to solve.
Returns to argument; focuses on choice of Image 1.	What makes Image 1 more effective, however, is the visceral impact of what we see as a burning lung. We may be reminded of some of the grim health warnings displayed on cigarette
Explains why the message behind Image 1 is more effective.	packages. The added implication of this image is that perhaps the effects of climate change, caused by humankind, are like a damaging disease inflicted upon our environment. It truly is an
Personal response to conclude.	image that affected me: its message is shocking in its simplicity, but it will stay with me for a long time.

Theme 6: Fragile Planet

🔔 Hint

Question A (ii) asks which image is more effective in conveying its message. You should not necessarily argue that the message of one image is powerful while the other one is not. Both images are effective in their own way. Indeed, if an image was considered to be ineffective, it would be unlikely to be chosen for an examination paper.

QUESTION B – 50 Marks

In the written element of TEXT 3, we read about billionaire Jeff Bezos' spaceflight company, Blue Origin, and its 'suborbital space tourism vehicle', New Shepard. Write an **opinion piece**, suitable for publication in a broadsheet newspaper, in which you argue either for or against the concept of space tourism. In your article, consider both the benefits and the disadvantages of tourism in space and describe what the future of space tourism might look like.

Exam Mechanics

QUESTION B

Read the question and highlight the main task. This task will inform your entire answer. It will indicate what **genre** you will be writing in, what your **purpose** is and what **layout/ structure** to use. Identify the type of **audience** you will be writing for, which will determine the appropriate **style and register** to use. **Number the points you need to cover** to make sure that your answer addresses all aspects of the question.

> In the written element of TEXT 3, we read about billionaire Jeff Bezos' spaceflight company, Blue Origin, and its 'suborbital space tourism vehicle', New Shepard. Write an **opinion piece**, suitable for publication in a broadsheet newspaper, in which you argue either for or against the concept of space tourism. In your article, consider both the benefits **(1)** and the disadvantages **(2)** of tourism in space and describe what the future of space tourism might look like **(3)**.

Genre: an opinion piece.

Purpose: to argue either for or against the idea of space tourism.

Layout/structure: use the standard layout for an article to be published in the print media – include a headline and byline. A date is optional but could be a nice touch. You do not need to write in columns.

Audience: this article is to be published in a broadsheet newspaper, so your audience will be people who read newspapers like *The Irish Times*, *Irish Independent* and *Irish Examiner*. They are a national audience of well-informed and critical readers. Your best strategy with these readers is to win them over with reason.

Style and register: you could take a discursive/detached tone when considering the benefits and drawbacks of space tourism, and then come out fighting on one side or the other when you make your argument. However, the more authentic tone for an opinion piece would be confident and fairly strident from the start. Argumentative language should be used throughout to develop a strong, logical and convincing case. Persuasive language and rhetorical techniques can be used as well. Remember that you can 'consider' the positives of something in such a way that it is clear they are vastly overshadowed by the negatives (or vice versa). Your register should be formal to demonstrate that you are keeping your audience in mind.

(1) Consider the benefits of tourism in space. We know from TEXT 3 that when Bezos experienced the 'overview effect' from his spaceflight, he was inspired to do more to save the Earth's atmosphere from pollution. Might others have similar experiences as space tourists? Could putting space exploration into the hands of private citizens instead of governments be a good idea? Might these privately funded scientists and engineers develop new technologies that will benefit us all? Private companies are not limited by government funding and do not have to worry about winning votes – is this positive or negative?

(2) Consider the drawbacks of tourism in space. Only the very rich will be able to access these flights. Is all the expense involved worth it so that millionaires and billionaires get to experience a few minutes of weightlessness and a view of Earth? What about the huge amount of pollution each of these rockets produces as it burns through tonnes of fuel to escape Earth's gravity? What about how dangerous spaceflight can be?

(3) Describe what the future of space tourism might look like. The best way to try to imagine the future is to consider the past and see if it has taught us anything. How did the air travel tourist industry evolve over time? Could the same happen with space travel and tourism?

Hint

Do not forget that you have an exam paper in front of you containing all sorts of information that you could use in your answer. Obviously, TEXT 3 contains information that is very relevant to this topic, but the other two texts could also be useful. Students are encouraged to use the resources provided for them.

SECTION II   COMPOSING   (100 marks)

Write a composition on **any one** of the assignments that appear in **bold print** below.

Each composition carries 100 marks.

The composition assignments are intended to reflect language study in the areas of information, argument, persuasion, narration, and the aesthetic use of language.

1. In TEXT 1, Greta Thunberg accuses world leaders of 'pretending to take science seriously'.
   Write a persuasive essay entitled 'Humanity's Three Greatest Scientific Discoveries'.

2. In TEXT 2, we read the phrase 'an apocalyptic sight of unimaginable grandeur'.
   Write a short story inspired by, and including, the words 'an apocalyptic sight of unimaginable grandeur'.

3. 'Bezos has taken some steps to help protect that fragile shell and the rest of our beleaguered planet.' (TEXT 3)
   Write a descriptive essay entitled 'Our Beleaguered Planet'.

4. World leaders, according to Greta Thunberg in TEXT 1, felt that 'the public pressure was too much' and that they had the 'world's eyes' on them.
   Write a personal essay in which you reflect on a time (or times) when you may have felt under pressure and as though the 'world's eyes' were on you.

5. In TEXT 3, Jeff Bezos tells us that 'Turning such bold dreams into reality starts with relatively small steps.'
   Write a speech, to be delivered at your Leaving Certificate graduation ceremony, in which you explore how to turn bold dreams into reality.

6. **Write a short story inspired by either, or both, of the visual images associated with TEXT 3.**

7. In TEXT 1, Greta Thunberg speaks at length on the theme of role-playing and hypocrisy. She observes that the 'gap between [world leaders'] rhetoric and reality keeps growing wider and wider'.
   Write a speech to be delivered at a public-speaking competition for second-level students in which you consider the 'gap between rhetoric and reality' in the world around you. Your speech can be serious, or amusing, or both.

Composing

In the beginning...

The Composing section of your exam is Section II of Paper 1. Remember that you can answer the paper in any order you wish: some students like to write the composition first. Your timing is the same either way.

You will be given seven composition titles, and you will choose one. The titles relate to the texts in Section I and to the overall theme of the paper, so it is vital that you read through the entire paper at the start of the exam.

As the composition is worth 100 marks, or 25 per cent of your overall grade for English, it is very important that you give yourself enough time to plan it, write it and read over it at the end. Allow yourself 1 hour and 10 minutes to plan and write this answer.

The average Higher Level composition is around 1,000 words or four to five pages in length (depending on your handwriting). As with all parts of your English examination, it will be marked using the PCLM system (see page xii).

Several different genres of writing will come up in this section. They usually include at least one:
• personal essay
• short story
• speech
• article.

Other genres that have come up in recent years include:
• discursive essays
• descriptive essays
• persuasive essays
• dialogues.

You should have the opportunity to write in each of these genres over the two years you spend completing your Leaving Certificate course, so when it comes to the examination you should know which you prefer. It is not a good strategy to go into your exam with your genre already chosen, however. You should be capable of tackling several different types of writing so that you can choose the best option for you from the specific questions on the paper.

Personal Essays

What is a personal essay?

Personal essays use a **first-person perspective** to explore and describe a significant personal experience or selection of experiences. The essay will be focused on a particular theme and the experience(s) discussed will be linked to that theme. The purpose of the discussion is for the author to share one or more important lessons learned. The language of narration is used to relate personal anecdotes, but the majority of the writing is discursive and reflective in style.

There are two key concepts that examiners are advised to look for in a good personal essay:

1. It should be reflective.
2. It should have confessional elements.

1. Reflective writing

When you look into a mirror, it reflects your image back at you, revealing certain truths about what is there. When you are reflecting on an idea, you are mentally holding it up to a mirror and searching for a deeper understanding. Reflective writing is generated by someone thinking deeply about something so that they can reveal significant insights about it.

2. Confessional writing

When your reader finishes your personal essay, they need to be left with the feeling that they have come to know you and that you have shared something quite personal about yourself. To achieve this, your writing needs to be honest and sincere. The best way to ensure that your writing is sincere is simply to write only about real experiences that actually happened. Avoid the temptation to invent anecdotes.

Preparing and planning

Carefully read the question, then take a few minutes to jot down your ideas.

Select which of those ideas you will focus on. Do not try to include lots of different anecdotes as this will make your essay choppy and less coherent than if you concentrate on a limited number. Is there one standout experience around which your discussion will centre?

A strong **introduction** can be achieved by going straight into an anecdote. Use the features of narrative language to make your opening paragraphs gripping: descriptive language and dialogue will immediately grab your reader's attention.

Remember that the bulk of your essay should be discursive: reflect on your experiences and what they have taught you; share those lessons with your reader.

To write a **conclusion** that leaves your reader feeling a satisfactory sense of closure, return to the anecdote you began with. Now, after reflection, are you able to look at that experience in a different light?

Sample Personal Essay

In TEXT 3, flight engineer, Ariadne O'Neill, explains how she takes pride in her work.

Write a personal essay in which you reflect on what you are proud of in your life. (2020)

What I Am Proud of in Life

Title indicates a clear response to the question.

The thing I am most proud of in life is how I've grown as a person. Over the last few years, I've really grown into myself. I feel like a fully fledged human being instead of just random fragments of one.

Vivid image acts as a hook to grab reader's attention.

Most of this growth has been in terms of my mental health. My younger cousin Erica had been diagnosed in July of 2014 with acute lymphoblastic leukaemia, a fast-growing type of cancer that affects white blood cells. She had a relapse in January of 2016 and passed away in August of that year after a bone marrow transplant.

Sums up subject of essay in a short anecdote.

This was a devastating and traumatic event for everybody in my family, and I, only being 12 and about to start secondary school, found it particularly trying. It was a time of change for me all around and I wasn't sure how to cope with it.

Confessional element brought into discussion early.

I tried to shut myself away from my family, afraid to get too close to anybody in case anything would happen to them too. I was the first grandchild on that side of the family, so I felt like I had to be the stable one, the secure one, the mature one. When I think about it now, I know that nobody was expecting any of that from me, I was still only a child and it had been a life-changing event. I felt so far removed from everybody else's grieving, like I was being left behind. While everyone around me picked up their pieces and continued with life, I was struggling to find the will to keep going.

Anecdote introduces further confessional elements.

Reflective element.

Echoes image in opening paragraph.

For Erica's birthday that year, my family and I decided to put together Erica's Fairy Forest in the amenity park near where we live. We didn't have long to do this, as her birthday was at the end of October, but together we managed to pull it off. Putting together fairy houses, painting fairy doors, and finding other magical and mystical items to put in the forest gave all of us something to focus our energy towards. It brought me closer to all my family members and gave us a way to keep Erica's memory alive. Even now, five years later, we all still enjoy adding new features to the Fairy Forest and putting up new decorations seasonally. I go down almost every Friday after school and see other children enjoying the area we all so lovingly created. It is always bittersweet, knowing who and what it all stands for.

Another anecdote, related to essay's central subject.

Imagery/aesthetic language – emotionally affecting.

Links to previous paragraph.

Further reflective and confessional elements.

Ties discussion back to the question.

Relates discussion of her mother to theme of pride.

Links to previous paragraph and introduces another anecdote related to central theme.

Narrative language.

Reflection.

Relates discussion back to the question.

Links to image in opening paragraph.

After work finished on the Fairy Forest, I fell back into that feeling of being alone. It was daunting for me to talk to anybody about what had happened to Erica and how it was affecting me. It took over two years for me to figure out that how I was feeling wasn't normal and that I really needed help. After that, I started going to counselling to try to feel better, and it really helped me feel like I wasn't so alone. I learned about all the different ways that people grieve, and that for some people it takes a lot longer to come to terms with a loved one dying than for others. I'm one of those people; it took a long time for me to come to terms with everything that happened, and I am still healing from it even now. I sometimes catch myself thinking I would have been better off getting help with my grief sooner, but I know I wouldn't have been ready for it. I'm glad I stopped trying to be the grown-up in the situation eventually and just let myself be sad. Looking at that today, I know it was the right approach to take; and it's what I'm proud of now.

Now, years after Erica's death, I know that my family will always be there for me, and that if I ever feel alone, I can go to them and be reminded of just how much they all love me and care about me. One of the people I am closest to is my mam. Anytime I miss Erica and anytime I'm feeling anxious, I know I can go to Mam to talk it out and she'll always listen, no matter how busy she is with work or anything else. Mam was Erica's godmother, so she was always particularly close to her, and she always made a huge effort to see her and do things with her. So, apart from the growth I personally experienced, I'm proud of Mam in the way she did everything she could. While Erica was sick and in and out of hospital, Mam would take us to Crumlin to visit her as often as was humanly possible.

These visits were hard sometimes, especially around the time of Erica's transplant. For eight days beforehand, she had to be almost completely isolated from the world, and the only people who were allowed in were her parents and our aunt Emma. When we went to see her then, we had to sit outside the window of the room she was staying in and talk to her through the phone. I wonder sometimes how we all managed to keep it together then, but I guess it's something we just had to get through. I really couldn't be prouder of my family for that, especially Erica's parents. They made it all seem easy, and they're doing a great job of keeping Erica's memory thriving in the Fairy Forest.

So, I'm proud of all of us for the journey we've all been on together; and I'm proud of myself back then for getting through everything, and myself now for learning from it. I think I've really grown up into the best version of myself I could: no longer just random fragments but a fully fledged human being.

Essay reproduced by kind permission of Hannah Moynagh.

Discursive Essays

What is a discursive essay?

A discursive essay considers an issue or topic from multiple sides. The writing should be as objective as possible. The style will tend to be quite formal and detached. For this reason, it is best not to use a first-person perspective. Instead, use the **passive voice**: 'It is believed that …', 'It is thought that …', 'It has been argued by some', etc.

 For more information on the passive voice, see page 177.

The key purpose of a discursive essay is to demonstrate the breadth of the author's knowledge about the topic in question. The language of information is used extensively. All the possible perspectives on the issue are weighed and measured in a dispassionate manner. Often the question will require you to choose one side; however, make sure you present all sides first before finally choosing, with a logical rationale, a particular position.

Preparing and planning

A tool that many students find helpful when planning a discursive essay is known as GEEP SMASH:

Geographic

Environmental

Economic

Political

Scientific

Media

Aesthetic

Social

Historical

 Hint

Not all the elements of GEEP SMASH will be equally helpful for all topics. It is simply a tool to encourage you to look at an issue from different perspectives. Once you have thought through the ramifications of your subject, select the most useful ideas and plan your essay around them.

Using this mnemonic will help you consider any topic from multiple angles. For example, the discursive essay question in Theme 1 requires you to discuss the topic of third-level education. Applying GEEP SMASH to this topic will spark off some ideas, such as:

Geographic

• Is third-level education similar or different depending on where you are in the world?

• How does being a student in Ireland affect how we value third-level education?

Environmental

• What are the environmental ramifications of third-level education? Is a highly educated society likely to be more or less environmentally sustainable?

• Are environmentally conscious third-level courses going to affect climate change in the future?

Economic

• What are your views on the costs involved in receiving a third-level education? Are the costs offset by potential earnings in careers that require this level of qualification, or are other careers just as well rewarded?

• Does our economy need more university-educated people, or should students be encouraged to learn other skills, such as trades?

Political

- What are the government's policies regarding third-level education?
- Are students involved in political movements or demonstrations?

Scientific

- What is the science behind the kind of learning that takes place in universities and colleges?
- What does the research say about the value of third-level education?

Media

- How is third-level education reported on in the newspapers and on radio and television programmes?
- How is it represented on social media platforms?

Aesthetic

- How is third-level education presented in films or in music?
- How do third-level institutions contribute to the arts?

Social

- What are the social aspects of college life? Is the social life a particularly attractive element? What about the dangers involved with notorious excesses?
- How does society generally benefit from third-level education?

Historical

- How has the concept of third-level education changed over time? Are more people expected to go to college today than in previous generations?
- What roles have university settings had in history (for example, the student-led peace movements during the Vietnam War and the civil rights movements in the USA and Northern Ireland)?

For a captivating **introduction**, you could use a vivid and relevant quotation. You will have studied a Shakespearean play, numerous poets and the texts for the comparative question and may be able to draw a suitable quotation from one of them. Otherwise, start with an interesting fact or statistic, or a memorable image. To give your essay a sense of closure, return to this quote, fact or image in your **conclusion**.

Sample Discursive Essay

Robert Montgomery, whose work features in TEXT 1, sometimes uses advertising billboards to display his work.

Write a discursive essay in which you explore the positive and negative aspects of different types of advertising. (2017)

You are unlikely to lose marks without one, but an appropriate title indicates purposefulness.	### The Pros and Cons of Advertising

Is there a special place in hell reserved for the companies who interrupt YouTube videos with adverts? Or, are those companies obliging us by buying the advertising space that funds the media platforms? Or, is it simply an inescapable fact that if something is 'free', then the product is actually you? Perhaps companies like YouTube are not actually in the business of offering us free video content at all. Perhaps their sole concern is selling viewers to global corporations, ensuring that millions of consumers are constantly exposed to their advertisements. Welcome to the complex and perplexing world of advertising!

Strident opening statement grabs the reader's attention.

Opposing views presented to achieve balance.

Advertising has come a long way since Coca-Cola's early print ads, which simply stated 'Coca-Cola is delicious' and 'Have a Coke'. Nowadays, advertising companies tend to be a lot more sophisticated, subtle and inventive in their approach. There are many channels they can use – television, radio, billboards, internet, print media – and many methods they can adopt. Indeed, there is absolutely no escaping marketing strategies in our modern world. It is estimated that the average person is exposed to over 5,000 individual adverts every day.

Historical aspect of topic (GEEP SMASH); example illustrates how advertising has developed and become more sophisticated.

Fact given using language of information and passive voice.

How does advertising benefit us? The money provided by advertisers allows us to access content on the internet without having to pay for it directly. Instead, we 'pay' for access by being exposed to advertisements from sponsors. Waiting five seconds to skip an advert seems a fairly small price to pay to watch the video of your choice. Furthermore, adverts inform people about a product's unique selling points. Without this information, the buying public is at a disadvantage. Advertising allows us to compare competing brands; competition exerts downward pressure on the prices paid by consumers. In addition, advertising promotes economic growth on a local level. GAA clubs, for example, benefit from being affiliated with businesses, both local and otherwise. Without this kind of funding, local clubs simply could not survive.

Rhetorical question focuses discussion on first part of the task – exploring positive aspects.

Economic aspect of topic (GEEP SMASH).

Linking phrase shows continuation of a line of thought.

Social aspect of topic (GEEP SMASH).

Linking word demonstrates change in direction – second part of the question (negative aspects) to be addressed.

Passive voice.

Media aspect of topic (GEEP SMASH).

However, some argue that advertising might bring the objectivity of our media outlets into question. On top of the money derived from the licence fee, RTÉ, for example, generates income by selling advertising space on its television and radio channels. While RTÉ is ostensibly a public service provider, the gap between licence fee income and operating costs means that this public service is part-funded by commercial revenue. Newspapers and magazines likewise rely on advertising in order to remain commercially viable. The consequence of this is that big businesses will, inevitably, enjoy a significant influence over the news we receive. This fact brings into question the whole concept of an independent media.

Linking phrase shows discussion is returning to the positive aspects.

Geographical/ political aspects of topic (GEEP SMASH).

On the other hand, it is worth bearing in mind that it is only in a free society that competing perspectives can advertise. Through their advertising campaigns, businesses exercise their constitutional right to free speech in order to promote their commercial interests. Free-market capitalism thrives on personal liberty, which is not something readily found in North Korea.

Linking word indicates change in viewpoint.

Nevertheless, most people consider advertising to be an inconvenience at best and a loathsome imposition at worst. It is impossible to navigate the internet without encountering ads. Whether scrolling through a news feed or looking up something on Google, an internet user is exposed to hundreds of brand slogans daily. The sidebars are filled with images of shoes, lawnmowers and pension plans. Pop-up ads suggest buying anything from bicycles to timeshares in Lanzarote. Once a search has been performed for, say, a type of shoe, adverts for them will pop up for weeks afterwards; whatever site happens to be open.

Social aspect of topic (GEEP SMASH).

Rhetorical questions address and involve reader directly; passive voice.

Rhetorical question appeals to a common experience and creates rapport.

Many people are suspicious of multinational corporations and the power the internet has given them. How often do we hear it said that after having a conversation about a particular item, people suddenly find themselves inundated with adverts for that product? Were their phones listening to them, or is everyone just becoming paranoid? Perhaps this is an indication of just how extensively companies trade our personal information.

Rhetorical question identifies a common difficulty to which the reader may relate.

There is also a considerable amount of white noise associated with advertising. When companies make competing claims, it can be nearly impossible to ascertain which information, if any, is correct. Every brand claims to be the best, but which one really is? How can we tell without a significant investment of personal time researching and reading user reviews? Can these even be trusted?

Composing

Annotation	Text

Linking phrase; focus remaining on the negative aspects. Social aspects of the topic (GEEP SMASH). Passive voice.

Many people are concerned by how adverts target children. Toys are advertised on daytime television for one specific purpose: the 'nag effect', where adverts encourage children to pester their parents. Daytime children's television contains hours of action figures, dolls and all their accessories.

Linking phrase, continuing on the negative theme.

Likewise, children are targeted by fast-food companies that offer toys and games with their 'happy' meals. Apparently, children as young as two can have significant brand recognition. They learn what the symbols behind brands like McDonald's, KFC and Coca-Cola mean before they can even read.

Quotation and named expert are fictitious.

'Children as young as three are feeling social pressure and understand that certain brands can influence their popularity among their peers,' said marketing researcher David Hobson of Cambridge University. The pressure towards consumerism is being felt earlier and earlier.

Linking word; train of thought continues in the same direction.

Furthermore, there is the issue of product placement, which many consider to be a scourge on modern cinema.

Aesthetic aspect of topic (GEEP SMASH).

Purists of the art form are repulsed by the obvious plugs for popular brands. From the sponsorship of Nike in *Back to the Future* to James Bond's Nokia, product placement in films and television has become an everyday reality. In the past, programmes paused for a message from the sponsors, but now, the message is almost subliminal: you only notice it if you are aware it is being delivered to you. Many would argue that this is morally questionable; especially as such films and TV programmes are routinely seen by children.

Language of information.

For example, the popular series *Stranger Things* promotes Crush Orange, Coca-Cola and Pizza Hut all in the same episode (Season 3, Episode 4, if you are interested).

Paragraph briefly presenting a positive and a negative aspect in order to introduce the conclusion.

The advertising industry is a multibillion-dollar business with the singular aim of parting us from our money. However, advertising can positively affect communities throughout the world. There are soccer pitches in Africa that would never have been built without Coca-Cola or Vodafone. We must also remember that the advertising medium can deliver not just commercial endorsements, but laudable public service messages such as road safety campaigns.

Advertising has become an inescapable element of modern life. We simply need to be sufficiently media-savvy to recognise when we are being manipulated, and learn to live with them – even if you think there really

Conclusion refers back to opening.

should be a place in hell reserved for those who interrupt your YouTube videos.

Descriptive Essays

What is a descriptive essay?

In a descriptive essay, the author attempts to depict an experience (or experiences), place, object, person or event in such a vivid manner that the reader is transported and beguiled. The pace tends to be slow and considered. Aesthetic language is used throughout to appeal to as many of the reader's senses as possible.

> ## Hint
> Describe not only how something looks, but also how it feels and what it sounds like. Is it something you can taste or smell?

The language and imagery should be original. Figures of speech give your writing colour and vibrancy, but you must try to always invent fresh imagery. Avoid clichéd or overused images such as describing something as being 'as old as the hills' or indicating hot weather by saying 'the sun was splitting the stones'. Such images have been used countless times before. Good aesthetic writing is always innovative and original.

Obviously, you will be using adjectives in your description, but be careful: a long list of adjectives in front of a noun is generally viewed as poor writing. Choosing the right adjective is the key to success. For example, instead of describing a dress as 'beautiful, brightly coloured, expensive and revealing', you could use a word like 'electrifying' or 'voluptuous', or a phrase like 'elegantly vivid'.

 For more information on adjectives, see page 15.

The nouns you choose are also important. Generally speaking, try to avoid generic terms in your writing (of all genres). For example, do not use the word 'car' when you could use 'Nissan Micra' or 'stretch limousine' because those are far more specific images to evoke in a reader's mind. Similarly, do not use 'tree' when you could say 'ancient oak' or 'sapling'. Remember that the aim is crystal-clear communication of ideas.

 For more information on nouns, see page 42.

Students sometimes decide to formulate their descriptions in a narrative. This approach is fine, as long as the focus is clearly on the aesthetic language and the author does not get too caught up in a plot. There is no requirement to have a narrative if you do not wish to.

Preparing and planning

Past questions have asked students to write descriptive essays on a topic such as a night scene, or to take the reader on an urban journey, or to celebrate dawn and dusk. Whatever topic you are given, take a few minutes to jot down some ideas. For example, if you drew up a mind map with 'urban journey' as the focal point, what kinds of ideas would this generate? 'Urban' might make you think of glistening wet pavements, perhaps reflecting the changing colours of the traffic lights in the rain. It might make you think of busy shopping and congested streets, roaring engines, diesel fumes and litter. Or perhaps it might make you think of pigeons being fed in a park, donut kiosks or ice-cream vendors in the summer, bright lights and optimism. Whatever images come to you, write them down just as they are. Often if you let your ideas flow without filtering them, you end up with some interesting word associations that could be useful.

Quickly check over your ideas and identify which senses have been included. You are likely to have a lot of visual images, so ask yourself how you can bring in all the other senses. You may have noticed that the examples above mostly work on the sense of sight, however, 'diesel fumes', 'donut vendors', 'ice-cream' and 'roaring engines' appeal to other senses too.

Sometimes the best way to describe something is by making a comparison. Do your images present an opportunity to make a memorable simile, metaphor or personification? For example, cranes on a building site might be compared to lumbering giants, dinosaurs or whatever best serves the mood you are trying to convey.

When portraying sounds, poetic techniques can be very useful. For example, instead of 'the loud noise of brakes', you could use the onomatopoeic 'screech'. If you wanted to convey the sound of workmen using heavy machinery, alliteration, assonance, onomatopoeia or all three might come in handy; for example: 'the cacophonous clamour of crashing jackhammers'.

Then you will want to string all these vivid descriptions together somehow. Many writers like to use a first-person narrative voice to lend the writing intimacy. Using the first person 'I' and imagining yourself experiencing the things you are describing may help to focus your writing. Or you might prefer a slightly more objective standpoint. If you use an omniscient narrative voice, the imagery can flow without being tied to any specific observer.

 Hint

For examples of a writer describing ordinary things in an extraordinary way, why not read Sylvia Plath's poem 'Black Rook in Rainy Weather', Emily Dickinson's 'There's a certain Slant of light', Derek Mahon's 'A Disused Shed in Co. Wexford' or Eiléan Ní Chuilleanáin's 'Fireman's Lift'?

Sample Descriptive Essay

In TEXT 2, Fiona Mozley writes 'it was during this summer in the woods, that Daddy told us these stories'.

Write a descriptive essay in which you capture how the landscape reflects the transition of the seasons. You may choose to include some or all of the seasons in your essay.

(2018)

Indicates essay's theme: the symbolic wheel of the changing seasons; although optional, a title demonstrates purposefulness and cohesion.	

Refers to question and explains symbolism used in title.

Personifies snowdrops and winter: flowers portrayed as fragile; in contrast, winter portrayed as threatening.

Alliteration suggests gentle nodding of flower heads.

Metaphor conveys whiteness and coldness of winter sky.

Personification and assonance.

Alliteration conveys noise of branches knocking against each other in flurries of snow.

Metaphor adds elements of menace.

The Wheel of Nature

There is a forest park that was, long ago, the Barony of Rossmore. The castle that once stood on the crest of a hill has since been torn down, but the forests remain. I walk its pathways and trails with my little red terrier, Molly, the whole year round. Together, we witness Rossmore Park transform from the depths of icy winter to sweltering summer heat and back again as the great wheel of nature turns and turns.

When snowdrops first push their delicate white heads through the frosts of January, they herald the loosening of winter's iron grip. They seem bashful about flowering so early, so they stoop and bow, and cluster coyly in the shadows of the forest floor. An alabaster sky throws flurries of snow, and the beech trees' bare branches are fractures against whiteness.

Soon, the snowdrops are gone. The days are warming slowly, imperceptibly. The shadows of the evening grow longer, and at the feet of the bare beeches are the charmingly fragile wood anemones. Like the snowdrops, they echo the snow with their whiteness. They cover the deeps of the forest. Their moss-green leaves carpet the gloom of the woods; the little stars of their flowers nodding.

> Personification and metaphor convey a positive image: nodding in affirmation.

Now, the desire to awaken takes hold as February slips into March. There is an urgency within the earth and a briskness infuses the sleepy bulbs nestled there. Last year's leaves lie blackening, mouldering as the first shoots of the bluebells begin to insist their way into the air. Wild garlic begins to swell its roots and beneath the beech and spruce trees there are waves of green. The oaks, hazels and ash trees all begin to draw their sustenance from the burgeoning earth; their roots drink deep of the thawing soil and the sap surges skywards to feed their budding leaves.

> Personification encourages a certain affinity for the trees in the reader.

> Sibilance and assonance convey the liquid movement inside the trunks.

Then the flowering cherry trees bloom in an explosion of pink. The sad transience of life is symbolised in their quick fading. Their exquisite, sweet fragrance is only kept a few short spring days before the roads are filled with a profusion of their tragic petals. The harsh gusts of a late winter wind send them spiralling in eddies along the kerbstones. Then every hedgerow becomes magically transformed as the hawthorns bloom; as if their branches have been spun in, and now are groaning under the weight of, cotton floss. The pussy willows burst forth with their fragile wispy seeds, and the pathways look as if they have been dusted with frosting.

> The word 'explosion' causes a quickening of pace, symbolising start of spring.

> Appeals to sense of smell.

> Imagery of petals 'spiralling' echoes theme of a wheel.

> Similes appeal to senses of sight and taste.

The blackberries, with their tangles of fearsome barbs, are the playgrounds of a multitude of butterflies. Orange-tips, peacocks, painted ladies and red admirals teeter and flit as if drunk on sweet nectar. Later summer days produce the deliciously tart berries that cluster temptingly amongst the leaves. Their juices stain the fingers and mouths of generation after generation of children. The fields lie under the heavy almond fragrance of meadowsweet.

> Onomatopoeia conveys erratic flight of butterflies. Simile and personification appeal to sense of taste.

> Sensuous language appeals to sense of taste.

> Synaesthesia – different senses appealed to in a single image.

The Rossmores had their estate planted with exotic laurels and rhododendron bushes. Like many of the Victorian gentry, they had a remarkable affection for hunting, and these bushes make ideal ground cover for pheasants. The Rossmores are gone, but the rhododendrons remain and have grown into enormously labyrinthine entanglements through which visitors may wander. In the height of summer, the noise of honeybees feasting on the rhododendron nectar is like the drone of an aeroplane's engine. As we make our way along a dappled pathway, I may find myself suddenly waylaid by the stunningly sweet perfume of laurel blossom. The air beneath the beech trees now is thick with the savoury scent of wild garlic; its delicate white flowers have replaced the wood anemone and the bluebells to dominate the forest floor.

Across the lake, a family of aloof swans cruises with cool composure. They deign to accept scraps from a picnic thrown to them by giggling children. The water lilies flower with profusion, turning the lake's surface into a patchwork of ivory and gold. Dragonflies flick and skitter over the water as they hunt; if you listen closely, you'll hear the quiet clicking of their wings as they turn and dart and strike.

Summer slowly slips towards the autumn; the days begin to shorten, but there's still warmth left in the retiring sun. Now, amongst the spruce needles on the forest floor, it is the turn of the fungi to fruit. The blushing and speckled toadstools nestle between the roots of spruce and feast on dark autumn earth. A miraculous little fungus-staircase climbs up the trunk of a stricken beech. And mushrooms, white and egg-like at first, appear overnight as if by magic. They gather in the shadows in mysterious circles, and it's not difficult to imagine an assembly of fairies having used them for a midnight soiree. Listen closely and you may hear slivers of tiny laughter caught in the clinging twigs.

Margin annotations

- Multisyllabic words convey maze-like image of twisting pathways.
- Simile and onomatopoeia.
- Sensuous language appeals to sense of smell.
- Alliteration conveys gliding movement of swans.
- Onomatopoeia and assonance convey sound of children laughing.
- Metaphor appeals to sense of sight; 'patchwork' evokes a spread quilt; colours convey richness.
- Assonance conveys quick, darting movement.
- Assonance and onomatopoeia convey sound of dragonflies in flight.
- Sibilance conveys smoothness of the changing season. The mystical and mysterious tone is appropriate for the shrouded days of autumn.
- Personification implies both the sun's increasing distance from the Earth and the idea of it growing older.

Composing

The limbs of the rowan trees, the hawthorn and the noble mountain ash are bowed over with the weight of their flame-red berries. The hazels, oaks and sweet chestnuts, too, are bursting with fruit. If you are lucky, you will find red squirrels hard at work gathering their winter stores because they know their time is short. The blue jays clatter and squawk among the shrubbery, bickering and grumbling. The magpies chuckle at their foolishness.

Alliteration, onomatopoeia and personification bring sounds to life.

The first frosts proclaim the coming winter. Across the lakes and hollows, mists shroud the morning in mystery. The sycamores have long since lost their leaves; now the other forest trees follow. The mighty beeches turn golden; then slowly, sedately, allow their leaves to spill. The towering trunks become the pillars of a colossal cathedral, their leaves the confetti of a great autumnal fiesta. The aisles soon become cloaked in their golden debris, and every footfall is a crunch and flurry of leaves.

Alliteration and metaphor. 'Shroud' adds a slightly sinister, perhaps otherworldly, element to the image.

Metaphor implies semi-spiritual connection with nature.

Onomatopoeia conveys sound and movement.

The world freezes as winter returns once again. The pathways become iron, under an ivory sky. Sometimes Molly and I are treated to the sight of a hoarfrost covering the landscape in a magical dusting of crystalline glitter. When the snows come, children with their toboggans converge on the hill where the Rossmores' castle once stood. I imagine people have used that hill for sledging for hundreds of years. After nights of bitter cold, the lakes themselves will freeze. A rock flung across the icy surface makes it ring like a giant drum: each little shock wave chimes weirdly through the ice.

Metaphor conveys coldness and hardness. There is an implicit echo of the essay's opening images.

Assonance conveys enchanting sight of hoarfrost.

Simile and onomatopoeia. Assonance mimics bouncing of a rock across the surface.

Through every season, Molly and I experience the forest park where the Rossmores once called home. No two walks in this enchanting place are ever the same. Whether sweating under an August sun, or bundled up against the cold of Christmas, we explore the pathways together, watching the ever-turning wheel of nature.

Conclusion returns to opening image.

Articles

What is an article?

An article is a type of essay written about a particular topic with a specific audience in mind. The purpose of an article is to be informative, entertaining and/or interesting. There are different types of article; for example:

- News articles are informative, convey key facts about a recent event and are usually written in a formal register.
- Feature articles tend to focus on a subject with human interest – a newsworthy person, place or event – and can be more informal in tone.
- Opinion pieces are articles in which the author argues a case for or against something using the language of argument and persuasion.

 For more information on feature articles, see page 3, and on opinion pieces, see page 46.

All articles in magazines and newspapers will be published with a headline and a byline.

Increasingly, articles appear online. Most newspapers and magazines have an online presence. Many people have essentially become self-publishing journalists and authors by creating their own websites and blog pages.

Preparing and planning

Read the question carefully to determine what type of publication your article will appear in and/or who your audience will be. The tone and content of your article need to be appropriate for your readership. You will often be told whether the tone should be serious or humorous. If the tone is serious, there should be more emphasis on informative language. If the tone is light-hearted, then the focus shifts to be more entertaining. Remember that even though you are addressing a mass audience, they will each, individually, be reading your words. Therefore, speak to them as if it is a one-to-one dynamic between author and reader.

Depending on the topic, the GEEP SMASH technique (see page 139) can help focus your ideas when planning your article.

Use the following advice as a guide when writing your article.

- All print articles need to have a headline. Some authors leave that until last when they have a clearer picture of the article's focus. Do not forget to fill it in.
- Try to start with a captivating opening paragraph. A quotation, a startling image, even an anecdote could be effective.
- Develop from your opening with illustrative examples, using the language of information, facts and expert opinions. If you are writing a feature article or opinion piece, put forward your own opinions and experiences too.
- Conclude by returning to however you began. Pick up on the question you posed and supply the answer. Or go back to your anecdote/news story and reappraise it in the light of your discussion.

 Hint

The best way to prepare to write an article is to read as many different types as you can. Any daily or weekly newspaper will be full of examples. Many newspapers will allow you to read articles free of charge online.

Sample Article

In TEXT 1, Alan McMonagle writes about allowing room for, among other things, discovery, invention and re-invention in life.

Write a feature article, suitable for publication in a popular magazine, offering some ideas for new inventions and discoveries you think would improve your life or make the world a better place. Your article may be serious or humorous or both. (2020)

Alliteration makes headline memorable.

Byline – fictious author.

Striking opening image grabs reader's attention. The serious tone of the article is indicated from the outset.

Language of information.

Rhetorical question.

Language of information – statistics invented.

Sums up the contention of the article.

The Discovery We Desperately Need

By Patsy McCaffrey

At this very moment, floating somewhere between California and Hawaii, is an island of garbage three times bigger than France. Alternatively named the Great Pacific Garbage Patch, or the Pacific Trash Vortex, it is estimated this enormous agglomeration contains at least 800,000 tonnes of plastic, or 20 billion individual pieces. Some scientists are referring to this – without hyperbole – as 'The Eighth Continent'.

Why are we so wedded to plastic – something that is so damaging? Like addicts, we know the immense harm we are causing ourselves, and yet, we cannot stop. Plastic packaging is cheaper, stronger and more convenient to produce than anything else. Glass bottles break in transit and are more expensive to make than plastic ones. Paper bags are more environmentally friendly, but are not as strong, as flexible or as cheap to produce as plastic ones. So we end up with single-use plastic items such as the trays our supermarket fruit arrives on, the Styrofoam cups our coffee is served in and the soft drink bottles we constantly find thrown under hedges. A report released by the Environmental Protection Agency (EPA) in 2022 states that around 390 million tons of plastic were produced worldwide in 2020 alone. That is up from 2 million in 1958. The same report also estimates that two-thirds of all the plastic that has ever been produced has been 'released into the environment' – and is still there.

The innovations we so urgently need right now are twofold. First, we need to invent a way to remove all this plastic and reverse the damage it is causing. Second, we need a cheap, viable alternative to plastic; something that will biodegrade harmlessly but offer all the flexibility, strength and convenience that has made plastic such a ubiquitous presence in our lives.

Cleaning up the Great Pacific Garbage Patch (GPGP) will be no mean feat. The items found there are fishing nets discarded from trawlers as well as waste thrown from ships and from land. It is estimated that the equivalent of a garbage truck full of plastic is dumped into the world's oceans every minute. Our invention will also have to cater for the fact that 94 per cent of the waste is in the form of microplastics, as large pieces of plastic have broken down into small pieces, which are particularly dangerous for marine life and seabirds. So, instead of an 'island' of rubbish, the GPGP is really more like a soup of pulverised and toxic slop. According to the National Oceanic and Atmospheric Administration (NOAA), a fleet of 67 ships, all trawling through the trash for an entire year, would be unlikely to remove more than one per cent of it. Our invention will need to be far more efficient than this.

One promising candidate for a solution to the world's plastic predicament comes from an unlikely source: mushrooms. British scientists recently revealed that a species of fungus that is often responsible for the fruit in your fruit bowl going mouldy might actually hold the key to ridding the world of all its unwanted plastic. Scientists working at the British Academy of Marine Research discovered that this particular fungus was able to break down most forms of plastic in a matter of weeks. The fungal cells secrete enzymes that break the chemical bonds between plastic molecules. As we all know, left to its own devices, plastic takes decades, or even centuries, to decompose. Perhaps, with a little genetic engineering, the species of fungus identified by the British Academy might become a kind of mushroom superhero, munching on all the plastic we have allowed escape into the environment. Perhaps it could be made into a salt-water resistant mutation; an organism quite at home in the sea, gobbling up every scrap of plastic it happens to come across. Perhaps we might engage a fleet of autonomous trash-seeking robots, each one large enough to hook and drag back to land the largest items it comes across. Each could also be armed with a payload of millions of fungi spores that can be administered where they are most needed.

Annotations (left margin):

- Startling facts maintain the article's serious tone.
- Language of information.
- Striking image using metaphor and assonance.
- Expert opinion.
- Offers possible solution based on real research findings.
- Fictitious organisation.
- Snappy image – appropriate for feature article.
- The serious tone of the article lightens slightly. More light-hearted diction is associated with a possible solution to the problem.

Composing

Descriptive passage illustrates ideas for new inventions – required by the question.

Such a robotic fleet could set sail across all the world's oceans; solar powered and fully automatic, they need never restock their supplies of fungi since the cultures each one is carrying would quickly reproduce and be, for all intents and purposes, immortal. When their host robot comes across floating garbage, the fungal payload could be injected directly into the clouds of microplastics. There they could happily gorge themselves, clearing the waters of our trash for us, before drifting peacefully and harmlessly to the ocean floor.

Inclusive language makes reader feel involved – persuasive technique.

The second invention – the question requires a discussion of 'inventions' (plural).

The other side of the coin in our two-pronged attack on plastic pollution is the invention of a viable alternative. We need to invent a substance that is strong, flexible and economically attractive to produce. It must be something that we can use to wrap food but also mould to make computer hardware, car interiors, mobile phones, toys, boats, medical supplies … In fact, we need to replace the plastic we use in almost everything. This would be nothing short of a revolution. Such an invention would rival the wheel, the printing press and the internet as a candidate for the most important invention in human history. Wherever we find our alternative, we need to accelerate our search as if our very lives, and the lives of all the creatures we share the Earth with, depend upon it – because they do.

Powerful imagery and a pithy statement to drive the argument home.

Returns to the image used in the opening.

Alliterative ending.

The Great Pacific Garbage Patch is growing daily, snaring sea life and poisoning the water. Our reliance on the plastics that comprise it must come to an end. We need to invent our way out of the muck of our own making.

152

Speeches

What is a speech?

A speech is a verbal address delivered to a particular audience on a specific topic. The kinds of speech you may come across range from formal debates in front of an international audience to informal talks to a class group. You might be writing the text of a talk for a radio broadcast, a television slot or a live-streamed speech to be broadcast online. Whichever form your speech takes, your style and register should be shaped by your purpose and your audience.

If the question indicates that you are competing in a **debating** competition, you can be fairly certain that you are required to construct a powerfully convincing speech using all the aspects of argumentative and persuasive writing to support your proposal. However, if you are taking part in a **public-speaking competition**, the task might simply be to construct an entertaining and informative speech. It all depends on the context as explained to you in the question.

Preparing and planning

Like all writing tasks, foremost in your mind when considering a speech question should be:
- What is the purpose of the speech?
- Who is the intended audience?

The answers to these two questions will indicate the appropriate register and tone to use.

You may be asked to write a speech in which you 'give your views' to a particular audience on a topic. In this context, your approach would be less combative and more discursive. However, if they are your views, you are still going to present them in a way that satisfies your audience that those views are the right ones.

If you are writing a speech in which you are arguing for or against a particular motion or trying to persuade your audience to form a particular point of view, you should follow the seven steps overleaf.

Keep your audience in mind throughout. Address them in your opening. If you are speaking at a competition, address the audience, the judges and the adjudicator(s). If it is your class, welcome them and your teacher. Show that you are keeping your audience in mind by inserting appropriate references to them throughout. Use rhetorical questions. Include international/ current affairs references for an international audience, or local/school-related references for your class.

> ### Hint
>
> If your task is to write a **persuasive essay**, then just like a persuasive speech, the aim is to convince your readership of something. However, the key difference is that when you are writing the text of a speech, you are conscious of a live audience, whereas in a persuasive essay, you are not. Therefore, you will not need quite so many rhetorical devices, and can employ more logic and reason. Normally, no specific audience is mentioned for a persuasive essay, so you simply adopt a reasonably formal style and write as if addressing a single individual; in this case, your examiner. When writing a persuasive essay, you should still follow the seven steps overleaf.

You should imagine that you are delivering the text of your speech to an audience in real time. For example, if you tell a joke, you could pause for the audience to laugh. If you reveal a startling statistic, or challenge the audience with a thought-provoking rhetorical question, you could pause to allow it to sink in. You might even address certain members of the audience directly or ask for a show of hands.

Composing

Seven steps to convince an audience

1. Hook

A hook is something that grabs your audience's attention. The type of hook will depend entirely on the topic you are addressing. Perhaps you should lead with a shocking statistic or a relevant quote from someone your audience will recognise. Or you could employ aesthetic language to evoke a powerful image that will inspire sympathy/outrage/indignation, etc. You could also start with a personal anecdote to draw them in.

Imagine you want to argue that the legal voting age should be lowered to 16. What hook could you use to grab your audience's attention?

- **Statistic:** The voter turnout for the 2021 Dublin Bay South by-election was just 37.4 per cent. At the Dublin Fingal and Dublin Mid-West by-elections in 2019, turnout was just 26 per cent!
- **Quote:** 'A great democracy must be progressive or it will soon cease to be great or a democracy.' – Theodore Roosevelt
- **Image:** Something to emphasise the injustice of a passionately political 16-year-old being denied an opportunity to participate in a democratic vote while the majority of adults who are legally entitled to vote do not bother to exercise that right.
- **Anecdote:** Do you belong to a political youth movement or the school's student council? Any relevant anecdote could work here if it demonstrates the ridiculousness of someone under 18 not being allowed to vote.

2. Contention

The contention is a clear expression of the thing you are arguing for or against. In the example above, your contention could be:

> *The voting age for the Irish electorate must be lowered immediately to include people over the age of 16.*

Notice that qualified terms such as 'in my opinion' or 'I think that' are not used. Instead, the more forceful words 'must' and 'immediately' are used.

3. Ethos

Ethos means character or values. For example, your school's ethos is a written statement of the values that your school holds dear.

In order to convince your audience, you first need to demonstrate that your opinions on the issue are relevant. Why should they listen to you? What experience do you have in this area? What do you actually know about this topic? In the voting-age example, perhaps simply being a young person establishes your ethos sufficiently. However, if you also happened to be a member of a political organisation, or have campaigned on this issue, or attend political rallies, providing that information would help bolster your ethos and satisfy any of the audience's doubts concerning your credentials.

4. Pathos

Pathos is where you appeal to your audience's feelings. Whether you provoke anger, fear or a sense of injustice, pathos exploits the audience's emotions rather than their sense of reason. For example, you could work on your audience's sense of outrage at the unfairness of denying the right to vote to tens of thousands of citizens. Use the stylistic techniques associated with persuasive writing: rhetorical questions, lists of three, repetition, a passionate delivery, etc.

5. Logos

Here is where you employ your argumentative language and your language of information. Facts, expert opinions and statistics logically build up a convincing case. For example, include statements from respected experts about the democratic benefits of lowering the voting age, or give examples of countries (such as Scotland or Austria) where the voting age has been lowered and explain what has been learned in these places.

6. Rebuttal/refutation

These two things are similar, but quite separate ideas:

- When you refute a claim, you show it to be false.
- When you rebut a claim, you show how the person making it may have misinterpreted the facts.

In your argumentative/persuasive piece, it is crucial you do not forget to include a rebuttal, refutation or both. Take your opposition's key counter-argument(s) and raise them in your own speech. Then prove them to be either false or mistaken. For example:

Some might argue that a 16-year-old lacks the maturity required to exercise the right to vote. However, consider that only two years later, on the very day they turn 18, they are abruptly able to not only vote, but also get married, run for office and serve on a jury. If every single 18-year-old suddenly becomes mature enough for all this, surely there are plenty of 16-year-olds with the maturity to decide on who they want to represent them in the Dáil?

7. Conclusion

Your conclusion sums up your argument and hammers home your message. One good way to conclude a piece of writing is to return to however you began (pick up on the image you opened with, revisit your quote, reappraise your personal anecdote, etc.). Otherwise, leave your audience with a powerful slogan, a catchy phrase, an image or anything else that will stay with them and promote your argument.

Note: the seven steps do not have to be addressed in the order they are presented here. The ethos, pathos, logos and rebuttal/refutation steps can be played around with. In fact, it would make a more cohesive whole if you mixed these areas up a little. The important thing to remember is that for most argumentative and persuasive writing, you will need to use all seven steps. Depending on the task, you can work out for yourself which steps need the most attention.

Sample Speech

TEXT 1 contains the statement: 'Language is a great weapon'.

You are competing in the final of a national public speaking competition. The topic to be addressed is: *Language is a great weapon.* **You are free to agree or disagree. Write the speech you would deliver.**

(2018)

Addresses audience – false name and school given.	Good evening adjudicators, fellow speakers, ladies and gentlemen. My name is Michelle and I am delighted to be here with you this evening, proudly representing St Bernadette's public-speaking team.

Addresses audience – false name and school given.

Good evening adjudicators, fellow speakers, ladies and gentlemen. My name is Michelle and I am delighted to be here with you this evening, proudly representing St Bernadette's public-speaking team.

Pauses can be as powerful as words – you can indicate them like this.

[pause]

Opening hook is a famous quotation – appropriate for an Irish audience.

Contention is stated boldly and confidently.

My favourite Seamus Heaney poem begins with the words: 'Between my finger and my thumb, the squat pen rests; snug as a gun.' Ladies and gentlemen, this simple image eloquently conveys our contention here tonight. Heaney's weapon of choice is the pen because he knew – as do we – that not only is language a great weapon, it is arguably the greatest weapon of all.

Highlights speaker's ethos.

You may be wondering what a Leaving Cert student could possibly know about the power of words. I am young and fairly inexperienced in the ways of the world. However, here I am at the final of this prestigious competition, using my language to compete against the best and brightest young minds in the country. To get here, we have all experienced the influence of the spoken word. We have also all learned to respect the vitality of the written word: how language is confined by neither time nor space; how when we read Heaney, Shakespeare, Brontë or Wilde, we listen with our inner ear to the whisperings of long-dead geniuses. Once you learn to listen to the dead, you learn the awesome power of language.

Vivid imagery helps the audience to visualise the point being made.

Image of vulnerable beings appeals to audience's sympathy – pathos.

Repetition – persuasive. References to human evolution – argumentative. Image of humanity triumphant and inspiring – pathos.

Ladies and gentlemen, it is language that sets humanity apart from the animals. The ability to speak and convey abstract thoughts to one another is the ultimate and defining characteristic of what it means to be human. Long ago, somewhere on the sweltering plains of Africa, huddled a wretched band of scavenging apes. They had no claws or fangs, and they could not run at any great speed. They had no thick hide to protect them or wings to help them escape the many creatures who hunted them. The one tiny advantage they had was the quickness of their wits. Then one day something momentous happened. One of them spoke – and was understood. Necessity forced them to communicate. Communication helped them organise. Communication helped them plan. Communication armed them. Now they – we – dominate.

Directly addresses audience with a challenging question.

To this day, language – whether written or spoken – is how we share ideas. Who here could argue that it is not ideas that shape the world we live in? Just as it was language that co-ordinated those first hunters, it was language that helped our ancestors spread to every corner of the globe. Language helped them adapt to every environment on every continent:

Vivid imagery and repetition.

from frozen expanses to blistering deserts. As they crossed the wide grassy plains and voyaged over the stormy oceans, our ancestors adapted, invented and communicated. Without language, none of this could have happened. Without language, we would be just helpless and naked apes.

Triad.

However, the ideas we communicate are not, of course, always laudable ones. Language also conveys hatred, prejudice and ignorance. A weapon may be used to save the innocent, but it

Rhetorical question using vivid imagery.

can just as easily be wielded for evil. Who here has not been that little child in the playground, sobbing and heartbroken at the vicious words someone has thrust at them, sharper than any knife? Does anyone need to be reminded of the devastating consequences of an unscrupulous maniac who happens to be

Historical example for context – logos.

gifted with words? Not very long ago, just such a madman plunged Europe and the world into a world war, the effects of which are still being felt. Just as Julius Caesar recognised two

Opinion from a well-known figure – logos.

thousand years ago: 'Language is a powerful weapon, and in the hands of a skilled man, it can be used to manipulate the masses.'

Expert opinion – logos.

Furthermore, Noam Chomsky, an American philosopher and linguist, once famously remarked that 'Language is a weapon of politicians, but language is a weapon in much of human affairs.' Ladies and gentlemen, my team and I wholeheartedly concur with this sentiment. While Hitler may have weaponised language and let loose a fervour of nationalism and hatred that scorched the world, there were those who stood up to it with a powerful rhetoric of their own. It could be argued that it was Churchill's steely resolve, coupled with his own considerable gift for oratory

Historical example – language of argument.

that helped Britain stand alone during her darkest hours. The stirring imagery of a valiant nation fighting a mighty foe 'on the beaches', on 'the landing grounds', 'in the fields and in the streets' perfectly captured their desperate situation and their unbowed resolve to fight till the last. More powerful than an invasion force, these words led their speaker to ultimate victory.

<table>
<tr>
<td>

This paragraph offers more historical evidence to support the point being made – language of argument.

Rhetorical question using a triad.

Sibilance creates rhythm – persuasive technique.

Rebuttal.

Engages audience through humour.

Returns to opening quotation.

</td>
<td>

Language has been used to fight injustice throughout history. Probably the most famous speech ever delivered was a passionate plea for justice and equality, delivered in Washington by Dr Martin Luther King. Who here has never heard the famous words 'I have a dream'? Is there anyone here who would claim that this speech served no purpose, that it did not shape a nation, that it left its audience unmoved? Barely six months after this speech was heard, in another part of the world, Nelson Mandela stood on trial for his life, accused of treason against the apartheid state. From the dock of the Rivonia Trial, the ANC activist delivered a three-hour speech to the courtroom; one of the most famous speeches of the twentieth century. He claimed he fought against white domination, and against black domination. Equality was an ideal, he said, for which he was prepared to die. That ideal was what transformed South Africa upon Mandela's release from prison 27 years later. His words, more than any weapons of sabotage or suppression, are what led that troubled country to a peaceful transition to democracy.

There are those who might argue that language is not actually that great a weapon. Who, after all, would charge into battle armed only with a thesaurus? [wait for laughter] This raises an interesting consideration, and yes, ladies and gentlemen, this is certainly food for thought. I admit: if I found myself cornered by a vicious-looking criminal with clearly evil intent, I would want to defend myself with something more than a witty rejoinder. [wait for laughter] However, we must bear in mind that physical weapons can harm only those within reach. Language, on the other hand, transcends both time and space. Ideas know no borders and no limits. They pass from generation to generation. Without language, there would be no weapons, because every weapon began as an idea. From the very first stone arrowhead to the atomic bomb.

And that, ladies and gentlemen, is why my team and I passionately believe that language is not only a great weapon, it is the greatest weapon we as human beings have at our disposal. Like all weapons, it may be used for good or for evil, depending on the character of the person who wields it.

Seamus Heaney, one of the world's greatest poets, certainly understood the power that coursed through the pen in his hand. Choosing to create instead of destroy, Heaney left behind a legacy of powerfully inspiring ideas. It is for us all to appreciate the power of language and to use it wisely.

Thank you.

</td>
</tr>
</table>

Short Stories

What is a short story?

A short story is a brief work of fiction. It deals with the elements of theme, character, setting, conflict and plot within a narrow time frame, with a limited number of episodes or scenes and very few characters. There is usually just one point of conflict. Typically, the protagonist of the story will be faced with a dilemma or must make some kind of decision. The conflict arises from the consequences of the protagonist's choices. The language styles used are predominantly narrative and aesthetic.

Preparing and planning

When planning a short story, you should consider: structure, plot, narrative voice, tense, setting, character(s) and dialogue.

Structure

A story has a beginning, a middle and an end. If events are told in chronological order from beginning to end, this is called a **linear plot**. Some authors like to start at the end and work back to the beginning: this is known as a **circular plot**. A circular plot often throws the reader in at the height of the action, thereby gripping their attention straight away. The reader may wonder how the character(s) came to be in their present predicament, and want to read on to find out.

The ending is all-important in a short story and you need to give it considerable thought. It should be as unpredictable as you can possibly manage. A genuinely surprising ending (or a **plot twist**) is the holy grail of short-story writing.

Do not forget to give your story a title. Many authors write the story first and then choose a suitable title.

> **Hint**
>
> For examples of short stories that contain a plot twist, read some of these:
> - 'Lamb to the Slaughter' – Roald Dahl
> - 'The Way Up To Heaven' – Roald Dahl
> - 'The Monkey's Paw' – W. W. Jacobs
> - 'An Occurrence at Owl Creek Bridge' – Ambrose Bierce
> - 'The Sniper' – Liam O'Flaherty
> - 'The Necklace' – Guy de Maupassant
> - 'The Gift of the Magi' – O. Henry
> - 'The Open Window' – Saki
> - 'Barney' – Will Stanton.

Plot

No two short stories are the same, but they all, broadly speaking, follow a certain shape. At the start, you normally find a main character in a particular setting – this situation is called the **exposition**. The character will encounter a problem or a conflict – this is the **inciting moment** that gets the plot moving. Attempts to resolve the problem often force the character to make a decision, which leads to a series of events and experiences. A **rising action**, characterised by increasing **tension** leads to a crisis or **climax**, which may be followed by **falling action** and a **resolution**. Put together, these events form the plot of the story and can be represented in a basic plot diagram (see overleaf).

Composing

Basic Plot Diagram

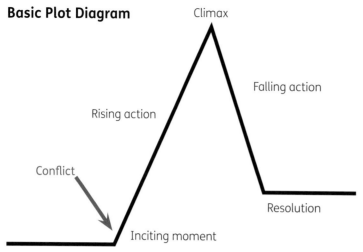

> **Hint**
>
> You will notice that the line representing the plot at the story's resolution has not returned to the original level. That is because in a good short story, the character changes or grows in some way: the events of the story have had a lasting effect on them.

A common mistake made by students is to write the narrative as though a series of events is the same as a short story. Such writing reads like a summary and is devoid of any tension. Very often, this error is a result of attempting to cover too much ground. It can be tempting to try to re-create a plot similar to a film, for example. However, a film script can easily be as long as a novel, so trying to compress all the action and the broad array of characters into around 1,000 words is just not possible.

Some students imagine that in order to create tension and suspense, the action of their story needs to be as dramatic as possible. Therefore, common themes are bank robberies, military raids, breathtaking crashes or other tragedies. However, some of the very best short stories have simple plots and feature characters going about their daily lives. It is the quality of the writing that sets them apart.

A short story needs focus. The events will tend to play out over a very limited time scale, sometimes only minutes of your characters' lives. Do not try to cram too much into your story. Cut everything that is not adding to your plot, your characters or the aesthetics of your narrative.

Narrative voice

One of the very first decisions to be made when writing fiction is choosing the right narrative voice for your story. (Joseph O'Connor speaks about this in his text on page 65.) You have four options:

- **First-person narrative:** events are told by one of the characters, using 'I'. It might be the main character, or a secondary character. This choice of narrator can present only the events that they witness and can share only their own observations and opinions. As in real life, they can only guess at the motivations and thoughts of others by listening to what they say and by reading their body language. Such a narrator can be unreliable – they could deliberately mislead the reader, they might misunderstand the situation they find themselves in, or sometimes they just don't have all the information.

- **Second-person narrative:** the narrator is 'you' (the reader). For example, TEXT 3 in the 2017 paper is an extract from Paul Auster's memoir *Report from the Interior*, which is written in the second person: 'Your earliest thoughts, remnants of how you lived inside yourself as a small boy. You can remember only some of it ... .' This choice of narrator

> **Hint**
>
> The second-person narrative voice is not commonly used and is a tricky choice to manage over an entire narrative successfully. That does not mean you should not give it a try; however, it would not be a good idea to do so in the exam without having experimented with it a few times first.

involves the reader very closely with the action and could help increase the tension.

- **Third-person narrative:** the narrative voice uses the third person: he/she/it/they. A *close third-person narrative* will follow one character as the story is told from their perspective. However, our relationship with this character is so close that we even know their thoughts.
- **Third-person omniscient narrative:** this narrative voice also uses the third person, but the voice telling the story is all-knowing and can tell you what each character is thinking, what their motives are, etc. It tends to allow a little more distance between the narrative voice and the characters. This type of narrator is presented as an authority of the story and can sometimes intrude to share their opinion or address the reader directly.

Tense

You must also decide what tense the narrative will be written in. Most writers opt for the past tense, but then must determine how far in the past that means. For example, if you are using the first-person narrative voice, does your narrator already know how the story ends? You need to think about where and when your narrator 'is' right now, at the moment they are telling us about their experiences.

Some authors choose to write in the present tense in order to increase tension and engage the reader. The present tense has an immediacy that the past tense might not offer.

Setting

Where the action is set can be what defines the narrative. Aesthetic language should be used to build up a vivid picture of the setting. Make sure you appeal to as many of the senses as you can.

Character(s)

When writing a short story, limit the number of characters because you do not have the scope or the time to develop them to any great degree. A short story can work perfectly well with just one or two characters.

Hint

A very common mistake made by students writing short stories is to be inconsistent in their choice of tense; and not deliberately so. Stories can slip from past tense to present tense and back again without any apparent reason. An examiner will mark such issues as language errors.

Hint

Basing your story on a place you know well usually makes the description easier to manage.

Hint

Many writers of fiction base their characters on real people they know, so remember that you do not need to completely invent characters for your short story.

Your character(s) should be described vividly for your reader. Try to make them unique because, in reality, that is exactly what all people are. One method of creating a memorable character is to give them a **character hook**. This is a shorthand way of making each character individual, and not just a name on a page. Perhaps they wear a leather jacket with chains that jingle. Maybe they are constantly flicking their long hair. A quick reference to this character hook every now and again immediately identifies them in the mind of your reader.

One of the most important rules to remember when writing is: *show, don't tell*. For example, instead of writing: 'Frank came in through the front door. He was very drunk', write: 'Frank stumbled through the front door clutching an empty bottle. His eyes were red and glazed.'

Dialogue

Not every successful short story includes dialogue, but it is a very good way to write characters vividly. Characters who are allowed to speak become memorable and unique. Dialogue allows the author to move the plot forward and gives the reader a better understanding of the characters' personalities and their motivations.

 For information on how to punctuate dialogue, see page 29.

Sample Short Story

In TEXT 1, John Banville recalls seeing, 'blear-eyed passengers off the overnight ferry from Fishguard in Wales' as he waited at the railway station.

Write a short story, set in a railway station, in which a passenger off the overnight ferry from Fishguard in Wales plays an important role. Your short story may be amusing or menacing in tone.

(2021)

Title represents the main character who finds himself at a 'loose end' (no home, prospects, etc.) and is echoed in the dialogue at the end of the story.

The first four paragraphs are exposition. They establish the setting and character. The opening sentence establishes narrative voice and tense: first-person narrative, present tense. The narrative is told as a stream-of-consciousness so the action feels immediate.

Location specified in question.

Narrator's backstory is given quickly, with broad strokes: important information for establishing character and plot.

Moves to the present: story's plot begins here.

Reader addressed directly to involve them closely with the narrator.

Auditory image adds to menacing tone – as required by the question.

Metaphor characterises main character's existence – an ex-mercenary reduced to hiding; being vulnerable and hunted.

Important context established.

Pithy sentences used for exposition of the story.

Hint towards the intended ending.

Loose Ends

I probably deserve this, you know. For the things I've done. This life, I mean. This day-to-day existence. Always looking over my shoulder. Never staying anywhere in the world long enough to put down roots. Going where people won't ask too many questions. Like this job at Connolly Station, Dublin, Ireland. I sweep. I mop. I pick up rubbish.

The mercenary life was fast and well rewarded. But there's no pension plan. And the enemies I've made, from Johannesburg to Havana, they don't forget. So here I am. Pushing eighty. No country is home. Hunted by the killers I crossed. Haunted by ghosts of the past. I've killed men of all colours, but now I'm mopping up needles and vomit. Shuffling around the concourse with my wheelie bucket, clutching my mop. To everyone passing through here, I'm just another old man in faded blue overalls. Hiding in plain sight.

But I notice things. It's what's kept me alive. Like now, for instance. Look across the station. It's a typical Tuesday morning. Listen to the distant shrieks of the trains braking. To most, crowds sound like babble. But not to me. I listen and sift; seeking information. I rely on instinct. I'm a rabbit in a forest: sniffing, listening, waiting.

And I'm in a city tearing itself apart. Drugs plus cash equals gangs and violence. There's a turf war going on; two families are slugging it out. Look at those headlines over at Frank's news-stand. Another guy got whacked yesterday. A tit-for-tat killing carnival. I've even heard rumours that the boss – the big dude – he's coming back to Ireland just to sort this out. To annihilate the opposition. It would be ironic, after all I've been through, if it was a stray bullet meant for someone else that got me in the end.

Annotation	Text

Second character introduced.

Complication/conflict introduced; begins rising tension of story's plot.

Character hook.

That's why I keep my eyes and ears open. Keeping two steps ahead. See that girl, for example? The one sitting on her own on the bench by the display board. The one with the long blonde hair. Twenty-ish. Maybe twenty-five? Mini-skirt. Nice figure. Can you see what's not right about her? Look again.

The woman is the complication: her behaviour marks her out as unusual.

Simile helps develop the menacing atmosphere mentioned in the question.

Use of character hook.

Oh, she's good-looking alright. That's not what I mean. Face like a picture in a magazine. But her eyes keep flicking from the arrivals board to the turnstiles to Platform 2. She's waiting for someone. So, what's unusual about her? No phone. Everybody else around this concourse has their head in their phone; faces weirdly lit like electric ghosts. But not Miss Blonde. She seems completely serene. But her eyes flicker between the great clock by the West Entrance, the display board and the turnstiles. The next train due at Platform 2 will be the 8:47 from Wexford. So she must be waiting on that. Boyfriend maybe? But when did you ever see a youngster like that without her face glued to a screen? Mysterious.

Combines alliteration and metaphor for aesthetic effect – the image will be returned to shortly.

Assonance – the sound combination echoes the passengers' bedraggled appearance.

Personification – the train 'disgorging' its passengers is compared to something regurgitating. A disagreeable image reinforces the unhappy appearance of the commuters and hints at the unpleasant nature of the one particular passenger on board.

Onomatopoeia – a sound effect developing aesthetic language.

Right on cue, the automatic voice crackles and blares. The 8:47 from Rosslare has arrived on Platform 2. Miss Blonde stiffens a little and her eyes lock on the turnstiles. I dip my mop in my wheelie bucket and casually move myself closer; out of the way of the great push of passengers about to stream onto the concourse. I position myself beside the gents' toilets to watch.

The first lot come through the turnstiles, all crumpled and grumpy. The midnight sailing from Fishguard disgorges fractious families and exhausted businessmen every morning. Now they all come blinking into the unforgiving fluorescent light of Connolly Station's main concourse, dragging their little wheelie suitcases that go *tucker, tucker, tucker* on the flagstones.

Third character – the passenger specified in the question.

Hints at the character's identity.

Miss Blonde is on her feet. She's walking with purpose. The man she approaches is not at all what I expected. Short, stocky, about fifty-ish, with a big paunch on him. Kind of arrogant swagger, too. The kind I've seen before; the kind a fellow develops when he's used to giving orders. And now that I think about it, his face is familiar. I never forget a face. Twenty years ago I would have put a name to him in a flash. Now, it takes a little longer; but it'll come.

She's talking to him now. She's right up close. He seems a bit testy, like he hadn't expected her. Is she flirting with him? Right there in the middle of the concourse? But who the hell is he? I know that face from somewhere.

OK. Now she's wandered off, and he's on his way out the East Entrance. What an odd little drama that was. She walks right past me and goes into the ladies' toilets just past Frank's news-stand. But wait. The fellow has stopped. Commuters stream past him left and right. He seems to be thinking something through, like he's weighing up some proposition. Then he turns around and walks back. He passes me so close I get a whiff of Old Spice and stale coffee and I hear the squeak of his patent leather shoes. Without a pause, he follows her right into the women's toilets.

I'm a broad-minded guy. I'm not going to judge. Each to his – or her – own, I always say. But just as I'm standing there, looking past the news-stand, that's when it hits me, where I've seen this guy before. It was in the papers. He's the head dude Interpol have been chasing all over Europe. The boss. The one ordering all the hits. He's come back to take charge of this war. Now I'm thinking Miss Blonde has bitten off more than she can chew and I've got to make a decision.

Look. I know I'm past my prime. But you'd be surprised what I can do with half a mop handle, snapped sharp. So that's what I do.

Just as I'm about to hit the door running, a woman comes out: short, dark hair, jeans and a t-shirt. I swerve around her and go in. The place is silent, flooded with harsh, flickering fluorescent light. There's the usual smell of bleach and urine. There's nobody else in here and all the stalls' doors are open. Except one.

Clutching my makeshift weapon, I go over and put my ear to the door. There's no sound except the electric hum of the lights. But then I look down and see the bright red pool forming around my boots. I take a step back and kick the door off its hinges.

He's sitting. His mouth is slack. In his hands is a blonde wig turning rust-red, just like his shirt, his pants and shoes. His throat has been cut from ear to ear. 'Don't turn around.' It's a voice from behind me. A woman's.

'You came back?' I say.

'You were watching me. You followed me.'

'I was worried for you. I know who this guy is.'

She hesitates a moment. I hear her breathing.

'That's sweet,' she says. 'But I'm afraid I can't leave loose ends. Sorry. It'll be quick.'

I probably did deserve that life. The one I was leading, I mean. But I'm damned sure I didn't deserve this death.

Annotations (margin notes):

- Revisits earlier metaphor describing the passengers.
- A first-person narrator can only guess at the motives and thoughts of other characters.
- Links to plot point included in exposition.
- Uses visual and olfactory (smell) imagery for vividness.
- Showing, not telling.
- Narration switches to dialogue to rapidly increase the pace towards the climax of the story.
- Conclusion returns to the opening line. The reason for the inclusion of the narrator's background is also revealed: if he had been an innocent caretaker, there would be no irony in his death.

Dialogues

What is a dialogue?

A dialogue is a spoken-word text written in order to be performed by actors in character roles. It can follow the conventions of a script, but a dialogue is more limited in length and scope than a stage play. Like a short story, there should be a sense of cohesion created by a beginning, middle and end.

There should be very few characters (there may be crowd scenes, but the number of speaking characters should be limited). There should also be a limited number of scenes (normally a single scene is sufficient).

Your script should inform the actors about not only what they say, but also how they should say it. For example, perhaps one of your characters needs to interact with a specific prop while they deliver their line. Or maybe you want them to say their line in a particular way (aggressively, tearfully, wistfully, etc.). This information can be given in stage directions. You should also indicate when characters enter or exit the stage. The setting, stage set-up, backdrop and props can also be included, but these are optional.

Preparing and planning

When planning your dialogue, think about how the stage itself should look. Is there a backdrop with scenery? Are there any props? Which characters can we see?

Decide how many characters you will include with speaking roles. Who are they? Draw up a rough plan for the ideas your characters will cover in the course of their conversation. What events will occur between them? How will you draw the dialogue to a close?

Begin your dialogue with a brief description of the setting. Stage directions are written in the present tense, so are conveyed as if occurring simultaneously with the reading.

Have a look at any of the dramatic texts you are studying to see how the written text is presented. Most obviously, you will notice that speech marks are not used. Nor are many of the narrative techniques associated with prose writing. Most vivid description will be confined to what the characters themselves say.

Remember to give your dialogue a title, but you might want to wait until you have written it all before doing that.

Sample Dialogue

Timothy Garton Ash alludes to the invention of the wheel in TEXT 2.

Imagine it is the Stone Age and you have just invented the wheel. Write a dialogue in dramatic form, in which you introduce and promote your new invention to your sceptical friends and neighbours. Your drama may be humorous or serious or both. (2017)

Title clearly establishes the focus of the dialogue in accordance with the question.

Sets scene.

Describes characters on stage; uses present tense. Audience is invited to wonder why Kevin has his head in his hands.

The Wheel

[Scene: Somewhere near the bend in the River Boyne, 3500 BC. Minimal set: three or four large rocks for seating.]

[Ms URWINA is on stage dressed neatly in animal skins. In her hands is a clipboard. She paces across the stage; she is waiting for someone. KEVIN is sitting with his head in his hands, a large wooden wheel beside him.]

URWINA: [speaking off] Hello. Hi, yes, this is the place. Come on in. You're very welcome. What? No, no, you're not late at all. Come in, come in.

[Enter THAGSON, BOGGINS and THIKKO. They are also all wearing animal skins, but soiled and worn, as if used for manual labour.]

URWINA: Yes, hello again. Nice to see you. How you keeping? Good. Lovely. Please take a seat. Help yourselves to some squirrel-on-a-stick cookies. They're really good.

[Pleasantries are shared for a moment until all except URWINA take their seats.]

Characterisation as a modern office training co-ordinator intended for humorous effect – as specified by the question.

URWINA: On behalf of Newgrange Construction, I'd just like to thank you all for participating in this project review programme. As team leaders in the Orthostat Transport Department, it's good to see you all back again. Today is just about touching base and seeing how you are getting on with the new tech.

[The others share glances, there's some muttering and whispering.]

Addresses task in the question.

URWINA: Now here's someone who needs no introduction: the inventor himself, a friend and a neighbour to all of us. Let's hear a wee hand for Kevin, shall we?

[Some unenthusiastic applause. KEVIN gets up and comes to STAGE FRONT.]

KEVIN: Um. Hi everyone. So, as you know, this is the very latest development in transportation technology. The 'Wheel' offers you the full 360-degree revolving experience. It is about to revolutionise the rock-freight industry *[waits for laughter at his pun – gets none, laughs uncomfortably himself, continues]* um – taking the hard labour out of moving megalithic structures. Why would you use old-fashioned roller logs when you can embrace the future with the sleek, durable and affordable custom-built wheel? Only the most high-end carbon-fibre materials go into the manufacture of the …

> Main character promoting his invention – addresses task in the question.

THIKKO: You mean 'wood', right?

KEVIN: Um, yes.

URWINA: *[laughing a little nervously]* OK, OK. Thank you, Kevin. Thanks for that. So, let's just see how we got on, shall we? Any volunteers to speak first? *[looks around]* No? OK then, let's just go to *[checks clipboard]* Mr Thagson, shall we? Could you tell us how your team got on with the 'Wheel' over the last few weeks? Any significant improvements at all?

[THAGSON coughs.]

URWINA: Sorry. Didn't quite catch that.

THAGSON: No. I said no. No improvement. Actually, it was worse than before.

KEVIN: Sorry? What? Using wheels to move your orthostat was worse than without?

THAGSON: Yes. The damned things kept falling off, so we had to stop every few metres and put 'em back on again. Can't see the point to be honest.

KEVIN: Sorry again. Could you just run through for me how the wheels we gave your team 'kept falling off'?

THAGSON: Right, OK. So you get your orthostat, right? A good five, six tonnes of high-grade greywacke rock. Normally you can do about a hundred metres a day, on a good run, with a full team. But with them fancy new wheels, what with them falling off every few metres …

> Colloquial language used for characterisation.

KEVIN: Falling off?

Character is sceptical – as required by the question.

THAGSON: Yeah. Bloody things are the wrong shape if you ask me. They won't stay up on the top of the rock. But what good they'd do there, I dunno.

KEVIN: Ah. Right. I see. You put them on top of the rock. Yes. Not to worry. Um. Did anyone else experience any difficulties?

BOGGINS: *[raises hand]* Yeah me.

KEVIN: Hi, hello. You also put your wheels on top of the rock you were trying to transport, did you?

BOGGINS: No, of course not.

KEVIN: Excellent. So how did you get on? Any improvement in your team's total distance covered?

Second character is also sceptical.

BOGGINS: No. Didn't get half as far as normal. These fancy new ideas ain't worth all the hassle. If anything, they just add drag, makes the whole job harder. I can tell you there's some in my team what ain't happy.

KEVIN: But you put them underneath the rock you were transporting, yes?

BOGGINS: Of course I did. Do I look like an idiot? – Sorry, Thag mate. No offence.

THAGSON: None taken.

KEVIN: OK. Just to be clear, let me just go and get the prototype *[he goes and fetches the wheel and rolls it across stage]* – now, could you tell me ...

BOGGINS: Whoa. Why'd you put it on its side like that? That's a health and safety issue right there. That thing could go anywhere, so it could.

KEVIN: *[slowly]* I see. So, you put the wheels underneath the rock you were transporting, but you laid them down flat? And this is why you were experiencing a bit of, um, 'drag'?

BOGGINS: Yep. We're talking tonnes of rock here. You can't just roll them around willy-nilly. Someone would get hurt.

KEVIN: Yes, OK. Fair point. Thanks for that. Um, and thanks for sharing, guys. Did anyone here follow the guidelines that came with the equipment?

THIKKO:	I did.
KEVIN:	Oh, thank the goddess. So, tell me, what did you think of the whole 'Wheel experience'?
THIKKO:	I thought it was great.

[URWINA and KEVIN share a meaningful glance.]

KEVIN:	Well, that's certainly good to hear.
THIKKO:	Yes, I wouldn't go back to how we used to do it. I reckon this 'Wheel' thing is the future.
KEVIN:	*[beaming]* Ah, now, well. I'm very glad. So, what kind of mileage did you and your team make?
THIKKO:	Mileage?
KEVIN:	Yes. How much further were you and your team able to pull your five-tonne rock using the 'Wheels'? Did you go double the distance? More than double perhaps?
THIKKO:	We were supposed to pull the damned thing as well?
KEVIN:	*[weakly]* You didn't pull the rock? Let me guess. You didn't push it either, did you?
THIKKO:	Ah, well now, that might explain a few things. One of the lads, he says to me one time: here, how come them wheels ain't moving the rock? I dunno, I said. I'm no good with new technology, so I'm not. But nobody complained. Best two weeks of work any of us ever had. *[To URWINA]* So listen, say thanks to Head Office from me, OK? Happy to help. Can I take the lads some of them squirrel cookies?

Returns to opening tableau.

[URWINA nods hopelessly. KEVIN quietly returns to where he was at the beginning of the scene, sits down and puts his head back in his hands.]

Composing Revision Table

Genre	Features	Language style	Sample questions
Personal essays	• Written in the first person • Explores significant personal experience(s) • Focuses on a particular theme • Author shares important lesson(s) learned	• Language of narration • Discursive • Reflective	• Theme 1, Question 1 • Theme 2, Questions 1 & 7 • Theme 3, Questions 1 & 4 • Theme 4, Questions 3 & 6 • Theme 5, Question 6 • Theme 6, Question 4
Discursive essays	• Considers topic from multiple sides • Objective • Passive voice	• Language of information • Formal	• Theme 1, Question 4 • Theme 2, Question 4 • Theme 3, Question 2 • Theme 4, Question 4 • Theme 5, Question 1
Descriptive essays	• Vividly depicts an experience, place, object, person or event • Appeals to as many of the senses as possible • Slow and considered pace	• Aesthetic language	• Theme 1, Question 7 • Theme 4, Question 1 • Theme 5, Question 2 • Theme 6, Question 3
Articles	• Written for mass audience on a particular topic • Informative, entertaining and/or interesting	• Formal (news) • Informal (feature article) • Language of information and argument (opinion piece)	• Theme 1, Question 2 • Theme 2, Question 2 • Theme 3, Question 6 • Theme 5, Question 7
Speeches	• Addresses audience directly • Anecdotes • Rhetorical questions • Facts/information	• Formal or informal depending on audience • Language of information, argument, persuasion and aesthetic language	• Theme 1, Question 6 • Theme 2, Question 6 • Theme 3, Question 7 • Theme 4, Question 7 • Theme 5, Question 3 • Theme 6, Questions 5 & 6
Persuasive essays	• Anecdotes • Rhetorical questions • Facts/information	• Language of information, argument, persuasion and aesthetic language	• Theme 6, Question 1
Short stories	• Structure and plot • Narrative voice • Tense • Setting • Character(s) • Dialogue	• Aesthetic language and language of narration	• Theme 1, Questions 3 & 5 • Theme 2, Questions 3 & 5 • Theme 3, Questions 3 & 5 • Theme 4, Question 2 • Theme 5, Question 4 • Theme 6, Questions 2 & 6
Dialogues	• Script form • Few characters • Limited scenes • Beginning, middle and end • Stage directions • Backdrop • Props	• Aesthetic language and language of narration	• Theme 5, Question 5

Spelling and Grammar

Imagine for a moment that the way you spelled words was optional; depending, perhaps, on your regional accent. Or that everyone invented their own punctuation style, or that syntax was a matter of personal whim. Written communication in those circumstances would be difficult, if not impossible.

The primary purpose of language is to communicate ideas effectively. There are certain agreed conventions that everyone who uses a language needs to observe for communication to happen efficiently. We call these conventions the rules of spelling and grammar. Without these accepted rules, communication would often be vague and baffling. How would a reader tell the difference between ewe, you and yew? Or between your genes and your jeans?

As in a sport, to become proficient in a language, it pays to know the rules: 10 per cent of every question in your exam is designated for *Mechanics* (spelling and grammar; see page xiv).

Spelling

When writers like Shakespeare and Donne were plying their trade in the sixteenth and seventeenth centuries, there was a far more relaxed attitude to spelling than there is today. Depending on where you came from, a word could have any number of spellings. It was only with the publication of the first dictionaries in the early 1600s that some kind of order came to bear.

For the vast majority of English words, there is now a single accepted spelling, and anything else will be counted as an error. There are two exceptions:

1. **In speech:** when writing dialogue, you may want a character to speak in a certain way – perhaps they have a heavy accent and say 'dis' rather than 'this' or they use contractions such as 'gonna' instead of 'going to'. Such spellings are perfectly fine and are often an indication of good characterisation. Here is an example from *Star of the Sea* by Joseph O'Connor:

   i am going to america shortly and will never come home again so i want to say what follows and hope ye and yeer men act on it. i know people in this christian county of hypocrites do be slightin about me spreading slurry and gossip on my name and i am going away so i do not give 'that' what is said no more but here is the truth and the full of it.

2. **American spellings:** there are certain English words that Americans spell differently. 'Ax' instead of 'axe', 'color' instead of 'colour', 'theater' instead of 'theatre', for example. They also tend to use a 'z' instead of an 's' in words with the '-ise' suffix, such as 'colonize', 'organize' and 'recognize'. In Ireland, our default is to use British spellings. However, since all examination papers are anonymous, an examiner has no way of knowing whether the script in front of them was written by someone who grew up in Navan or New York. Therefore, if you use American spellings, you should be given the benefit of the doubt.

Common errors to avoid

Everyone makes mistakes when writing; especially when they are under pressure (like when they find themselves in the high-stakes circumstances of a Leaving Certificate examination). However, certain words are misspelled so often, and by so many people, that English teachers and examiners alike have grown weary of correcting them. These are not difficult words: some people master them while still in primary school. Get the following spellings right, and your examiner will notice.

YOUR = belonging to you. For example: **Your** dinner is in the oven.
YOU'RE = you are. For example: **You're** going to have to heat it for five minutes.

THEIR = belonging to them. For example: **Their** bags have been put on the bus.
THERE = a place not here. For example: The bus is due to arrive **there** at midday.
THEY'RE = they are. For example: **They're** going to have to hurry to catch that bus.

TWO = the number, 2. For example: I'll be **two** minutes.
TO = a preposition. For example: Write these rules down **to** learn them. / Go **to** the board.
TOO = a modifier; can be used with or as an adverb or an adjective. For example: You drive **too** fast. We are going **too**. The watch was **too** expensive. It looks silly **too**.

OFF = the opposite of on. For example: Will you switch the lights **off**?
OF = a preposition. For example: It was cancelled because **of** the rain.

NO = the opposite of yes. For example: This is a 'yes' or '**no**' question.
NOW = indicating this precise moment. For example: What time is it **now**?
KNOW = knowledge or understanding. For example: Do you **know** where you are going?

OUR = adjective describing something as belonging to us. For example: That is **our** dog.
ARE = first, second and third person plural and second person singular present tense form of 'to be'. For example: We **are** going to the match. The children **are** there already. **Are** you going?

QUIET = describing an absence of sound. For example: The room was **quiet**.
QUITE = to a large degree. For example: It is **quite** easy.

BEEN = past participle of 'be'. Should be accompanied by 'has' or 'have'. For example: It has **been** a long time coming. We have **been** lucky.

BEING = present participle of 'be'. She was **being** friendly.

WEATHER = the current climate. For example: The **weather** does not look promising.

WHETHER = a conjunction. For example: Dad will decide **whether** the barbecue goes ahead.

HEAR = to listen. For example: Can you **hear** me over the music?

HERE = indicating place. For example: It is very loud in **here**.

IT'S = contraction of 'it is' or 'it has'. For example: **It's** the exception to the apostrophe rule. **It's** been a long time.

ITS = belonging to it. For example: This contraction has lost **its** apostrophe.

LOOSE = adjective describing the lack of tightness. For example: Your shoelace is **loose**.

LOSE = verb form of 'loss'. For example: You can **lose** marks in your exam for spelling errors.

TAUGHT = past tense of 'to teach'. For example: Spellings are **taught** in national school.

THOUGHT = past tense of 'to think'. For example: She **thought** she knew how to spell.

AFFECT = a verb – an action. For example: This medicine may **affect** your ability to drive.

EFFECT = a noun – a thing. For example: However, the **effect** should wear off soon.

ACCEPT = a verb. For example: Will you **accept** my invitation?

EXCEPT = not including. For example: The shop is open every day **except** Sunday.

WERE = second person singular past, plural past and past subjunctive of 'be'. For example: We **were** studying yesterday.

WE'RE = we are. For example: **We're** studying English.

WHERE = to, at or in what place. For example: **Where** were you studying yesterday?

One MAN, many MEN.
One WOMAN, many WOMEN.

Trys/crys/flys, etc. ✘   Tries, cries, flies ✓
Note: 'flys' is only correct if you are referring to zippers.

Should of, could of, would of. ✘
Should have, could have, would have. ✓
Should've, could've, would've. ✓

Please bring me them books. ✘
Please bring me those books. ✓

Alot ✘   A lot ✓
Infront ✘   In front ✓
Aswell ✘   As well ✓

I seen a film. ✘   I have seen a film. ✓   I saw a film. ✓
I done my work. ✘   I have done my work. ✓   I did my work. ✓

Write out the following sentences and insert the correct words.

1. (You're/Your) going to have to work much harder to improve (you're/your) grade.

2. (They're/There/Their) bags are over (they're/there/their) where (they're/there/their) going to be stored.

3. Is it (too/to/two) much to ask you (too/to/two) take the bus? You will easily make it back by (too/to/two) o'clock.

4. Because (off/of) our budget cuts, please make sure you switch all the equipment (off/of) after using it.

5. (No/Now/Know) that you (no/now/know) what you are doing, you should be able to perform your duties with (no/now/know) problems.

6. (Our/Are) you on (our/are) team or theirs?

7. Electric vehicles can be (quiet/quite) affordable, and they are very (quiet/quite) on the road.

8. It's (being/been) great (being/been) here.

9. We will still have fun, (weather/whether) the (weather/whether) is cold or hot.

10. Did you (here/hear) what time they close? I have to stay (here/hear) until nine o'clock.

11. (Its/It's) not a good idea to exceed the speed limit, especially during bad weather. Without (its/it's) grip on the road, a car is a danger to everyone.

12. Did the farmer (loose/lose) one of the herd? There was a cow (loose/lose) in the top paddock.

13. I have (taught/thought) of a way to improve our mealtimes: those children are going to be (taught/thought) how to cook.

14. We now know that it is human behaviour which (effects/affects) our climate. We are feeling the (effects/affects) of this change currently.

15. (Accept/Except) for one or two very rare instances, the majority of scientists (accept/except) the theory of evolution as fact.

Verbs and Tenses

Verbs tell us about an action or a state of being. The tense form of a verb indicates when the action happens. Things have either happened, are happening or will happen in the future.

 For more information on verbs, see page 56.

The root form of the verb without a tense is called an **infinitive**. For example: 'to be', 'to play', 'to speak'.

We can change infinitives into the three simple tenses by altering their form. For example:

• He **was** a very good writer. (past simple)
• She **cycles** to school every day. (present simple)
• They **will be** late for the bus. (future simple)

Infinitive	Past simple	Present simple	Future simple
To be	Was/were	Am/are/is	Will be
To play	Played	Play/plays	Will play
To speak	Spoke	Speak/speaks	Will speak

> Write out the following infinitives in the past, present and future simple tenses: 'to give', 'to go', 'to feel', 'to consider'.

There are subtle realities that our language needs to convey. For example, how do we talk about a specific moment in the past during which something was taking place? Or a precise moment tomorrow, or next week? What about something that is happening right now? For this, we need the continuous tense. For example:

• We **were working** on the project all night. (past continuous)
• She **is studying** journalism. (present continuous)
• This time next month, I **will be sitting** on the beach in Lanzarote. (future continuous)

Infinitive	Past continuous	Present continuous	Future continuous
To think	Was/were thinking	Am/are/is thinking	Will be thinking
To write	Was/were writing	Am/are/is writing	Will be writing

> Write out the following infinitives in the past, present and future continuous tenses: 'to judge', 'to pay', 'to amble', 'to worry'.

How do we convey the idea of a moment when the action has already occurred or has been completed? For this, we need the perfect tense. Imagine yourself at a specific moment in time – in the past, the present or the future – from which you are looking backward at an event that has been accomplished. This is where you need to use **have** or **had**. For example:

• I **had already sent** the message when I realised **I had forgotten** to attach the photo. (past perfect)

Spelling and Grammar

- I **have done** all my homework. (present perfect)
- By the middle of June, I **will have finished** all my exams. (future perfect)

Infinitive	Past perfect/ pluperfect	Present perfect	Future perfect
To be	Had been	Have/has been	Will have been
To walk	Had walked	Have/has walked	Will have walked

> Write out the following infinitives in the past, present and future perfect tenses: 'to have', 'to sit', 'to drink', 'to hurry', 'to concentrate'.

Do not forget that the words 'had' and 'have' can also be used as verbs; for example: I **have** four goldfish, or I **had** a skateboard when I was younger. This can lead to some unusual – but completely correct – constructions, such as:

- I **have had** my vaccination.
- The cat **has had** three litters of kittens.
- We were all tired yesterday because we **had had** a tough day at school.
- All the money she **had**, **had had** no effect on her.

In Hiberno-English, we sometimes see a different approach to the perfect tense. So instead of 'I have won the lottery!', we might hear someone say: 'I am after winning the lottery!' Remember that this form of the perfect tense is a uniquely Irish construct, and therefore an example of a colloquialism. English-speaking people from different parts of the world may misunderstand the meaning. For example: 'I am just after my dinner' would be interpreted by an Irish person to mean that the speaker has recently eaten. Someone from, say, England would probably assume the opposite and think that the speaker is hungry.

There is also a verb form known as the past conditional tense. This is where you are talking about something in the past that did not happen. You use the perfect tense here; for example: 'If I had studied, I **would have passed** the exam!'

There are also combinations of the above tenses. For example, the future perfect continuous tense: 'By the end of this year, I **will have been studying** for twelve years in a row.'

Active and Passive Voice

Whether your sentence is written in the active or passive voice depends on where you put the verb in relation to the subject.

 For more information on the subject/object of sentences, see page 107.

The boy kicked **the football.**

In the above example:

*   The boy = **the** subject
*   kicked = **the** verb
*   **the football** = **the** object – the thing that the boy kicked.

This sentence is written in the active voice because it is the subject of the sentence that is performing the action of the verb.

If we phrased the sentence in the passive voice, it would look like this:

The football was kicked **by the boy.**

The focus has shifted from the boy to the ball by turning the sentence around. In this case, the subject is the football, and it is acted upon, instead of doing the action.

So what is to be gained by choosing to write in the active or the passive voice?

Generally speaking, the passive voice can be seen as a weaker option, possibly because the active is understood to be more direct. However, sometimes you might want to present an idea less forcefully, or to convey a certain tentativeness. In such cases, the passive voice can be useful. The first sentence of this paragraph is an example.

The passive voice comes in handy when you may wish to obscure the identity of the person or organisation responsible for the action described by the verb. Politicians, for instance, tend to be quite adept at using the passive voice during interviews. There is a world of difference between 'we made mistakes' and 'mistakes were made'. Imagine hearing from your travel agent: 'An error has been identified with your holiday booking. Attempts are ongoing to remedy the situation.' What they actually mean is that they have made a mistake, which they are trying to fix. However, the way the sentence is formulated in the passive voice allows them to present themselves as less culpable.

Writing a sentence in the passive voice will tend to shift the focus, which can be an effective tool in writing. Compare, for example:

*   The hunter shot **the rabbit.** (active voice)
*   The rabbit was shot by **the hunter.** (passive voice)

In both cases, our attention is mostly with the subject of the sentence, while the object is secondary. Therefore, if your intention is to evoke sympathy for the rabbit, the second version would be the better choice.

However, if you are trying to convey ideas strongly, the active voice will probably serve you better. Consider these options:

*   This government must immediately introduce the reforms **we demand.** (active voice)
*   The reforms we demand must be immediately introduced by **this government.** (passive voice)

Both sentences convey the same message, but the second version does not have quite the same impact as the first.

Paragraphs

All sustained writing needs to be structured into paragraphs. A page of text without any paragraph breaks is a forbidding prospect for any reader, no matter how experienced. But what is the rationale for where the breaks should go? How do you know which sentences belong in which paragraph?

A few moments' planning before you start to write will help you to marshal your ideas into a logical and coherent order. In the Comprehending section of your exam, for example, once you have **simplified** the question and **selected** the ideas you are going to use, you then **sort** those ideas into the order in which you will present them. You will have focused your answer into three ideas for a 15-mark question (or four ideas for a 20-mark question). Three ideas will turn into three paragraphs, with every sentence in each paragraph relating to one particular idea.

The same is true for all your essay writing. Each paragraph contains sentences pertaining to a single idea. When you move on to the next idea, you start a new paragraph. This is why many writers will start a new paragraph with a **topic sentence**. In other words, the first sentence of the paragraph contains the main idea of that paragraph. All the following sentences develop that idea by adding detail or supplying examples.

Have a look at the paragraph below, which is taken from a speech made by Chris Packham in a video posted to his YouTube channel. In it, he is making an impassioned appeal to his viewers to sign his petition against the High Speed 2 (HS2), a proposed railway network in the United Kingdom.

Topic sentence establishes main idea.	Now, since 1970, we've recently learned that we've lost 68 per cent of all of the world's wildlife. And we already know that we live in one of the most nature-depleted countries in that world. And yet this project is going to plough through 108 ancient woodlands, 33 Sites of Special Scientific Interest, 21 local nature reserves, 693 local wildlife sites and 18 Wildlife Trust reserves. At a time when we should be looking after our biodiversity, this project is abjectly destroying it.
Develops idea from topic sentence.	
Provides factual information related to topic.	
Argument against HS2 made, based on topic sentence.	

One of the most common errors made by students is not structuring their writing properly. Perhaps ideas are not presented in a coherent order; or one paragraph contains several competing ideas. Or ideas are raised but not developed properly, or not illustrated with examples. Sometimes, there is no attempt to structure the writing at all. Such incoherently written answers tend to be heavily penalised.

Always plan before writing. Use a mind map to jot down key ideas. These ideas will develop into the topic sentences of your paragraphs. Organise those ideas into a logical sequence. Remember to refer to your plan regularly while you are writing. This will give your answer coherence.

Parts of Speech

Class	Function	Examples
Adverbs (see page 78)	• Modifying words • Give more information about verbs	Invisibly, insistently, quite, often, sometimes
Adjectives (see page 15)	• Describing words • Add information about nouns	Snowy, crimson, sprawling, beautiful, new
Conjunctions/connectives (see page 117)	• Joining words	But, if, or, and, then
Nouns (see page 42)	• Naming words	Chair, Mars, herd, love, money
Prepositions	• Give information about time and place	Since, after, on, before, inside
Pronouns (see page 107)	• Substitutes for nouns	I, me, him, she, their
Verbs (see page 56)	• Action words/state of being	Have been running, will be running, ran, runs, is running

Punctuation Marks

Punctuation mark	Use	Examples
Apostrophe (see page 70)	• Possession (singular) • Possession (plural) • Contractions	• The girl's blouse • The girls' blouses • They're, should've, doesn't
Capital letter	• At the start of a sentence • For the personal pronoun 'I' • When writing days of the week, months of the year, holidays, etc. • When naming countries, places, languages, nationalities, religions, monuments, companies, brands, organisations, etc. • When naming people and titles • For titles of (most) books, poems, plays and songs • To abbreviate names and titles	• **T**his is an example of a sentence starting with a capital letter. • Sinead and **I** went to class. • We will be carving pumpkins for **H**allowe'en on **S**unday 31 **O**ctober. • **I**reland, **P**aris, **L**atin, **S**wiss, **I**slam, **T**aj **M**ahal, **I**ntel, **K**errygold, **G**aelic **A**thletic **A**ssociation • **T**aoiseach **M**icheál **M**artin • *Of Mice and Men*, '**S**tairway to **H**eaven' • **GAA, RTÉ, Dr, Miss**
Colon (see page 94)	• To illustrate the thought that precedes the colon • To introduce lists	• I have only one wish: to become famous. • There are three things to remember: reduce, reuse and recycle.

Comma	• Indicates a short pause between clauses and ideas within a sentence • Separates items in a list	• 'A breeze slips invisibly, insistently through the streets, like a burglar seeking an entrance.' • 'You have to trust in something – your gut, destiny, life, karma, whatever.'
Dash (see page 125)	• Parenthesis • To pause for effect	• If you wait – and you should – you will see. • 'From that they can work out plausible scenarios of what it must have been like – or, more chillingly, would be like if it happened now.'
Exclamation mark	• Exclamation; to indicate a strong emotion • Commands	• I can't believe it! I won! • Get out of the water!
Full stop	• Indicates the end of a sentence • After initials in someone's name • Abbreviations that do not include the last letter of the full word	• 'To this day, Sabina haunts the castle's walls.' • W. B. Yeats, Iain M. Banks • Mon. (Monday), Prof. (Professor), etc. (et cetera)
Hyphen (see page 125)	• To join words	• Six-year-old boy, a light-hearted story
Question mark	• At the end of a question	• What is the weather forecast for tomorrow?
Semi-colon (see page 94)	• To link related clauses	• Eileen was starting to worry; Clive was later coming home than usual.
Speech/quotation marks (see page 29)	• To indicate words used in dialogue • To show quotations taken from written or spoken text • For ideas or words meant ironically or sarcastically	• 'I am not in the habit,' she said, 'of repeating myself.' • 'I am a man more sinned against than sinning' (*King Lear*, Act 3, Scene 2) • She was very disappointed with the 'meal' he prepared for dinner.

Acknowledgements

For permission to reproduce photographs and illustrations, the author and publisher acknowledge the following copyright holders:

Aidan Harte • Alyssa Carson • Bruce McGowan / Alamy Stock Photo • Kathy deWitt / Alamy Stock Photo • Metzger Cartoons • Phillip Roberts / Alamy Stock Photo. Other images from Shutterstock and Wikimedia Commons (public domain).

For permission to reproduce text, the author and publisher acknowledge the following copyright holders:

'Meet Alyssa Carson, the 18-year-old training to become the first human on Mars' by kind permission of TNW and Cara Curtis • 'Sculpting a brighter future for art' by Cristín Leach by kind permission of The Times/News Licensing • excerpt from *Love and Vandalism*, copyright 2017 Laurie Boyle Crompton, by permission of Sourcebooks • extract from *War Doctor* by David Nott by kind permission of David Higham Associates.

The author and publisher have made every effort to trace all copyright owners. If any material has inadvertently been reproduced without permission, they would be happy to make the necessary arrangement at the earliest opportunity and encourage owners of copyright material not acknowledged to make contact.

Notes

Notes

Notes

educate.ie

Redeeming Educate.ie ebooks

You are entitled to one complimentary ebook of this textbook.

To avail of this ebook, complete the following steps:

1. Visit Educate.ie and click the "**Redeem Ebooks**" button.

2. Select "**Sign in**" or "**Create Account**"ensuring
   you are using the correct email address*.

3. In your account, you will be asked to
   enter your redeem code. Enter this code ➜
   and select "**Check Code**".

   Hands On Paper 1 HL

   HOHSZGHTY

4. If the title is correct, select "**Yes, redeem
   my ebook**".**

5. Your title is now redeemed. To access your Educate.ie
   ebook app, select "**Ebook App**" or select "**Redeem Ebooks**"
   to redeem any further titles.

   ebook redeemable to one email address only.
   ** *If the title is incorrect, select "**No, contact support**".*

Free resources online

When you create an ebook account (see above), an account will also
be created for you on **educate*plus*.ie** – our free Digital Resource site.

You can also go directly to **educate*plus*.ie**, if you wish, without
redeeming an ebook and register an account there.

1. Visit **www.educate*plus*.ie**, and click "**Register**", completing the
   online form.

2. Once logged in, select your textbook and access your resources
   using the same redeem code above.

3. Each time you log in, your resources will be in your dashboard.

If you need any help, please contact us at **support@educate.ie** and
make sure to tell us what book you're using!